# ZERO YEN HOUSES
# 0円ハウス

Kyohei Sakaguchi
坂口恭平

Little More
リトル・モア

## CONTENTS
目次

## Nagoya
名古屋

### Around Shirakawa Park
白川公園周辺 ……………………………… 4

## Osaka
大阪

### Osaka-Jo Park
大阪城公園 ……………………………… 44

### Kamagasaki
釜ヶ崎 ……………………………… 62

## Tokyo
東京

### The Tamagawa
多摩川 ……………………………… 82

### Shinjuku Chuo Park
新宿中央公園 ……………………………… 132

### Toyama Park
戸山公園 ……………………………… 150

### The Sumidagawa
隅田川 ……………………………… 168

# Around Shirakawa Park

# 白川公園周辺

**A House Partitioned into Six Units**

六軒長家

ガード下に6軒の家が連なって建っている。この住居群のリーダーは50代の女性である。彼女が缶集めの仕事、食事すべてを指示している。

Six houses stand side by side under a girder bridge. The leader of this community is a woman in her fifties. She directs everything from dining to the task of can collecting.

壁には毎月、ベニヤ板に書かれた予定表が掲示される。

Every month a schedule is written on plywood and put up on the wall.

**An Almighty Reed Screen**
万能の簾

この家は簾をうまく利用している。簾は日除けになるが、ほのかに光が差し込み、風を通す。さらに内側から外の気配が伺えるため、この家の住人にとっては防犯にも役立つのだろう。

This house makes good use of a reed screen. It shades the sunshine while still allowing a little light and a gentle wind into the house. Also, since the inhabitant can see through to the outside, it is useful in crime prevention.

## A House with a Slide
## 滑り台のある家

この家は、玄関が滑り台である。子供の遊び場が完全に住居化してしまっている。防犯のためなのか、遊び心なのか。不便なように思えるが。

The entrance to this house is a slide. A children's playground has been completely turned into living quarters. Is this for protection or just for fun? It does look inconvenient, though.

## A House that Runs
## 走る家

車輪が付いている可動式の家である。動かないように車輪がヒモで固定されている。周りにも幾つか同じような家が見られた。家の形まで車そのものである。

This is a mobile home with wheels. The wheels have been fixed in place so that the house does not move. This same type of house was seen a few times in this area. Even the shape of the house resembles a car.

## A Japanese Restaurant!?
料亭!?

料亭のような佇まい、もちろん営業はしていない。男性1人が住む家である。植栽と拾ってきた公衆電話がさらに雰囲気を高めている。

Although this one resembles a Japanese restaurant, it is not open for business. A man lives alone in this house. The green plant and discarded public telephone help to further the atmosphere.

とにかく物が溢れ返っているのが名古屋の家の特徴である。高架下という立地条件を生かし、彼らは家の周りに物を配置し、自分の空間を大きくしていく。

A characteristic of Nagoya houses is that they simply contain a lot of stuff. Making the most of being located under elevated railroad tracks, the inhabitants of this house increase their space by placing many things around the house.

## A Huge Living Room
## 巨大なリビングルーム

この家も高架を屋根として利用している。しかし、ここの住人は、物を置くことを抑え、元々設置されていた水道やイスをも含めた広い空間を居間とみなしている。

This house also uses an elevated railroad as a roof. However, the inhabitant of this space keeps his belongings to a minimum. The wide space, including the chairs and preexisting waterworks, is used as a living room.

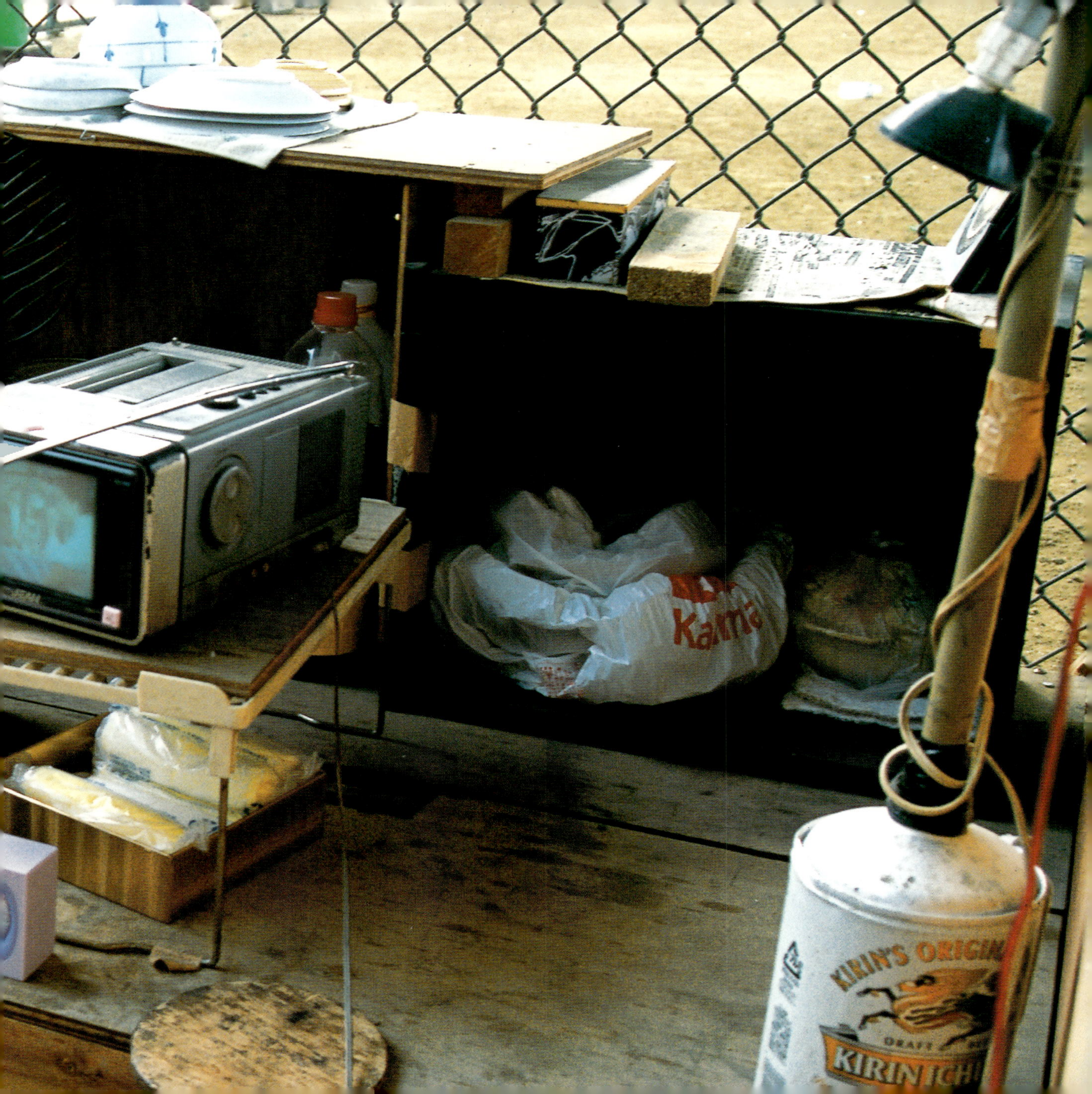

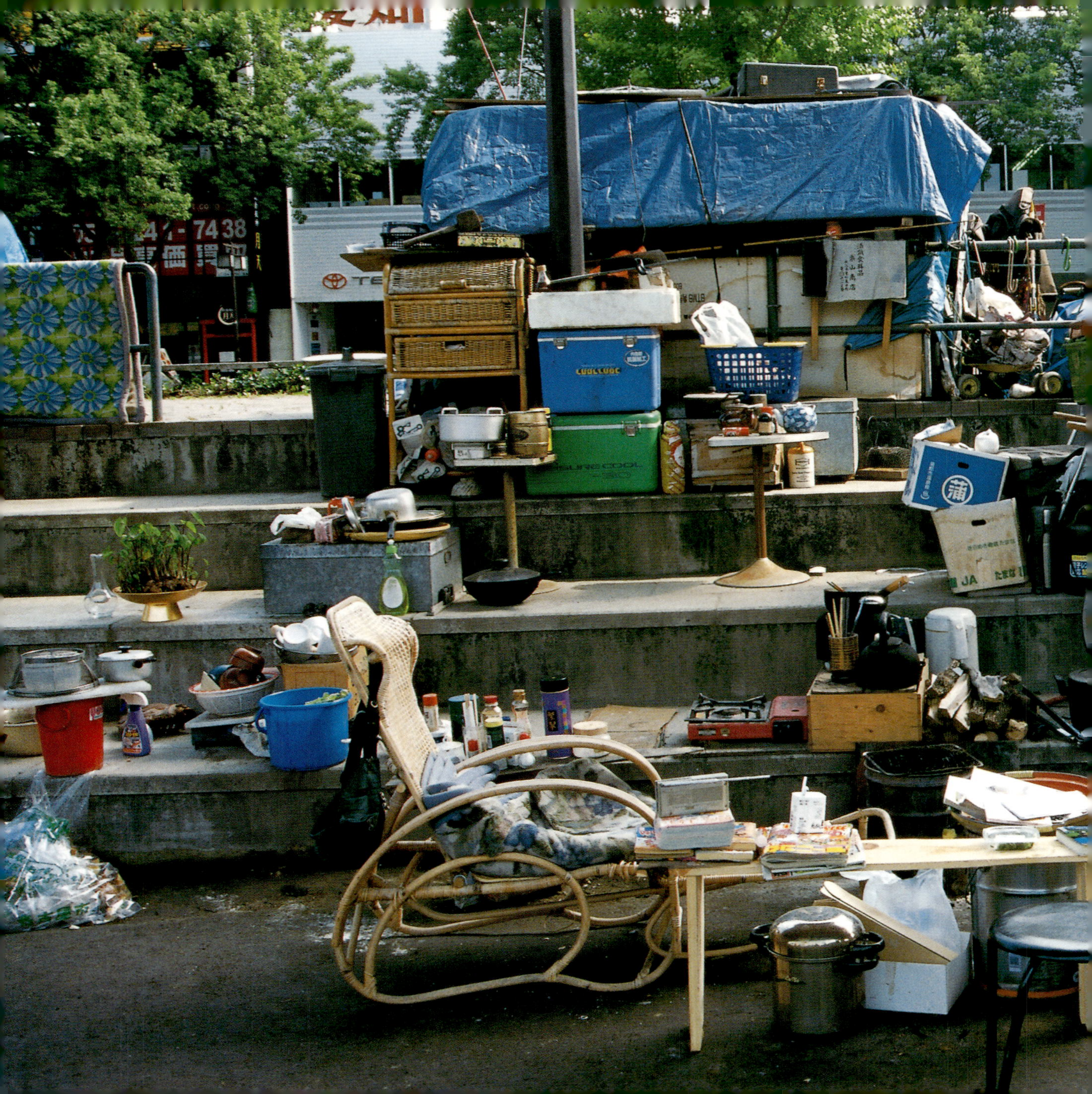

**A Stairway House**

階段の家

階段を居住空間とみなし家を作っている。階段はイスにもテーブルにも棚にもなる。

The dweller regards this stairway as a living space and is making a house on it. The stairs can be turned into chairs, tables and shelves.

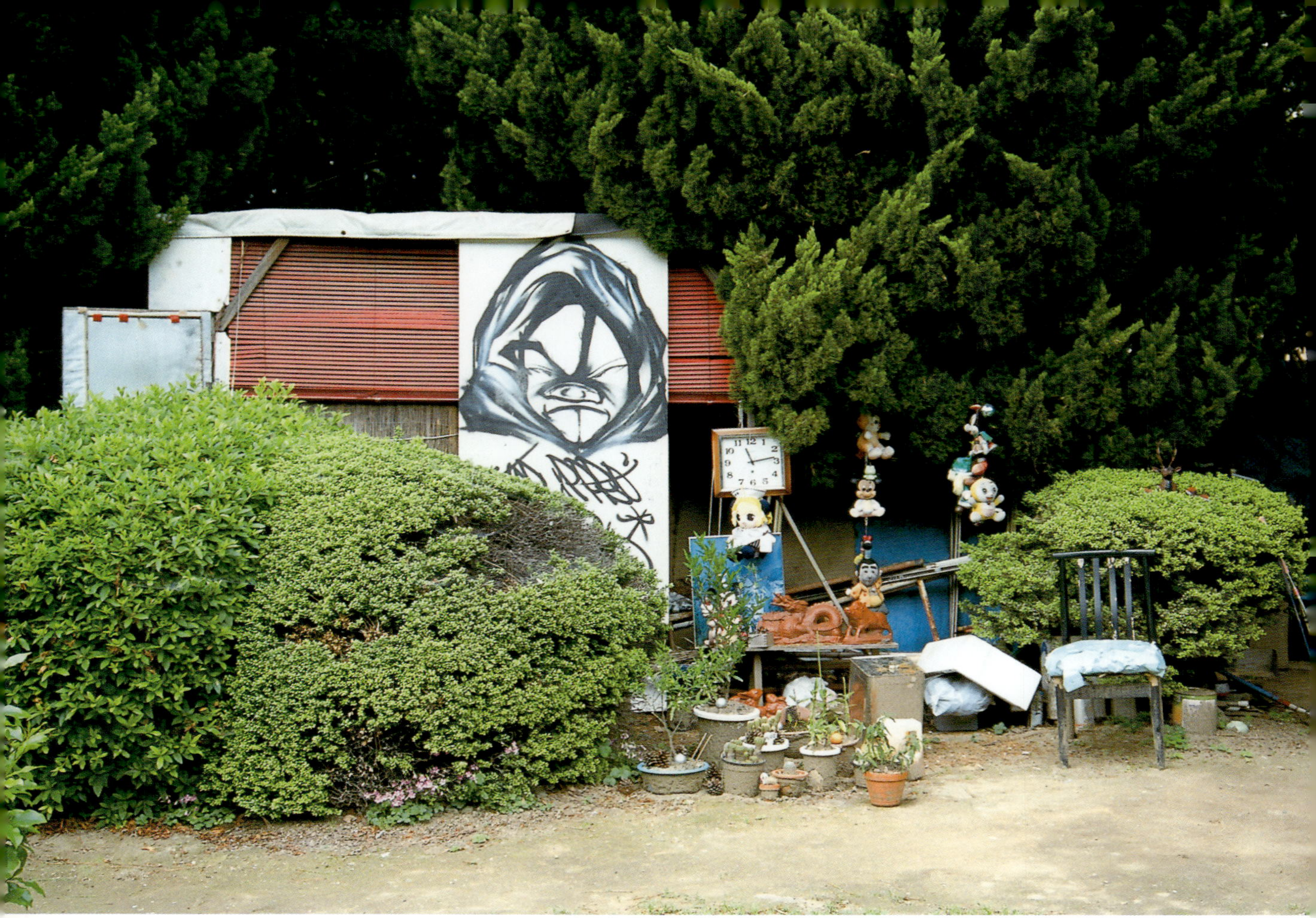

41

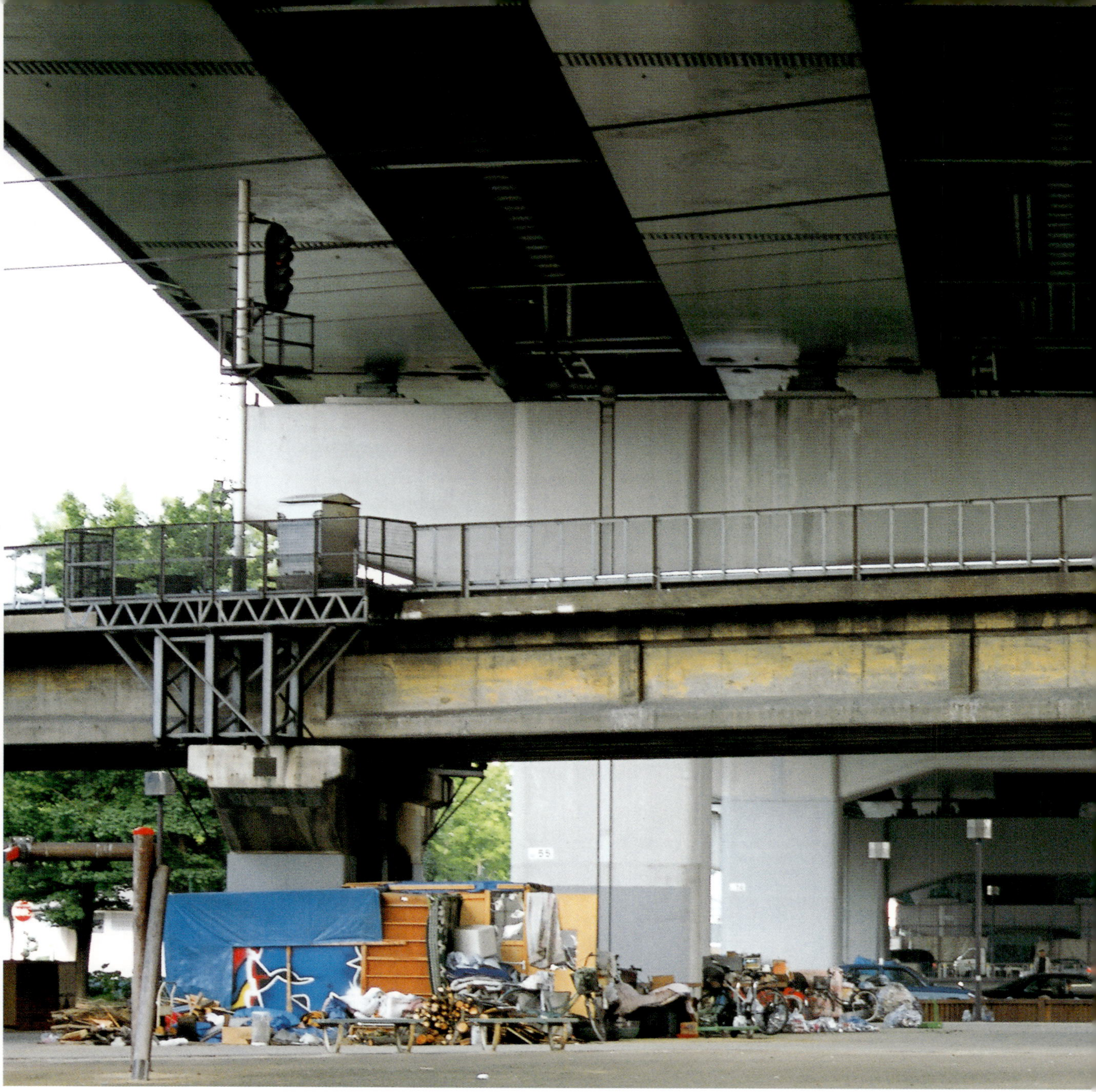
55

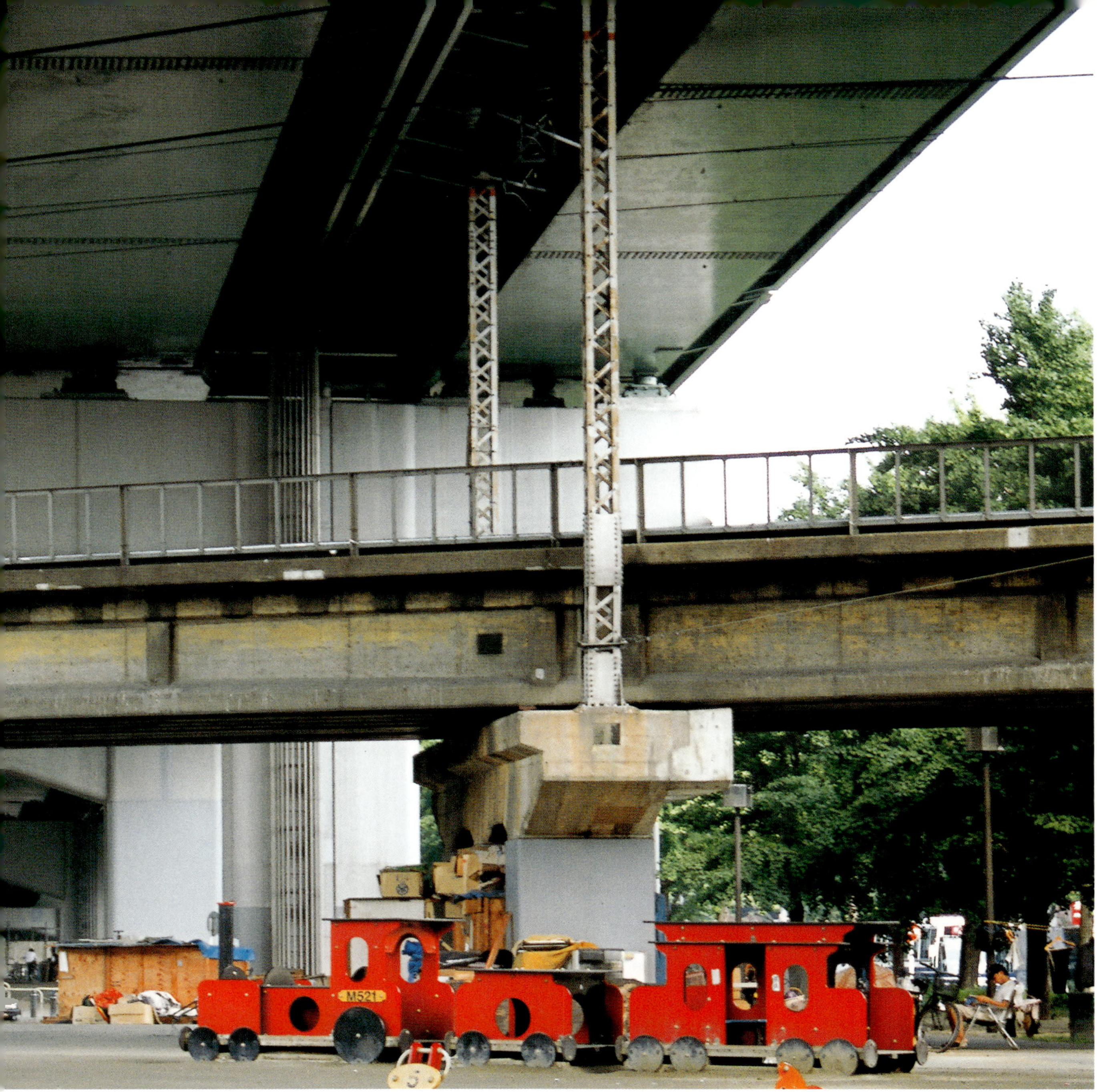
M521
5

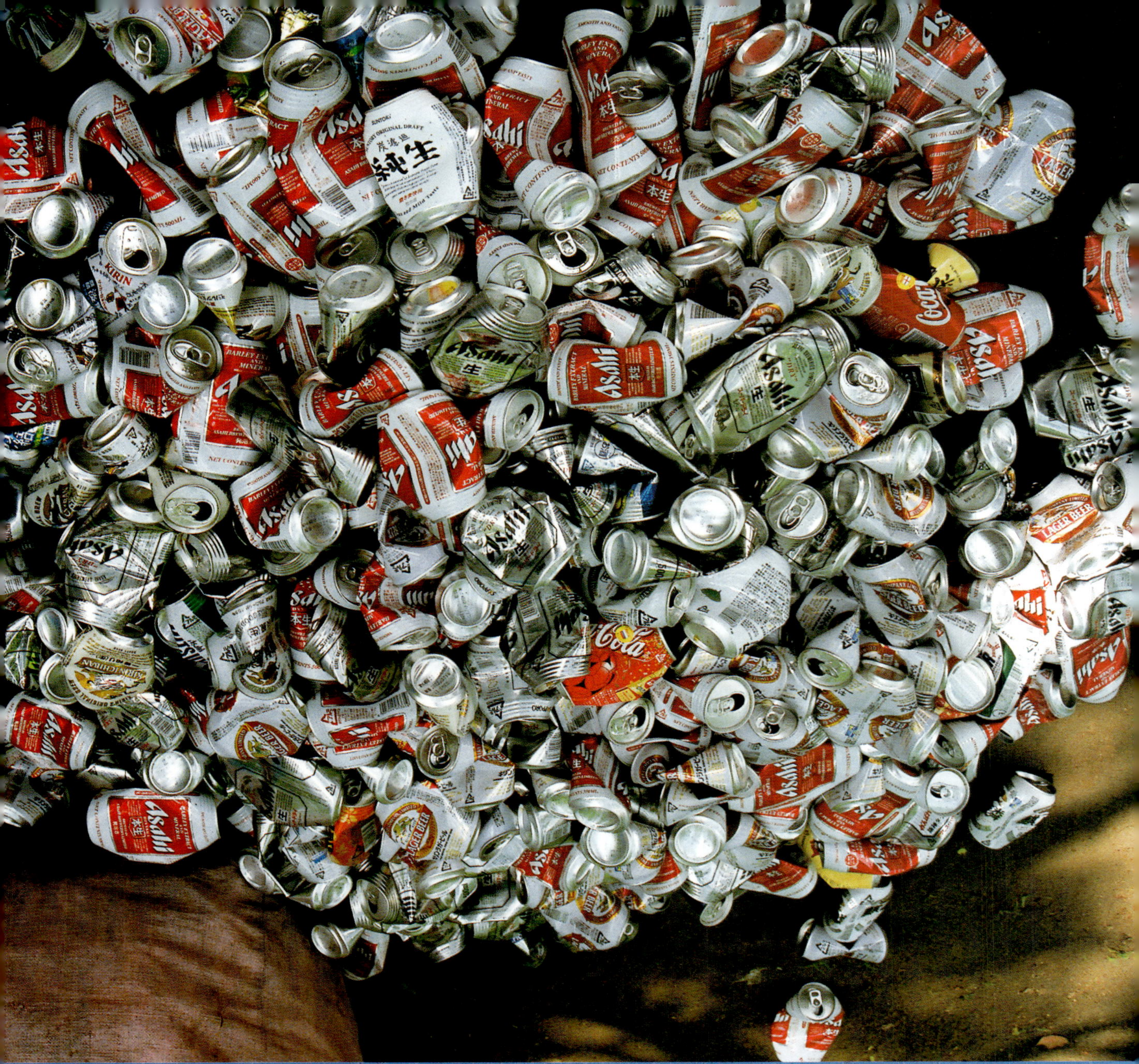
Asahi
本生
純生
KIRIN
LAGER BEER
Coca-Cola

# Osaka-Jo Park
# 大阪城公園

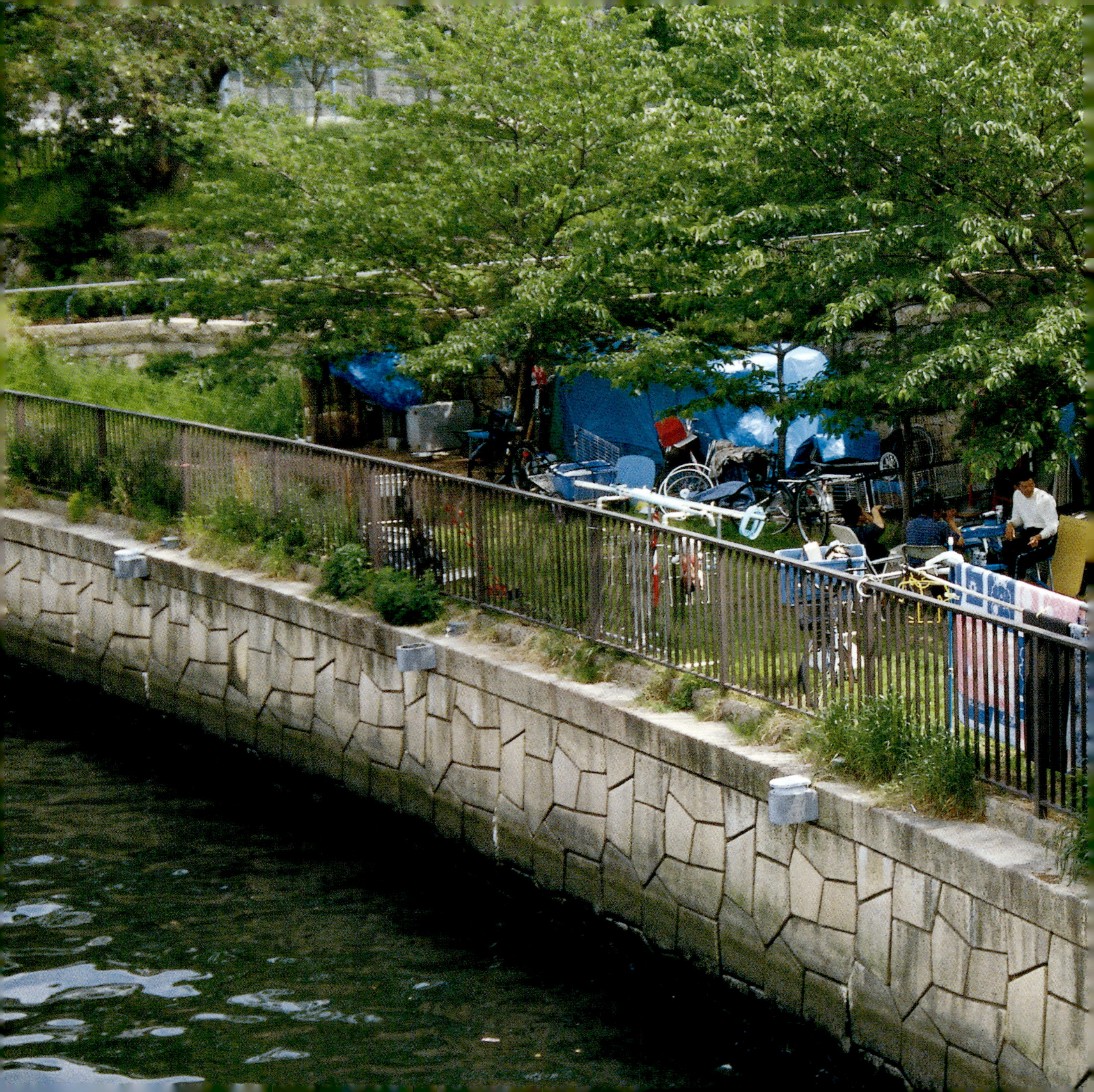

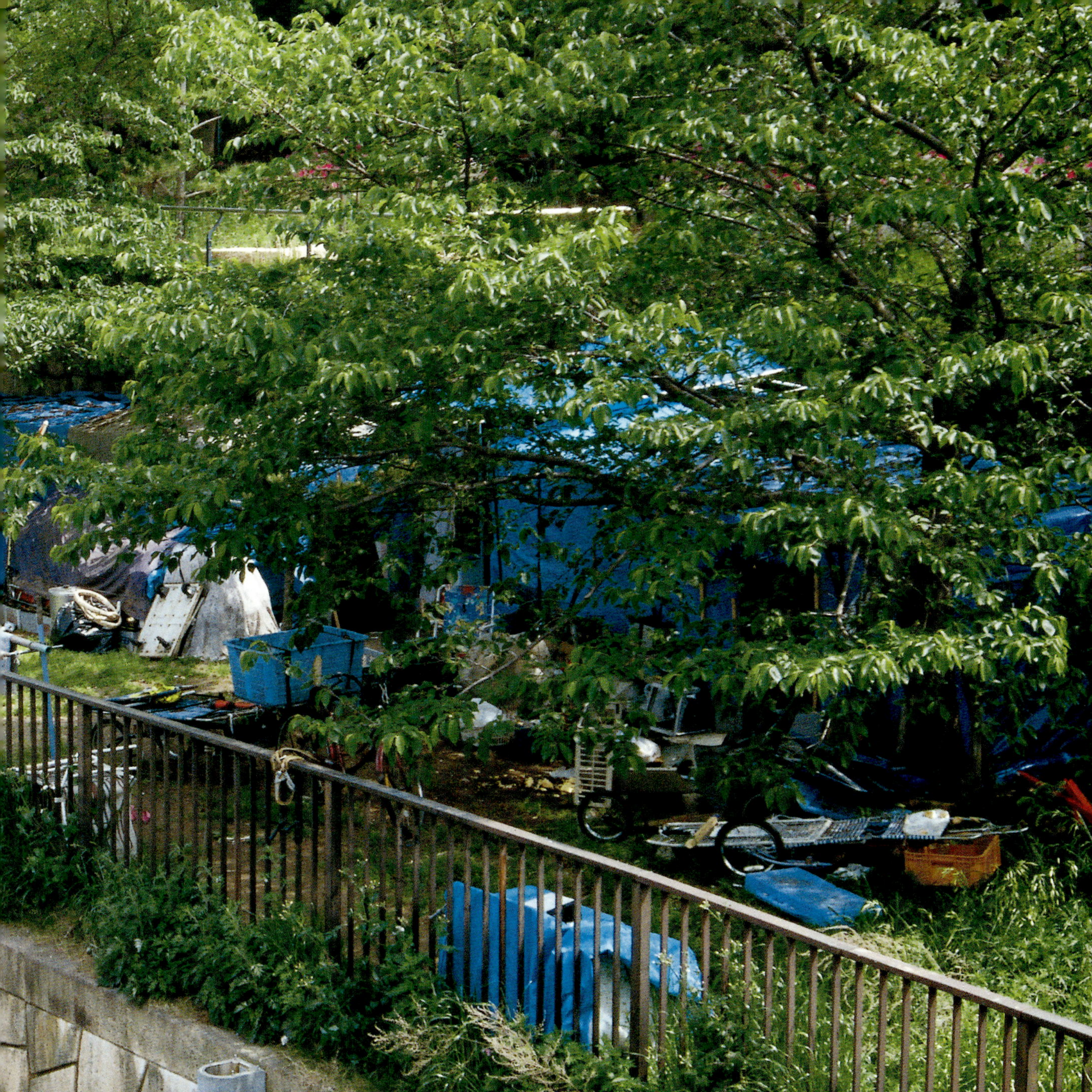

**A House of a Dog**
犬の家

この家の住人は犬と共同生活している。犬にもきちんと部屋が与えられ互いに寄り添って暮らしている。このタイプの家は大阪に多く見られた。

The owner of this house lives with a dog. The dog has a room of its own, but the two live in close quarters. This type of house is often seen in Osaka.

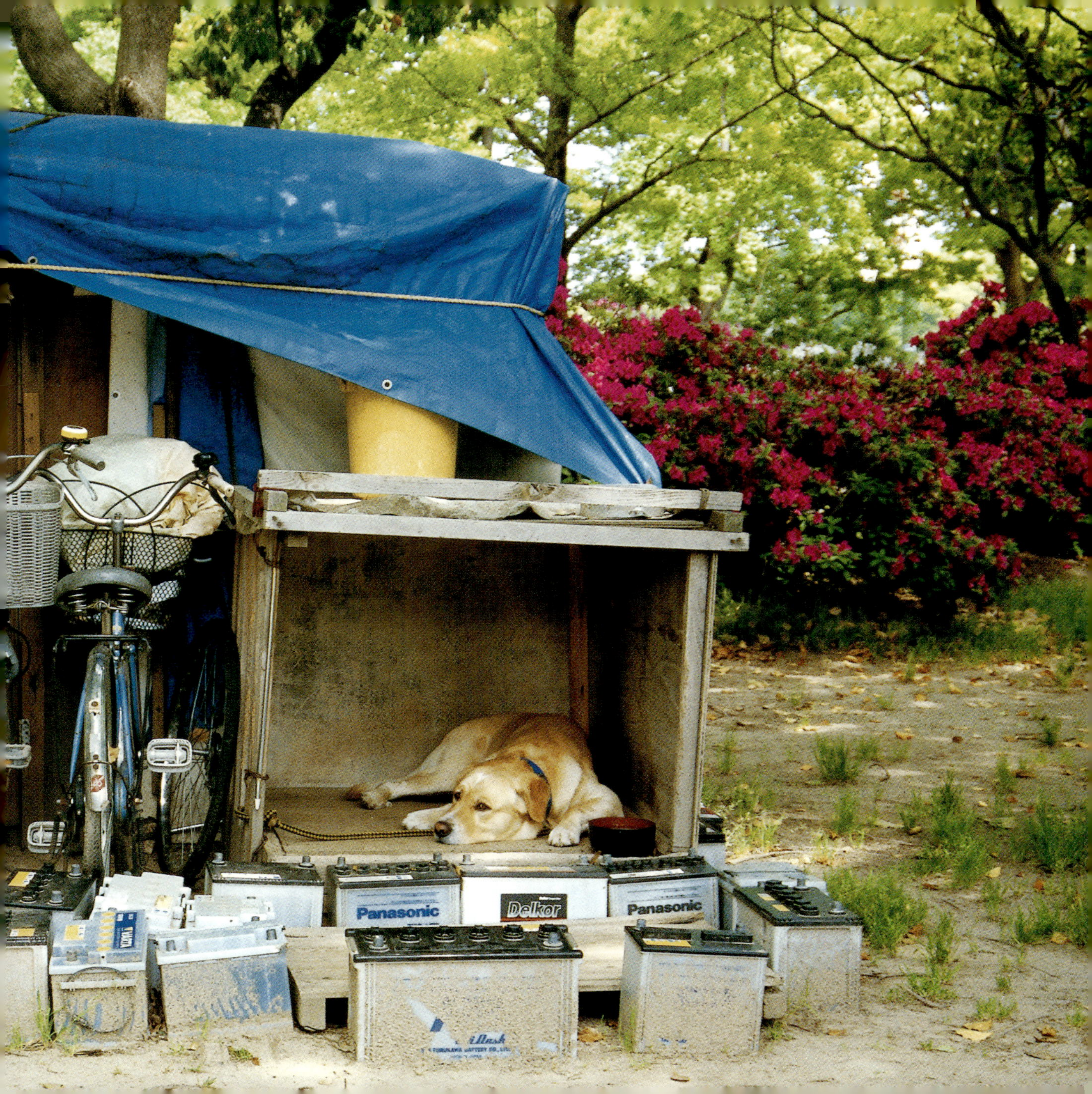
Panasonic
Delkor
Panasonic

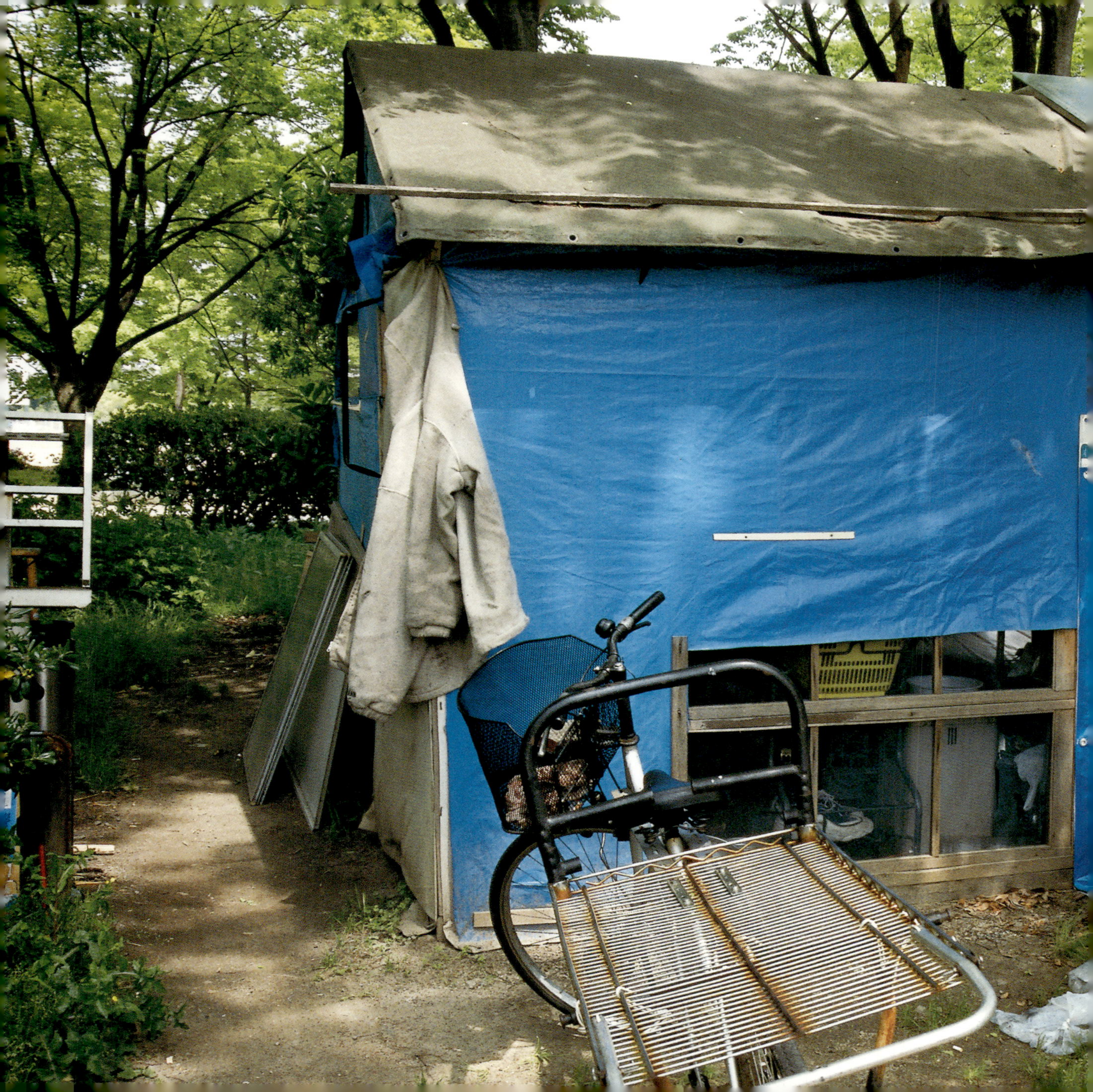

## A Light House
光の家

この家にはガラスが多用されている。屋根にもガラスがはめ込まれ、日中には室内にたくさんの光が射す。住人は拾ってきた物を器用に組み合わせ、いろいろな家具や道具を作り出している。

This house uses a lot of glass. Glass is even fitted into the roof so that in the daytime, sunlight floods through it. Its inhabitant makes furniture and tools by dexterously assembling things he collects.

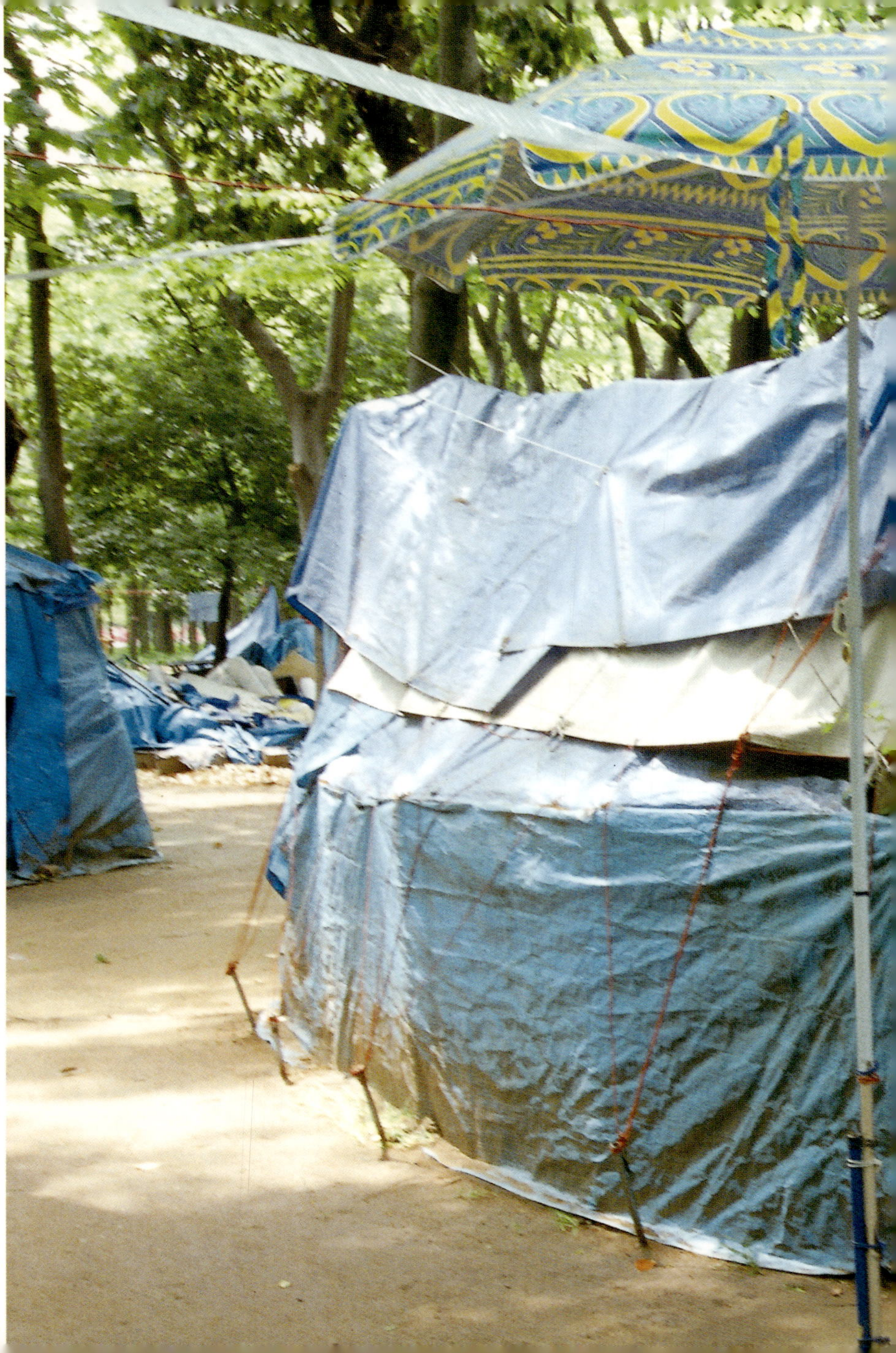

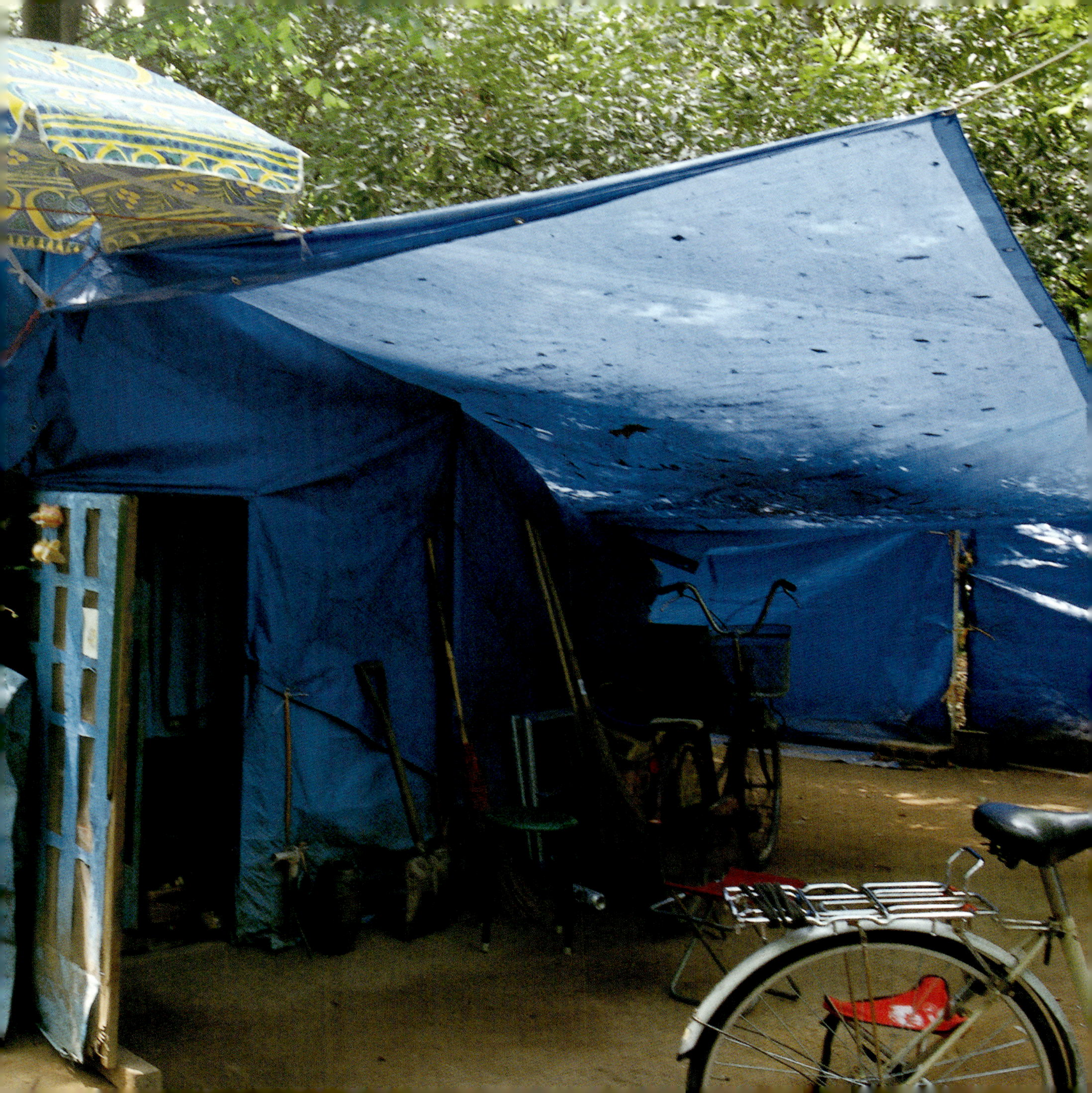

**A Double House**
二重の家

1軒の家のように見えるが、実はこれは目隠しで、中には2軒の家が存在する。

This appears to be a single house, but in fact there are two houses inside.

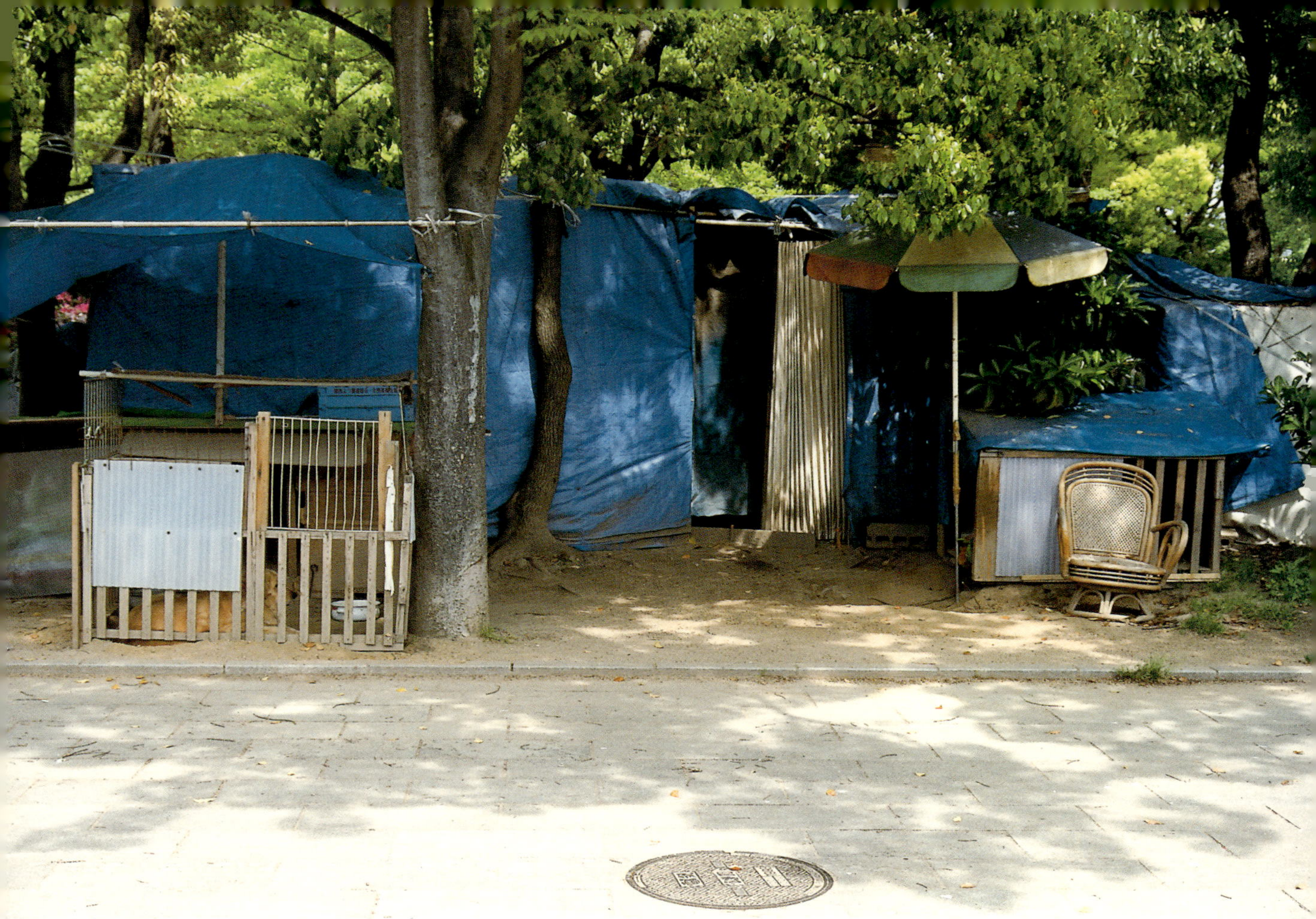

**An Open-Air Bedroom**
開放的な寝室

隣には住人が寝起きする部屋がある。来客用の寝室か?

The owner sleeps in the next room. Is this the guest bedroom?

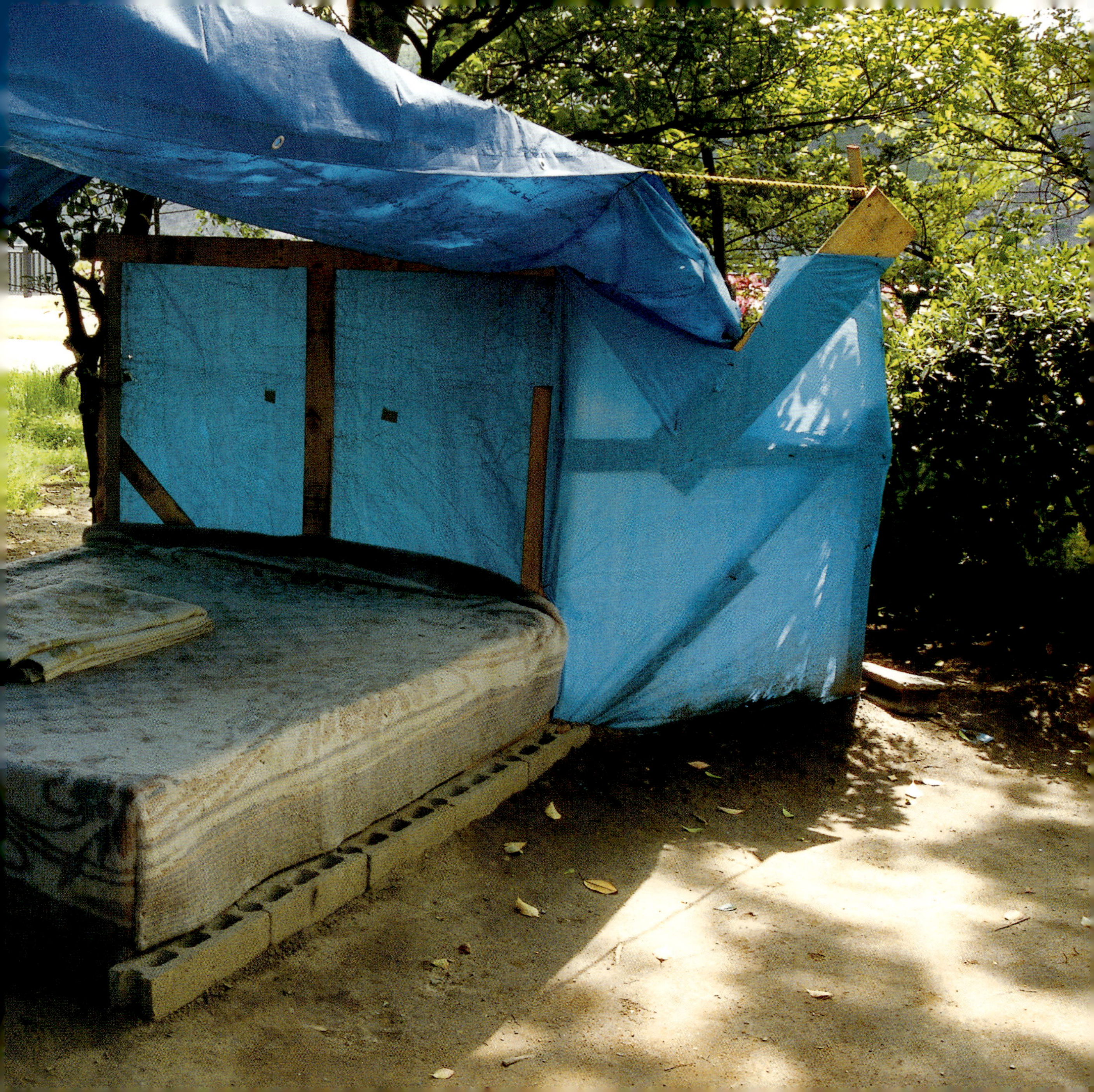

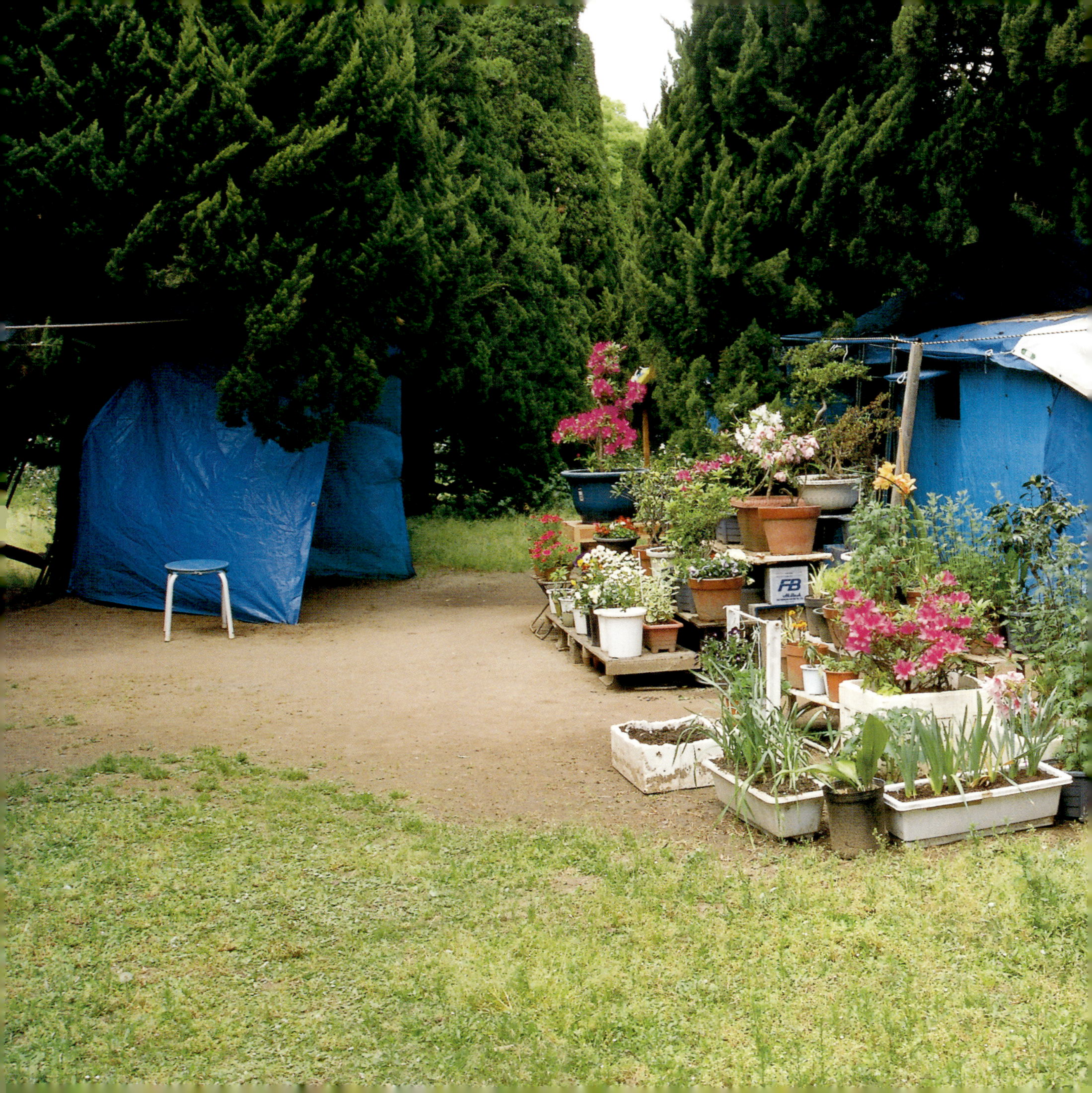
FB

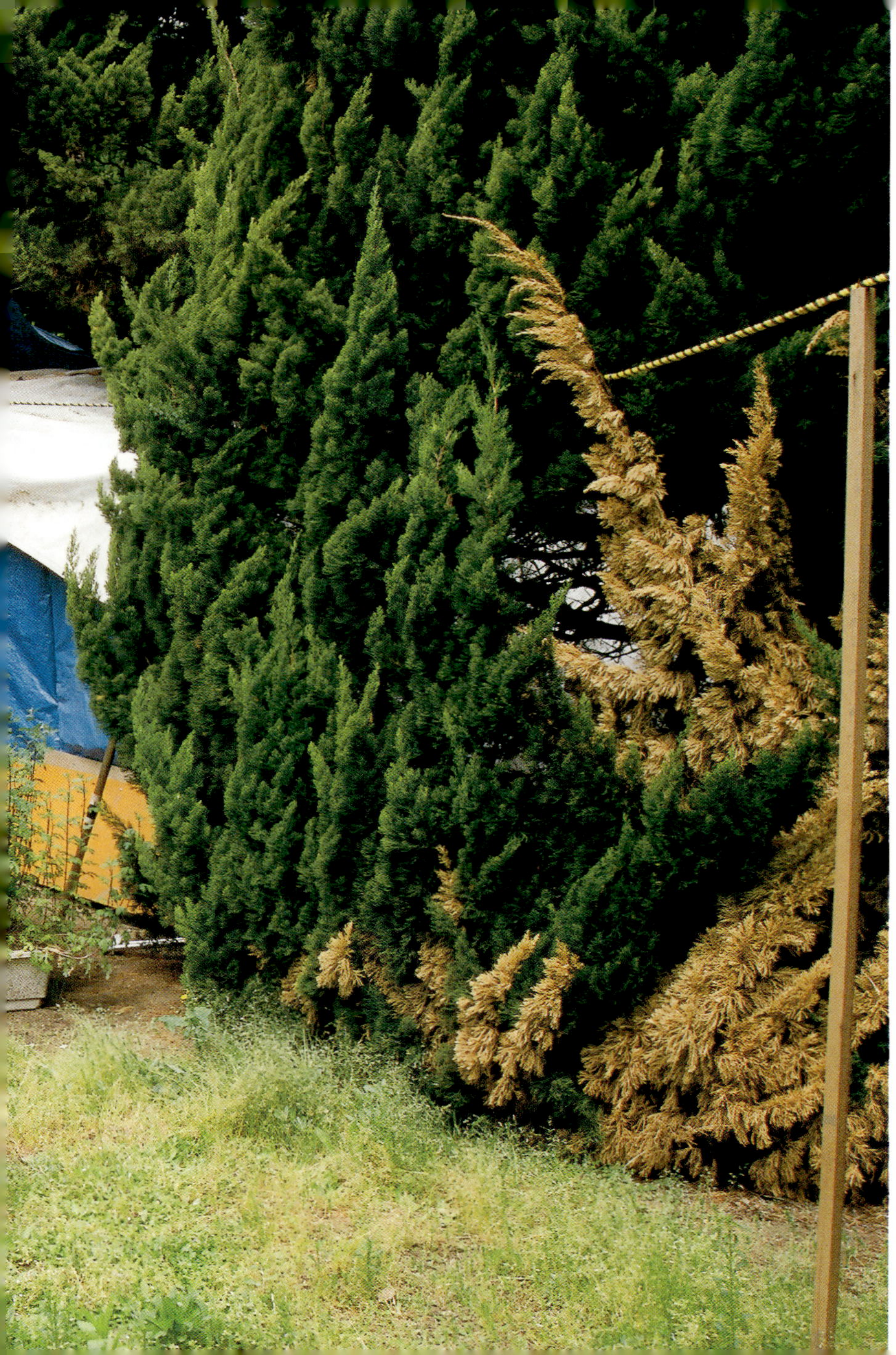

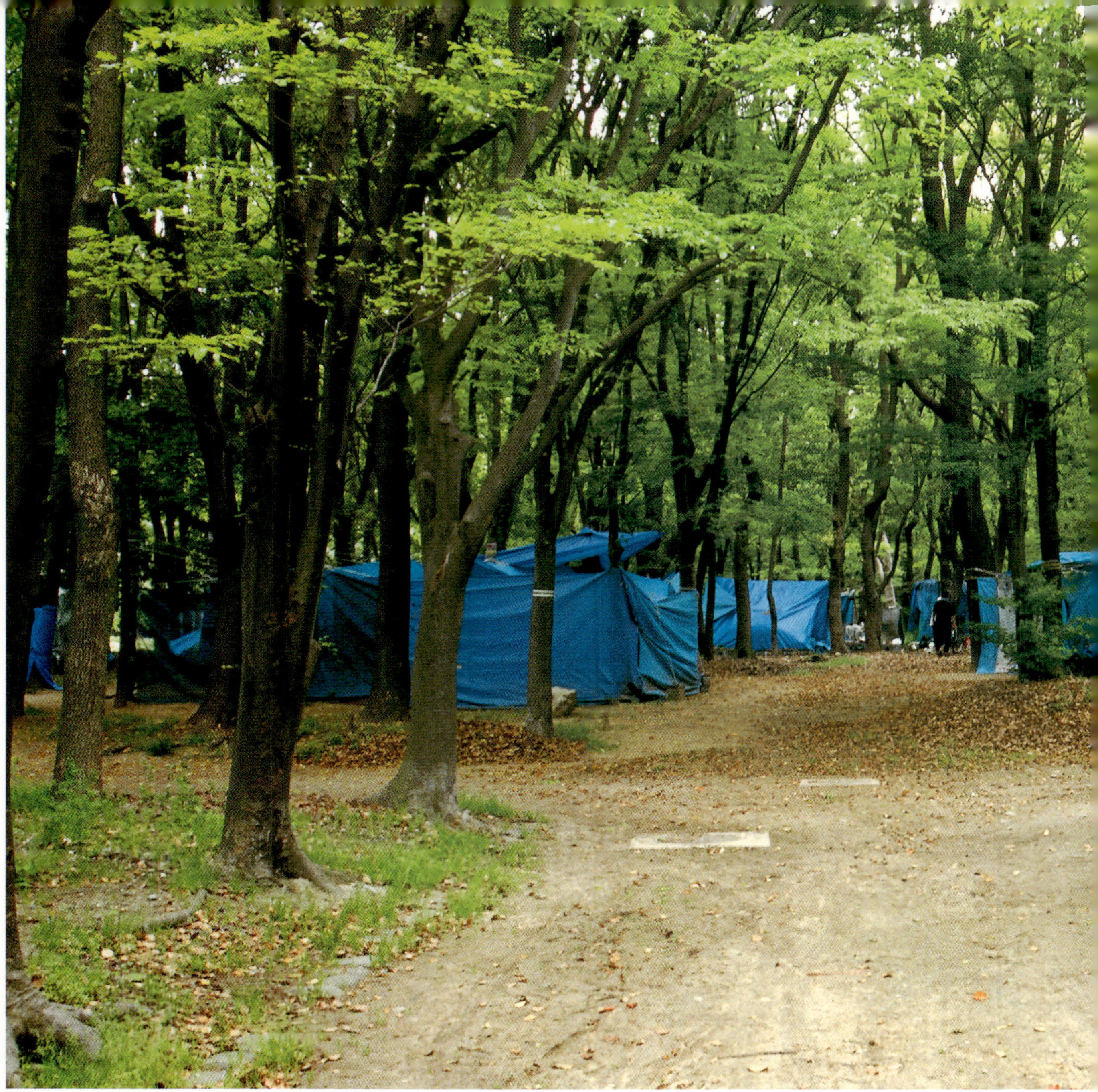

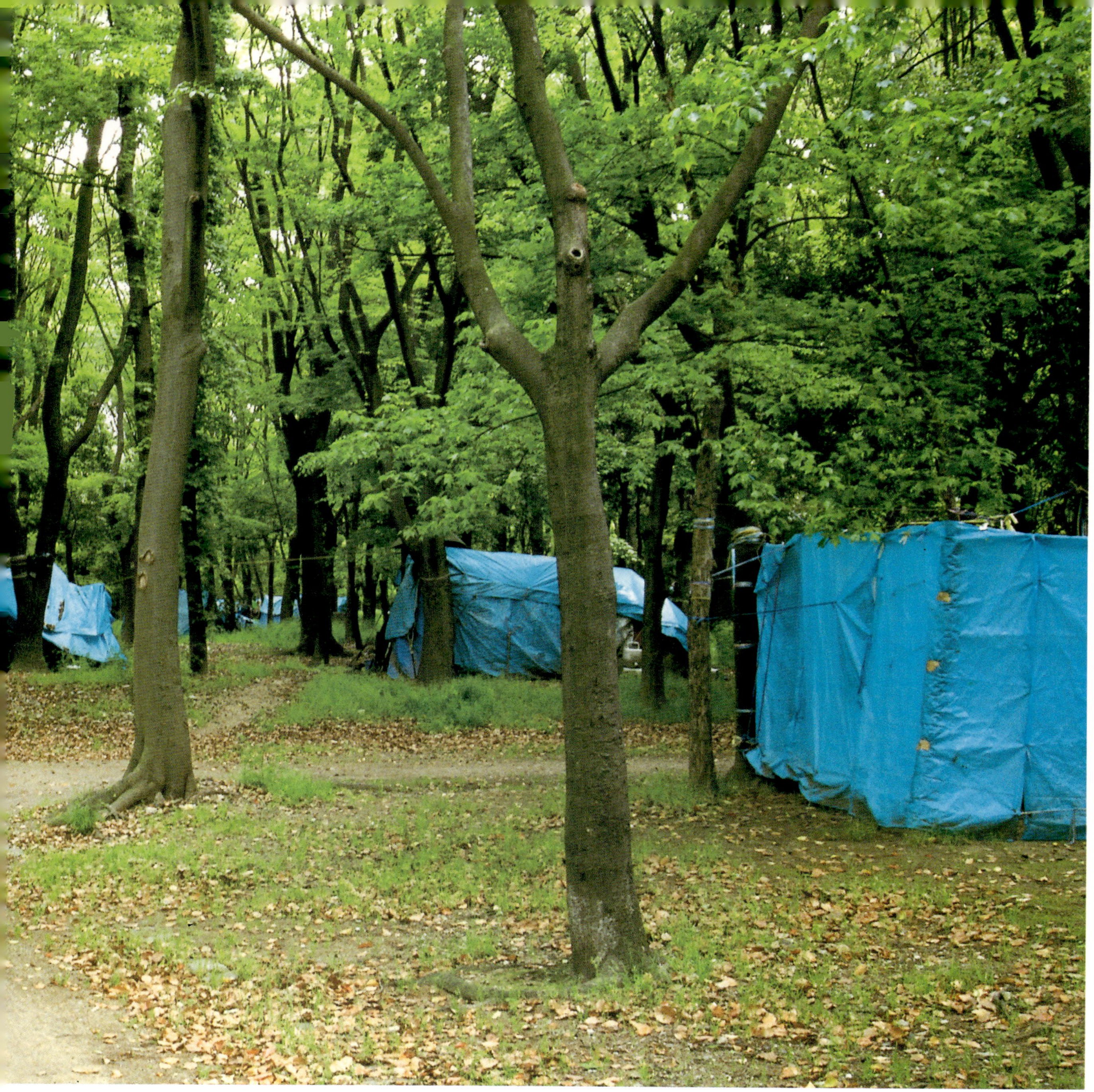

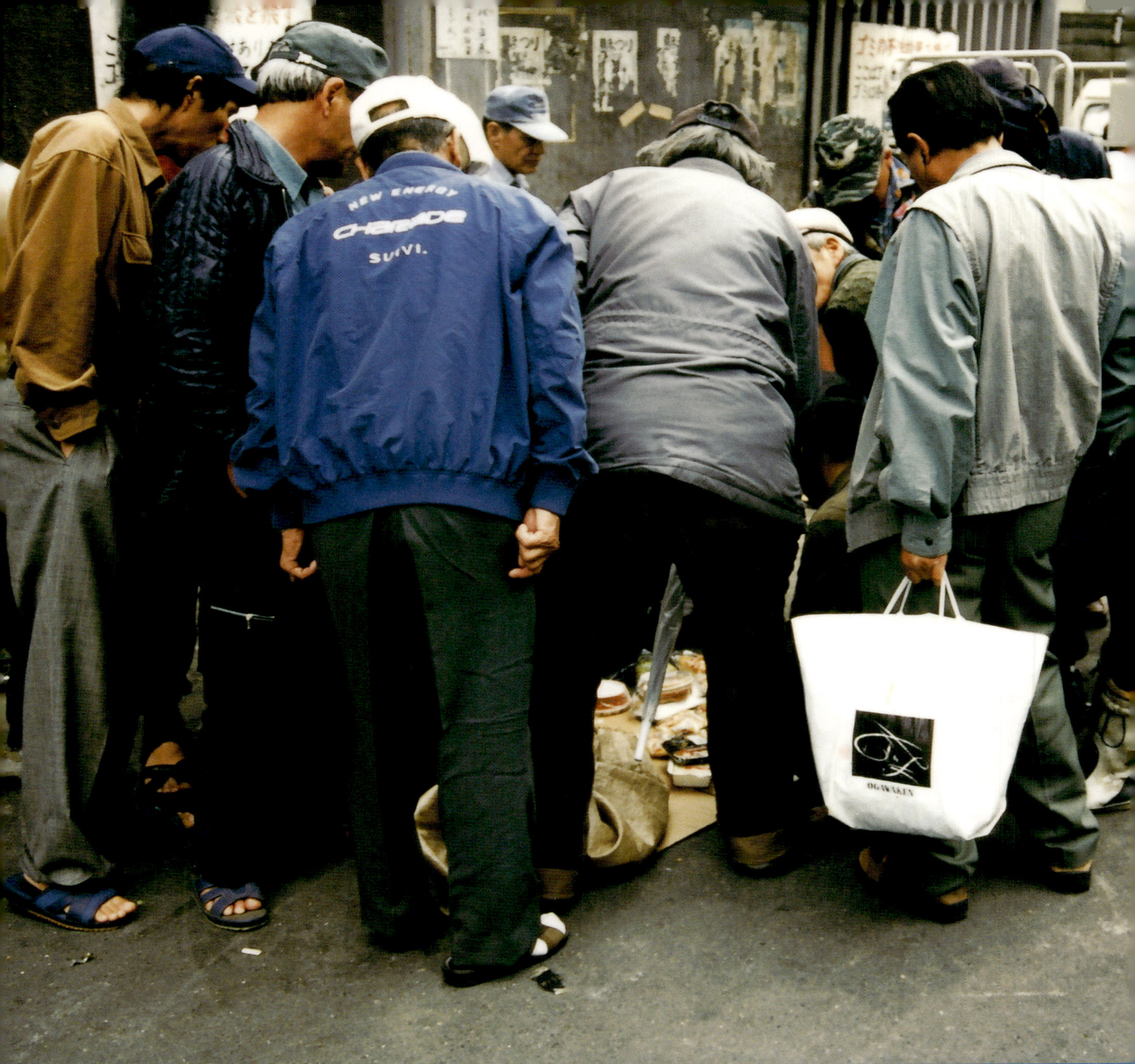
NEW ENERGY
CHARADE
SUIVI.

# Kamagasaki

釜ヶ崎

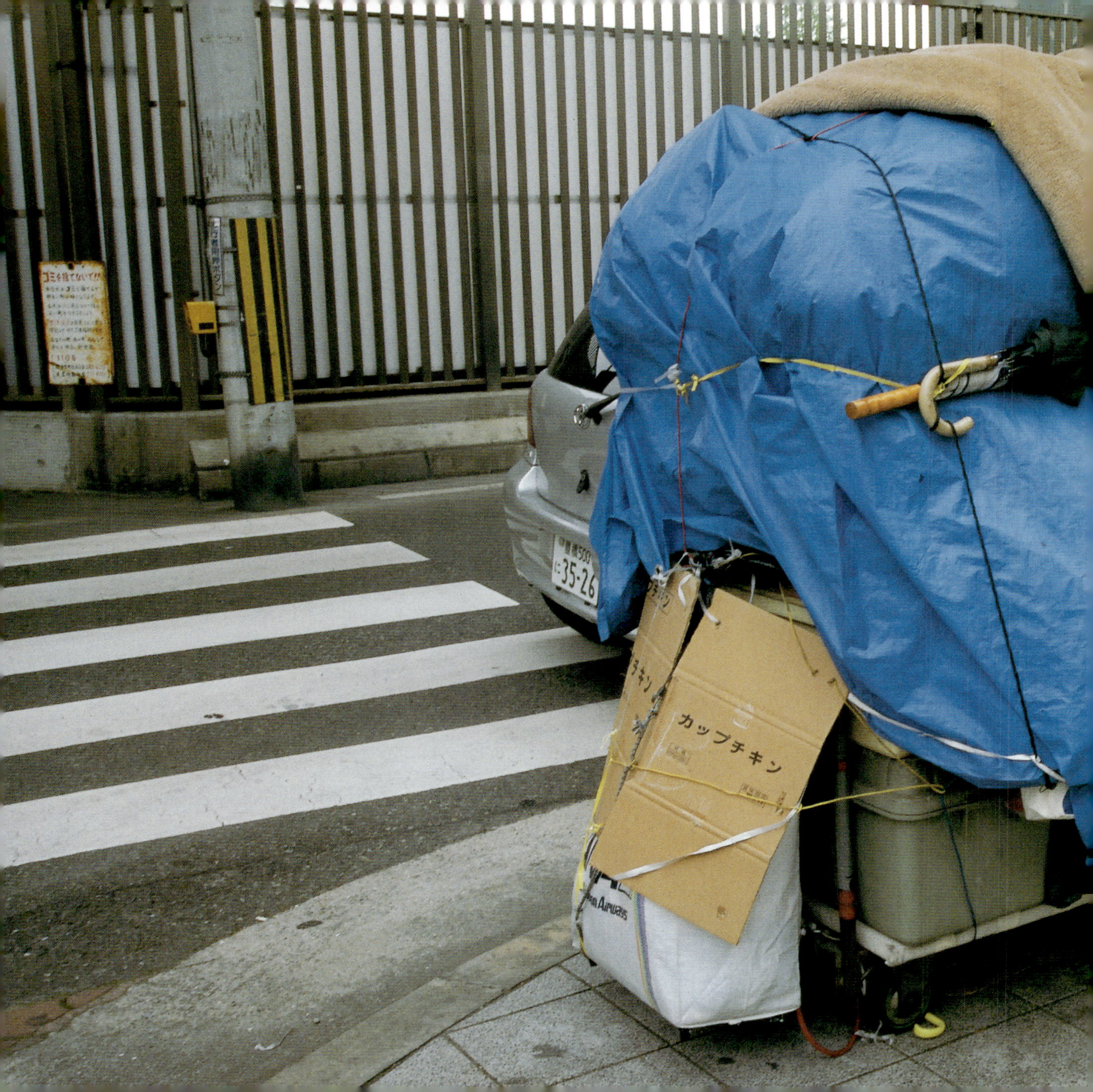
カップチキン
35-26

このカート1台に生活に必要な物すべてが収められている。

All of the daily necessities are contained in this one cart.

**A Streamlined House**
流線形の家

白いビニールシートで完全に梱包されている。屋根には、なぜか車載アンテナが見える。

This house is completely wrapped in a white vinyl sheet. For some reason there is a car antenna on the roof.

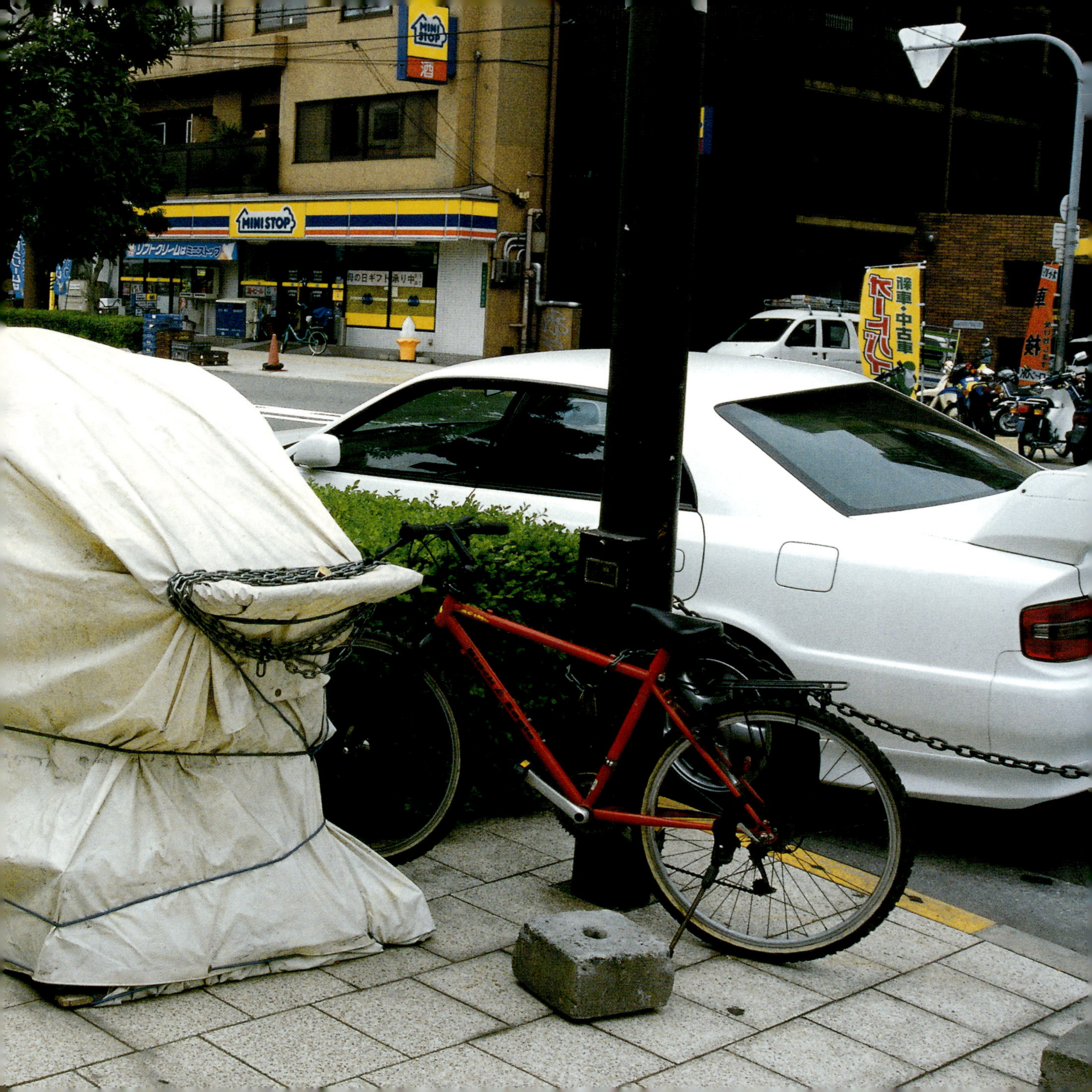
MINI STOP
酒
MINI STOP
ソフトクリームはミニストップ

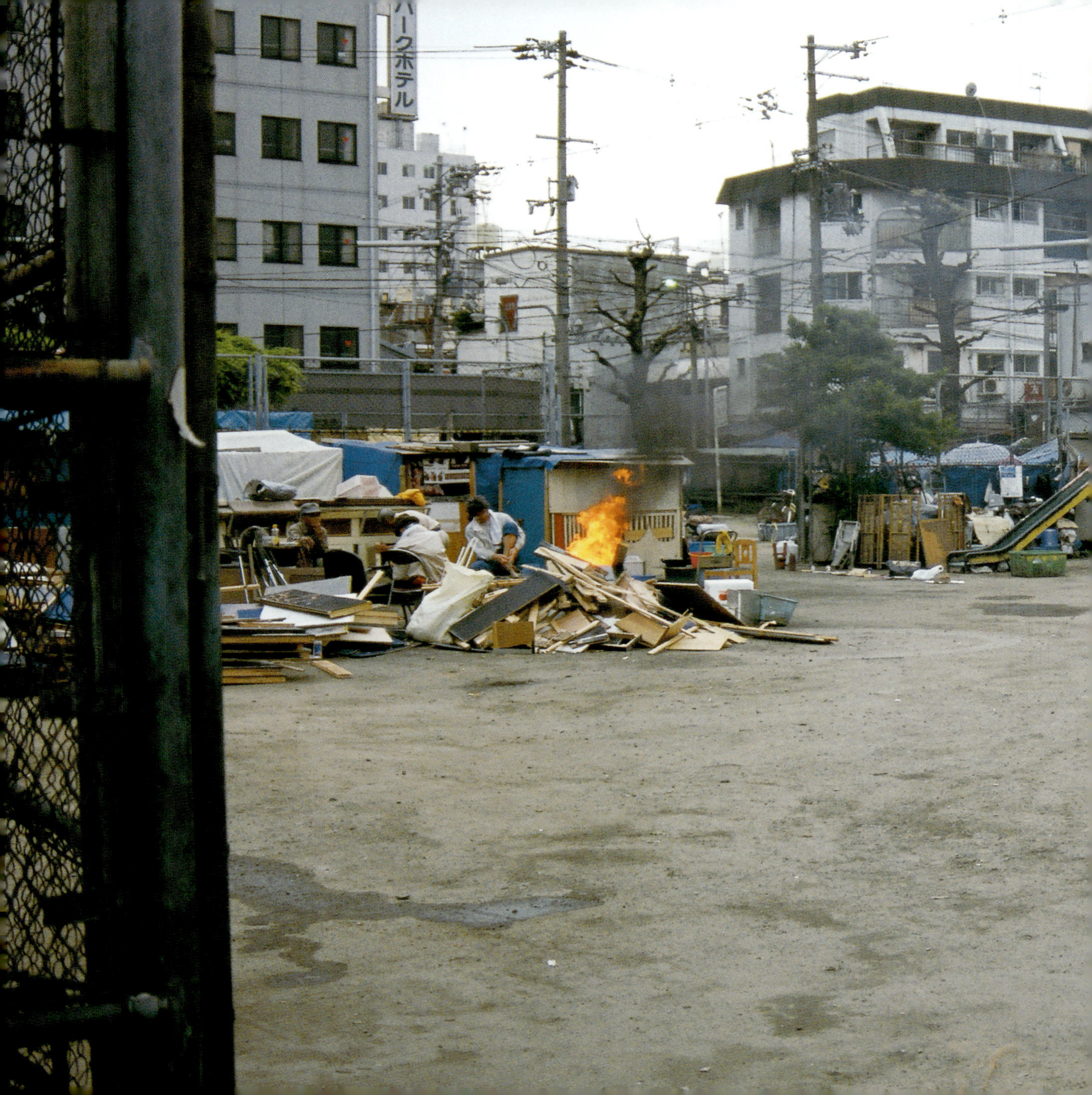
ハークホテル

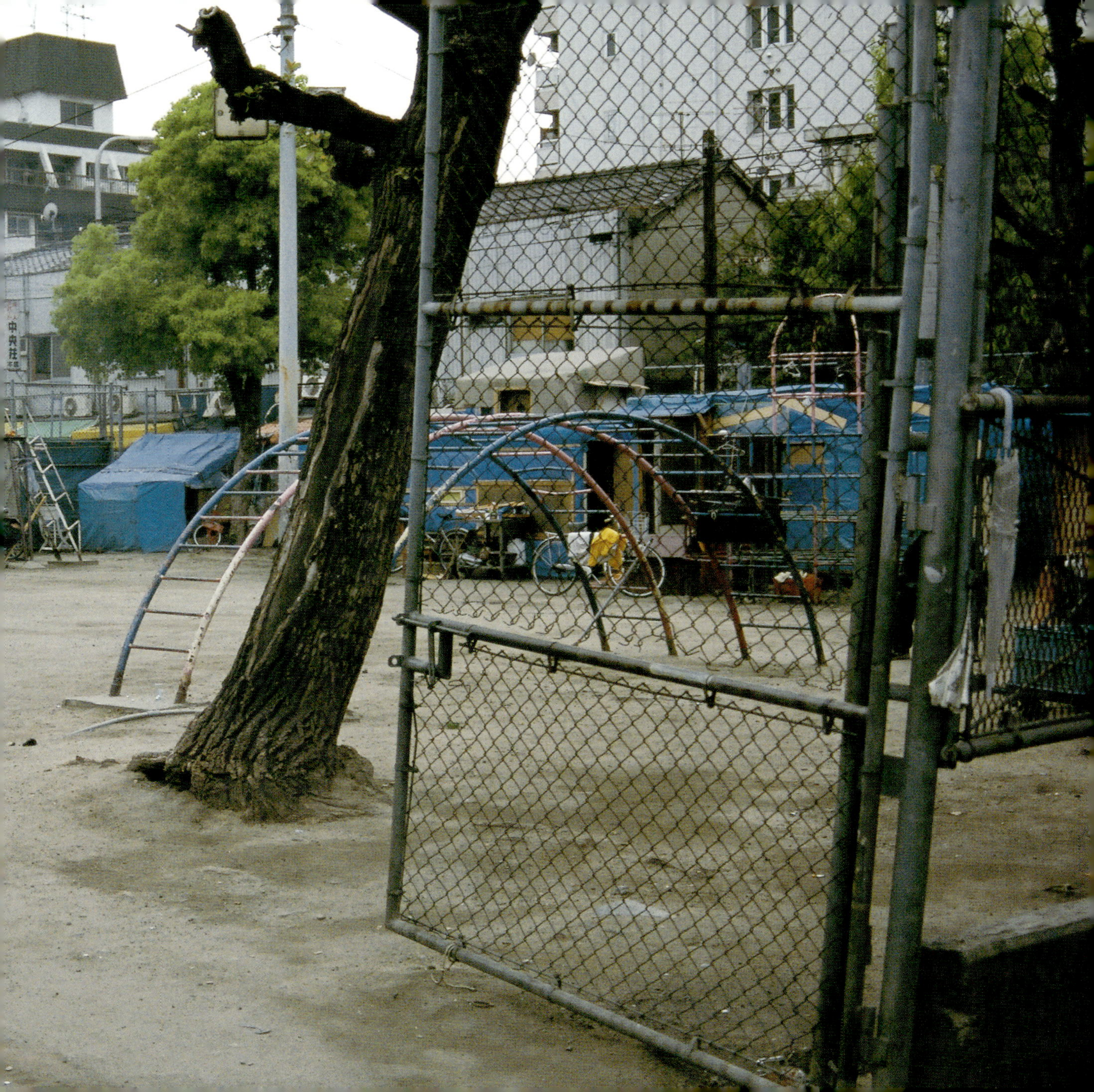
中央荘

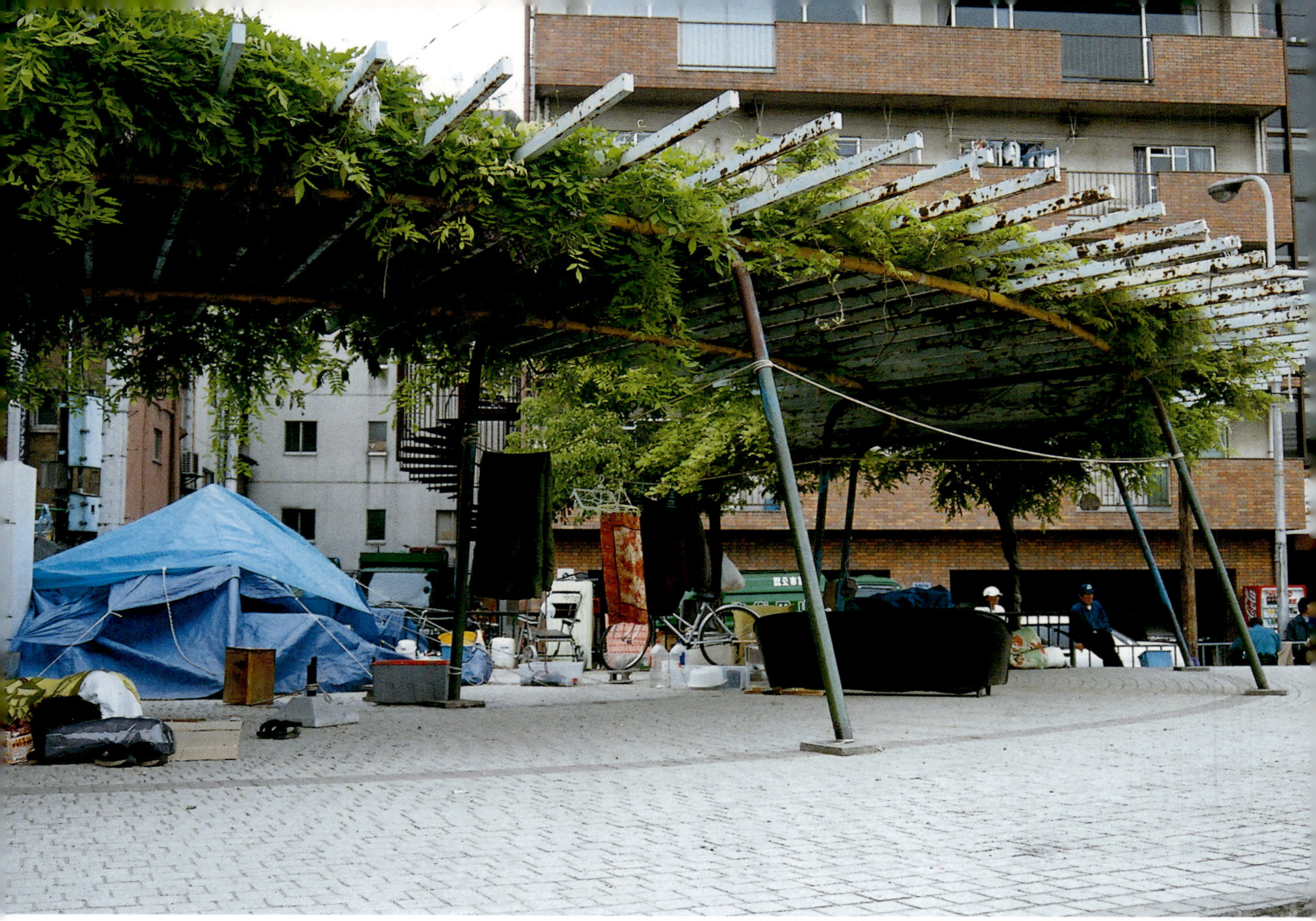

**Collective Housing**

集合住宅

円形の藤棚の下に幾つもの家が寄り添い合っている。

Here several houses are nestled close together under a round wisteria trellis.

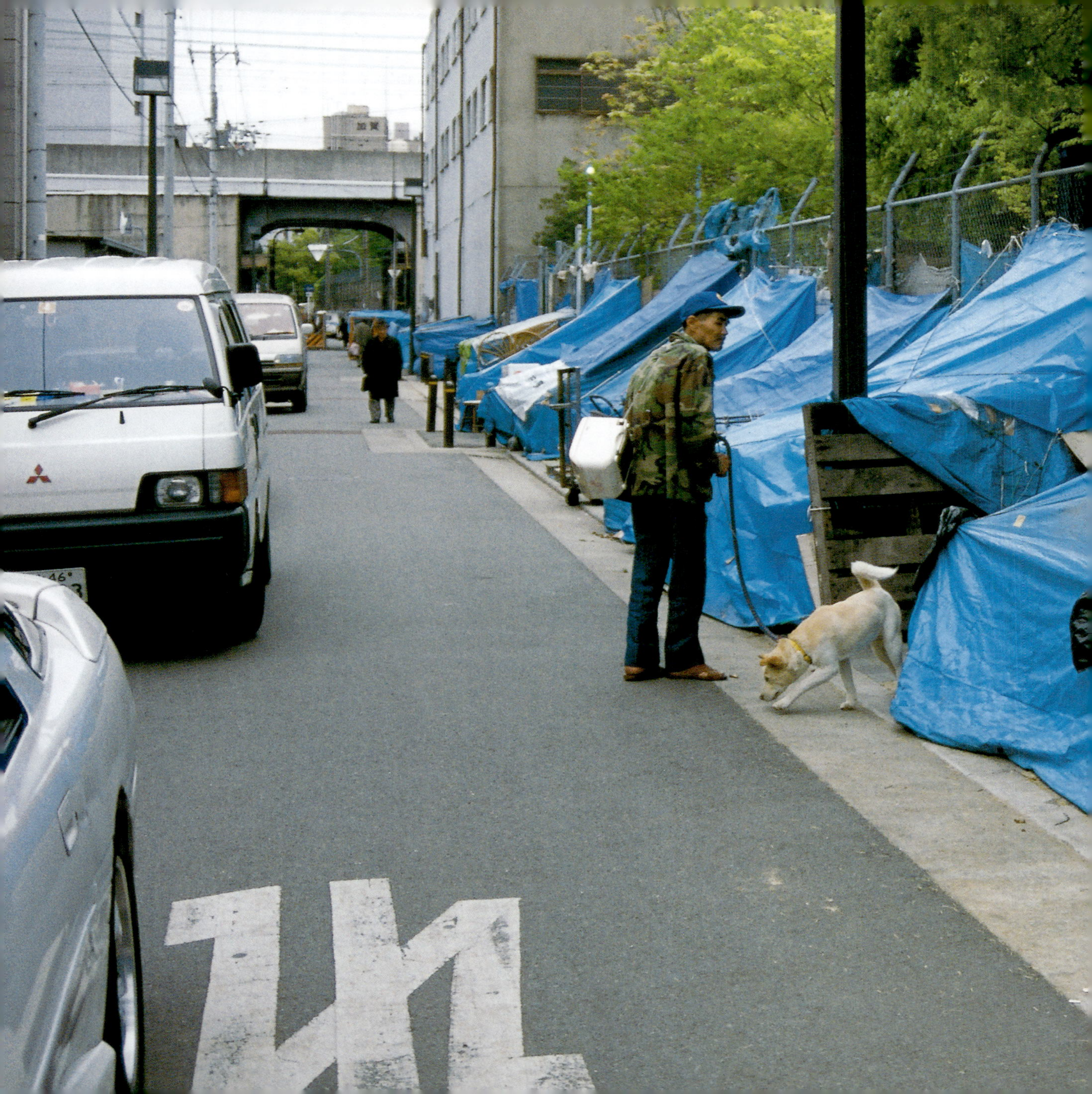

緊急車両の出
自転車等の
しないで

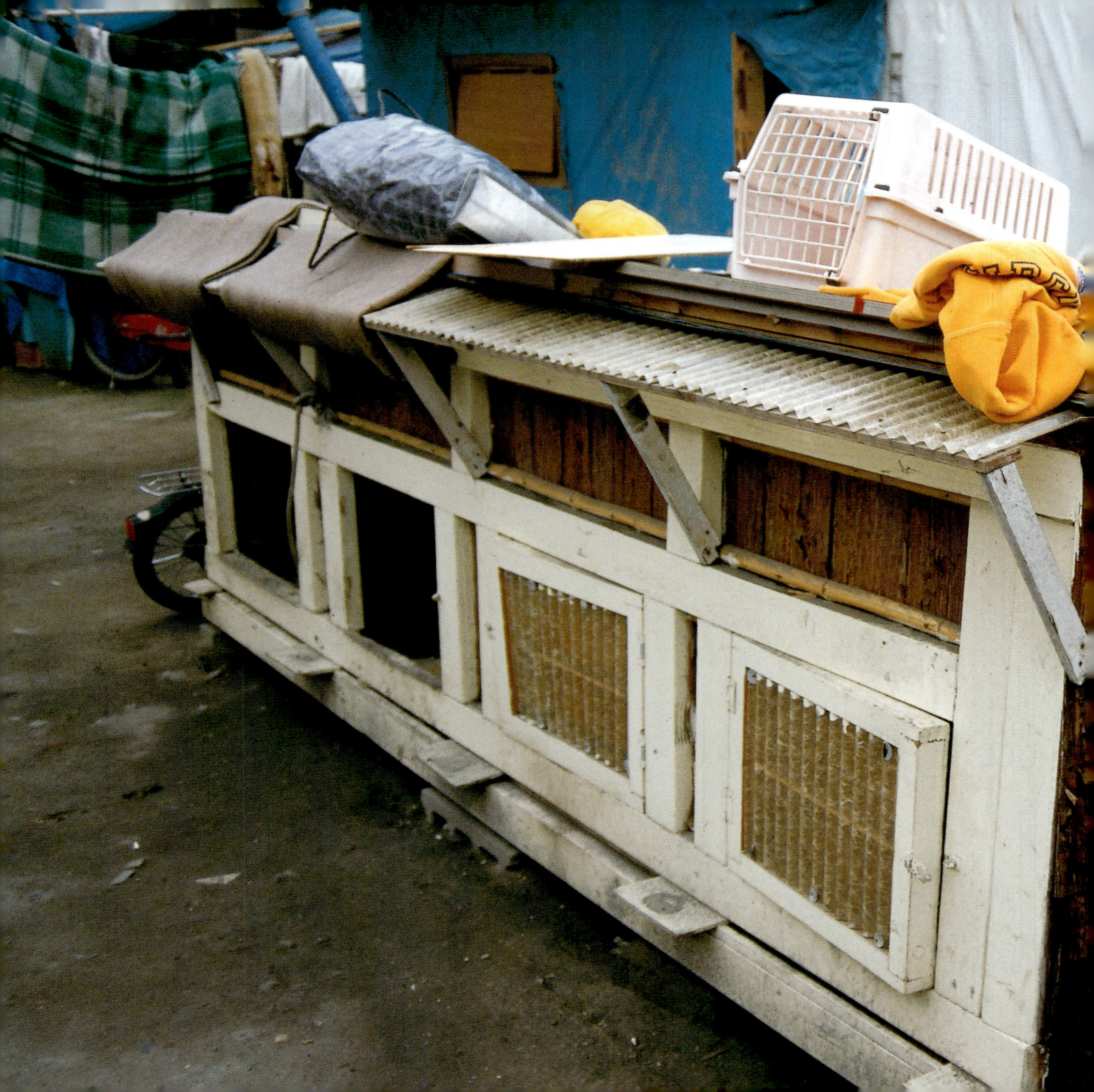

**A Doghouse**

犬小屋

4匹用の犬小屋。かなり頑丈な作りをしている。奥に見えるのは飼い主の家。

This is a doghouse for four dogs. It is quite solidly built. The house in the back belongs to their owner.

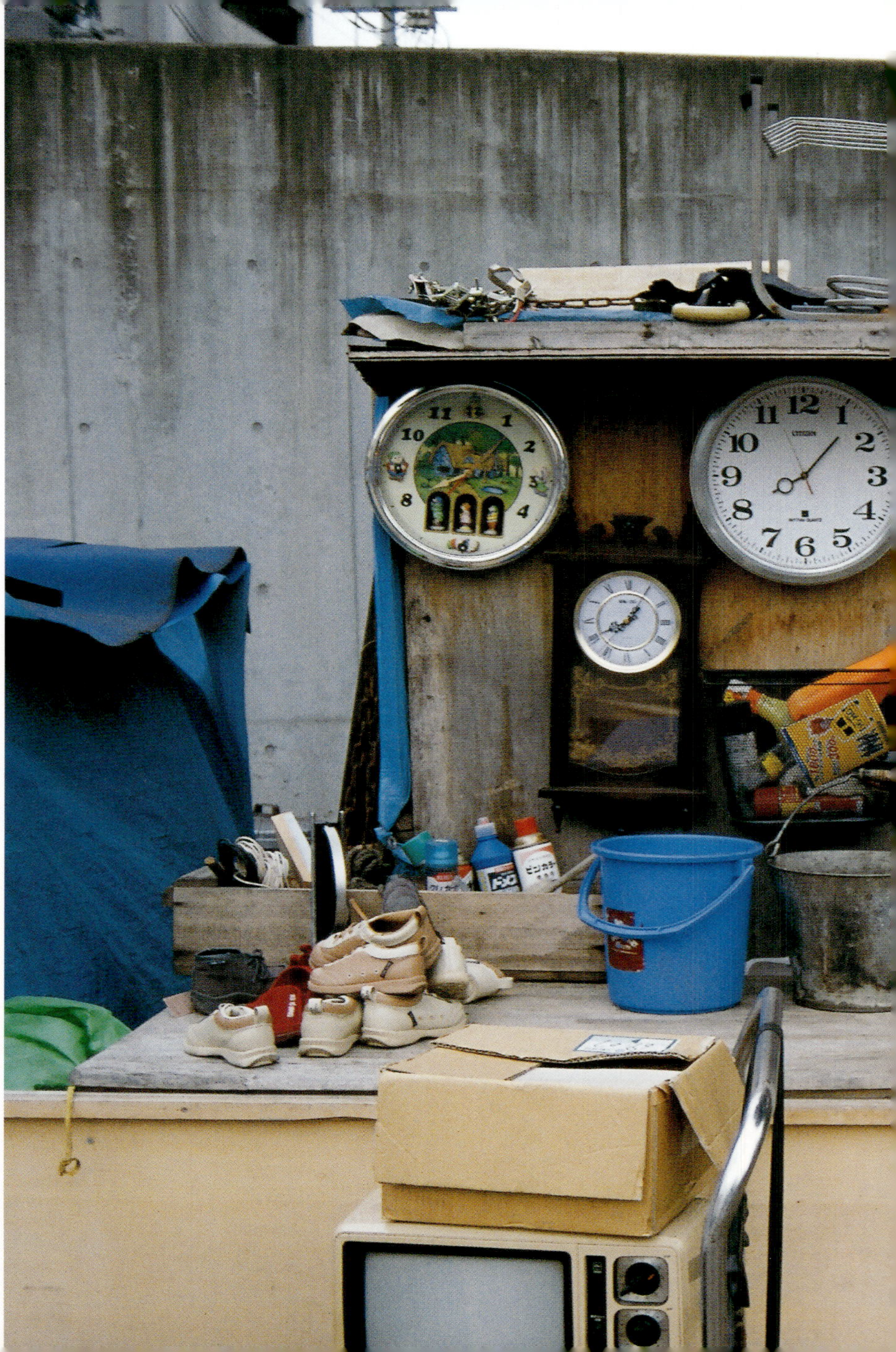

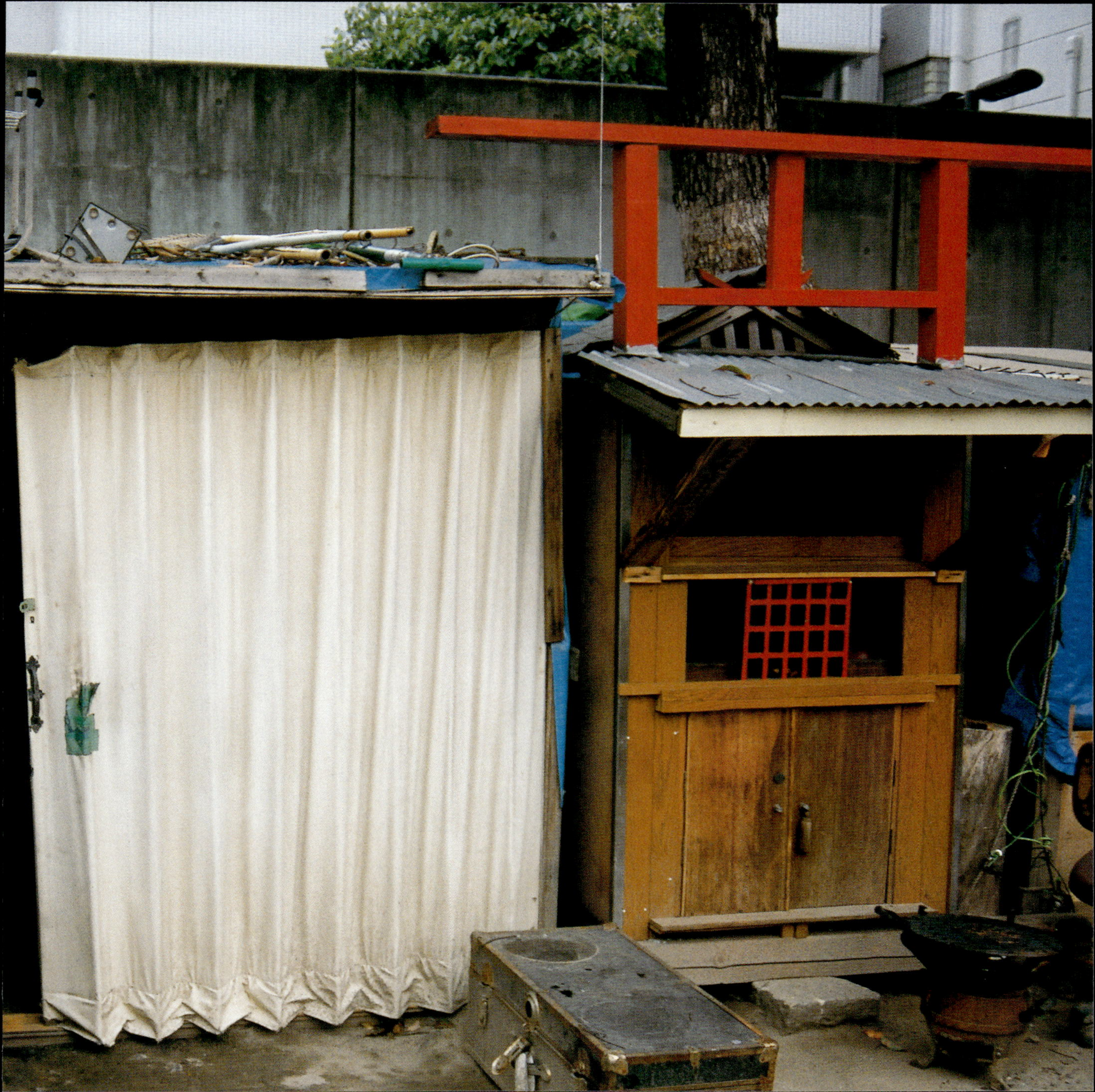

春です！フラワーポットを
近く、歩道両側に設置します
出張による各種修繕承りますので

茅ヶ崎土建機構

**The Room with a Picture of Flowers**

花の絵がある部屋

公道をリビングルームとして利用している。釜ヶ崎では、このような光景がよく見られた。

A public road is used as a living room. This sort of sight is often seen in Kamagasaki.

名古屋・大阪　2002年撮影

Nagoya and Osaka, photographs taken in 2002.

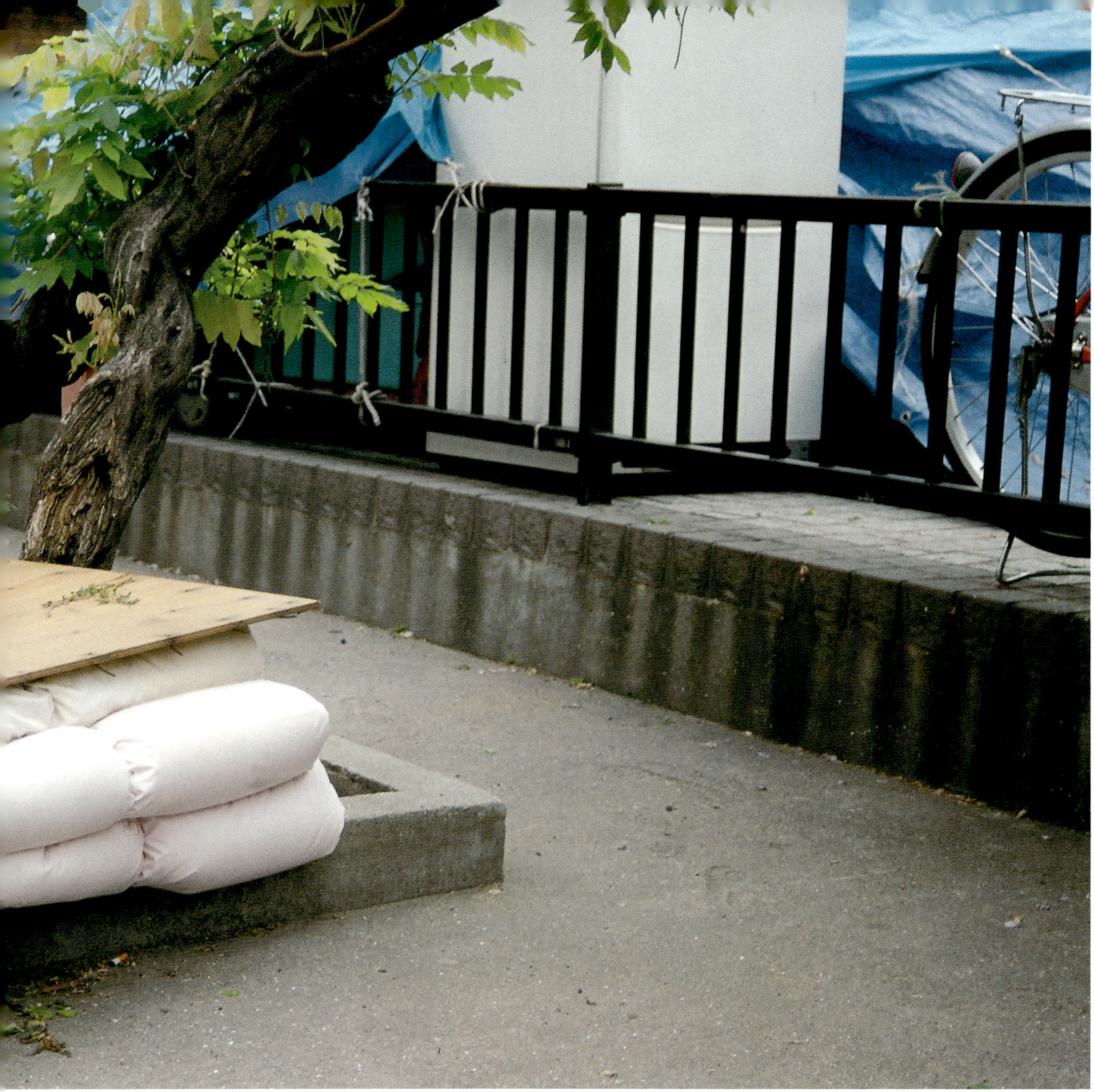

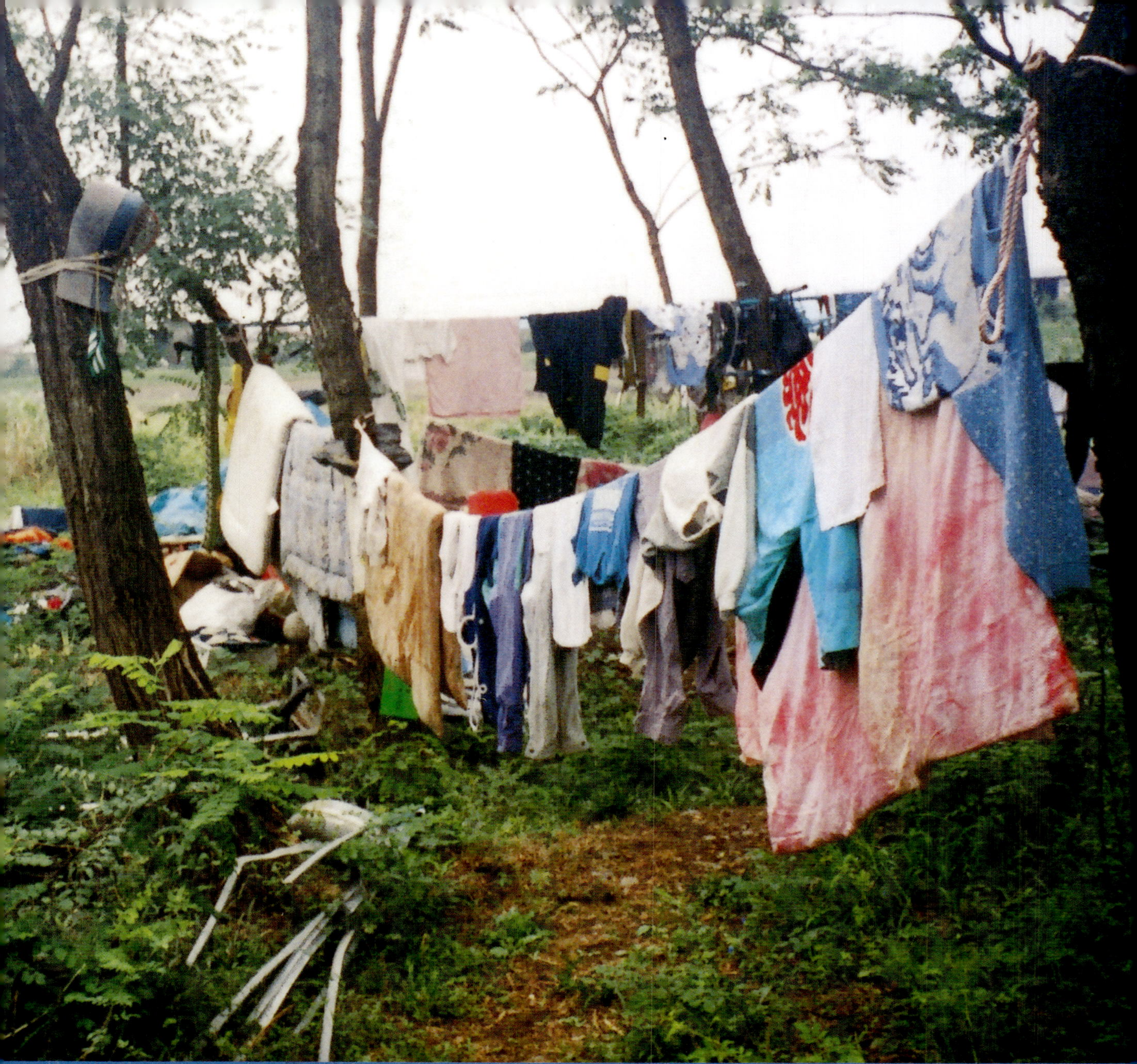

# The Tamagawa
# 多摩川

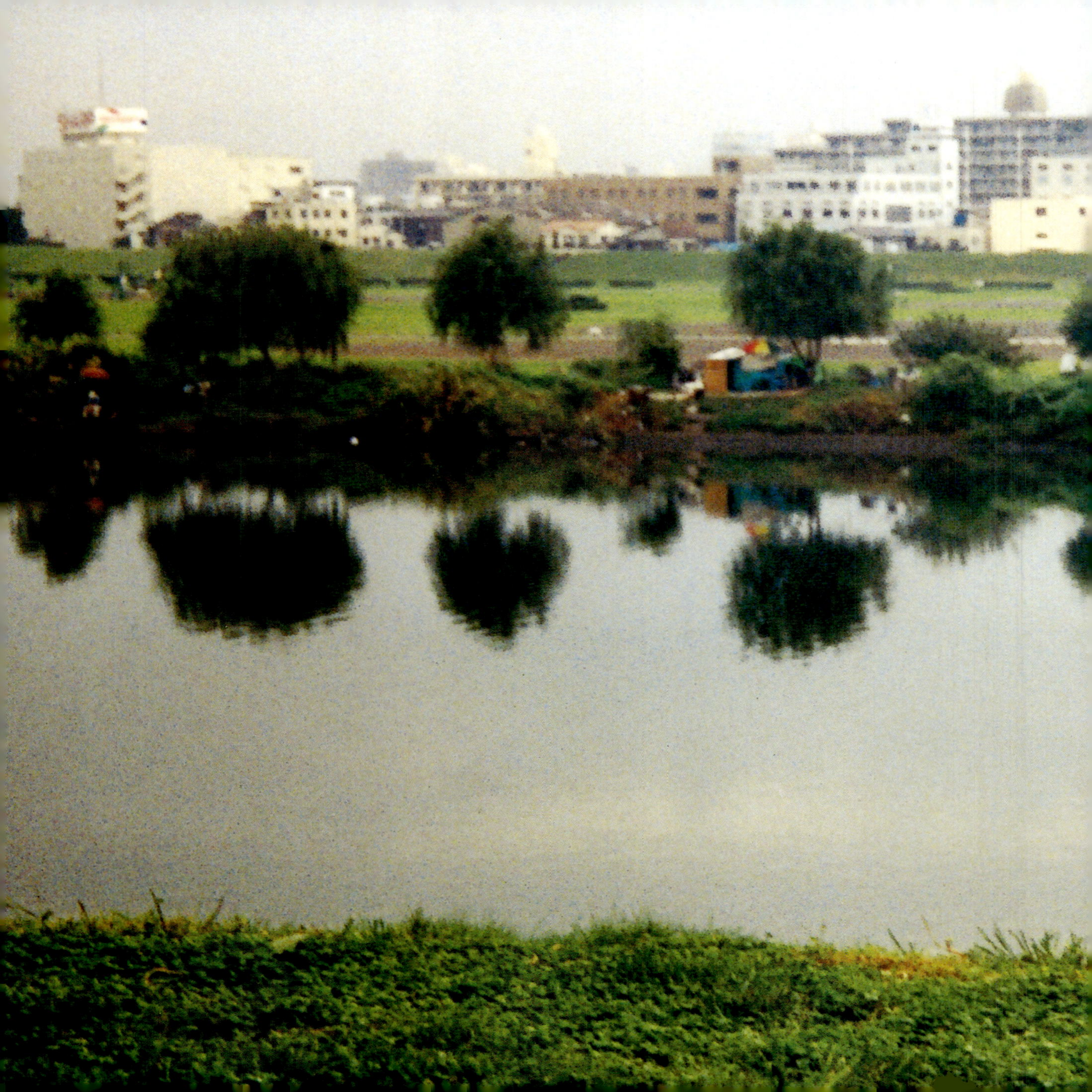

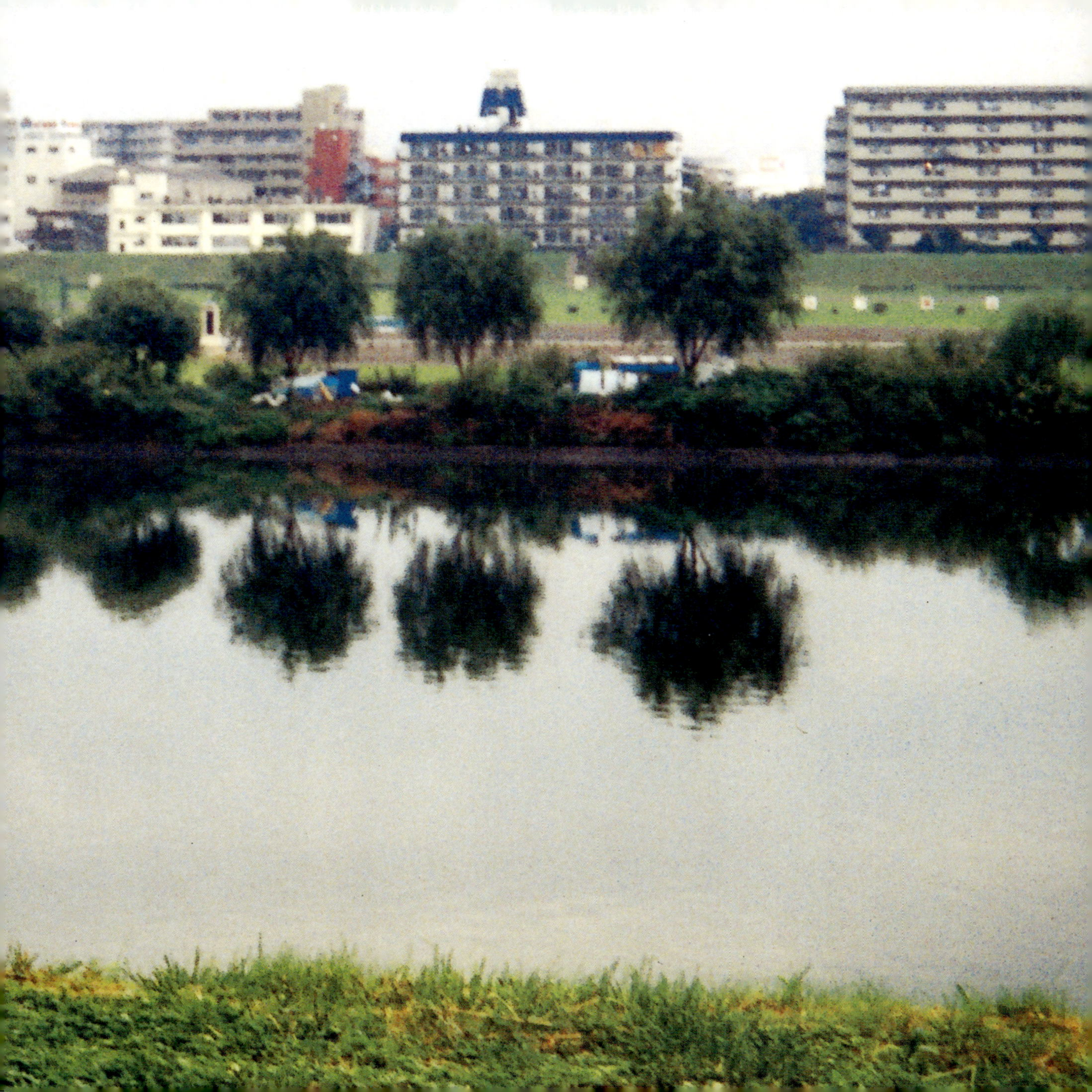

## The Growing House
## 巨大化する家

第3京浜が通る橋の下に建つ巨大な建造物。その姿はビニールシート・ハウスという言葉から程遠い。単管パイプで組み立てられた2階建ての家で、50代の男性が一人暮らししている。驚くべきことにコンクリートで基礎を作っている。多摩川が洪水になった時は、1階部分はほとんど浸水したが、家自体はびくともしなかったそうだ。1階が倉庫で2階が居間になっている。周辺は、拾ってきた廃品で埋め尽くされている。その量は止まることなく増え続け、彼の家は巨大化していく。

This enormous house stands under the Daisan Keihin Expressway Bridge over the Tamagawa River. It is a far cry from the typical houses of blue plastic sheets. A man in his fifties lives alone in the two-story house constructed with single pipes and, surprisingly, on a concrete foundation. When the Tamagawa River flooded, the man says, the first floor was almost inundated, the house itself was completely undamaged. The first floor is for storage and the second floor is a living room. The house is surrounded by discarded items he has collected. As the number of items increases, his house continues to grow.

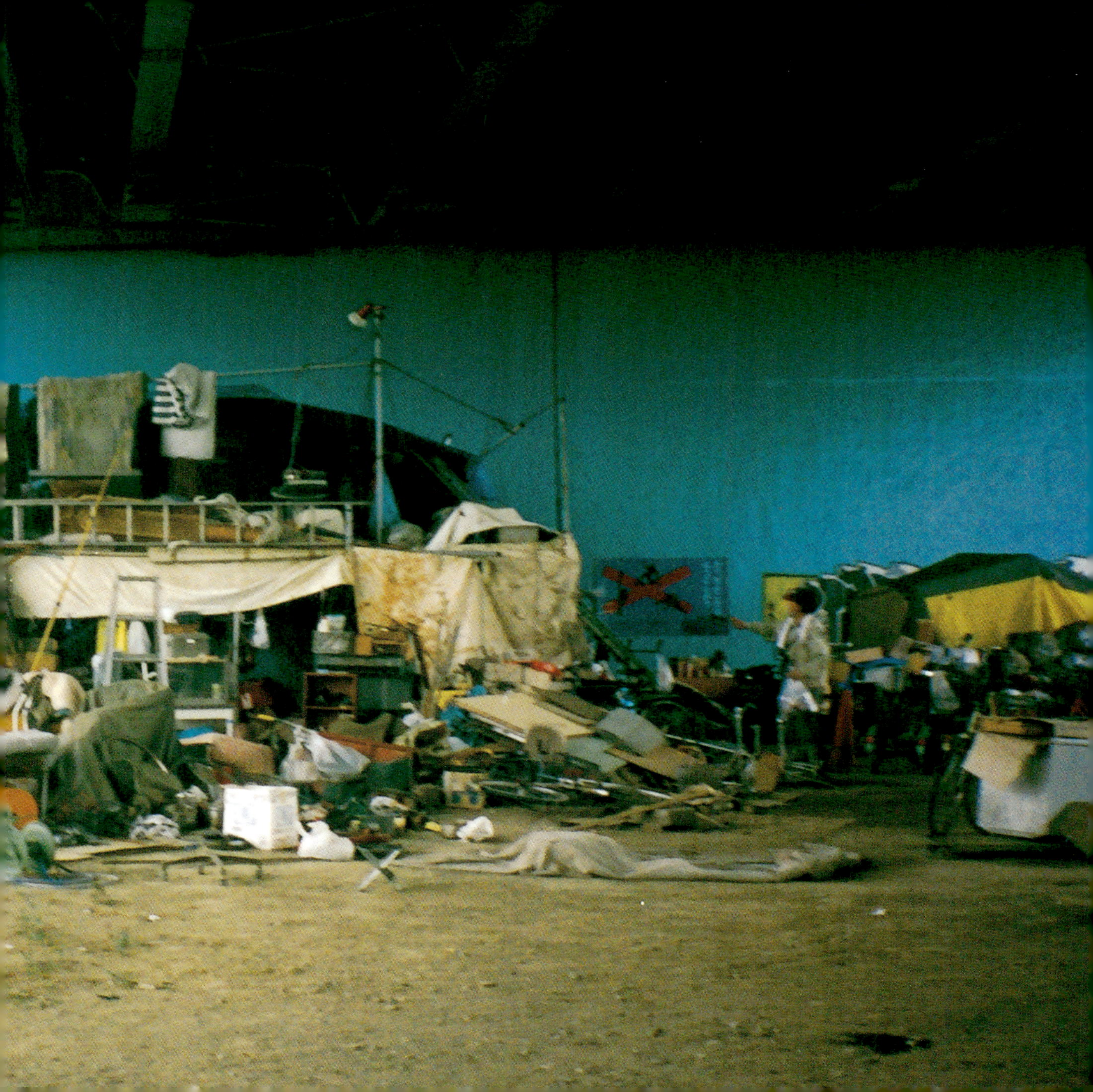

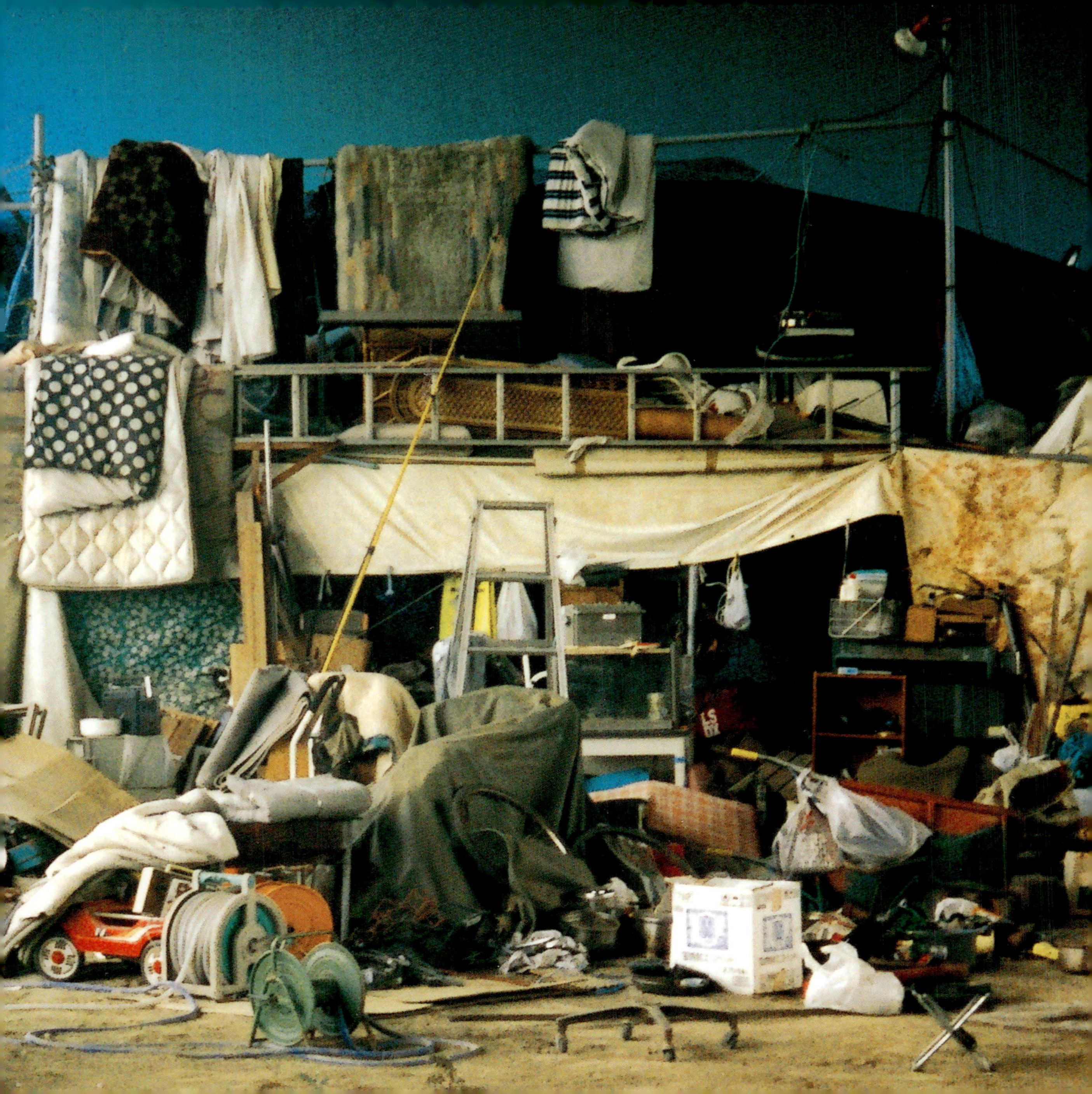

黄色いテントは"離れ"。積み上げられた袋の中には収入源となるアルミ缶が入っている。この場所は台所として使われている。

The yellow tent is an "annex". The piled up bags contain the aluminum cans that are his source of income. This area is used as a kitchen.

二階部分

Second Floor

## A Rising-Sun Waving House
### 日の丸が揺れる家

五重塔、金のシャチホコ、NTT DoCoMoのジャンパー、自由の女神の仮面、ライフジャケットなどが無秩序に並べられている。日本国旗が知らない国の旗にみえてくる。

A five-story pagoda, a golden *shachihoko* (a fabled fish with a lionlike head and an arched tail that points skyward), an NTT DoCoMo jacket, a mask of the Statue of Liberty, a life jacket... All of these items are lined up at random. Here the Japanese flag looks like the flag of some unknown country.

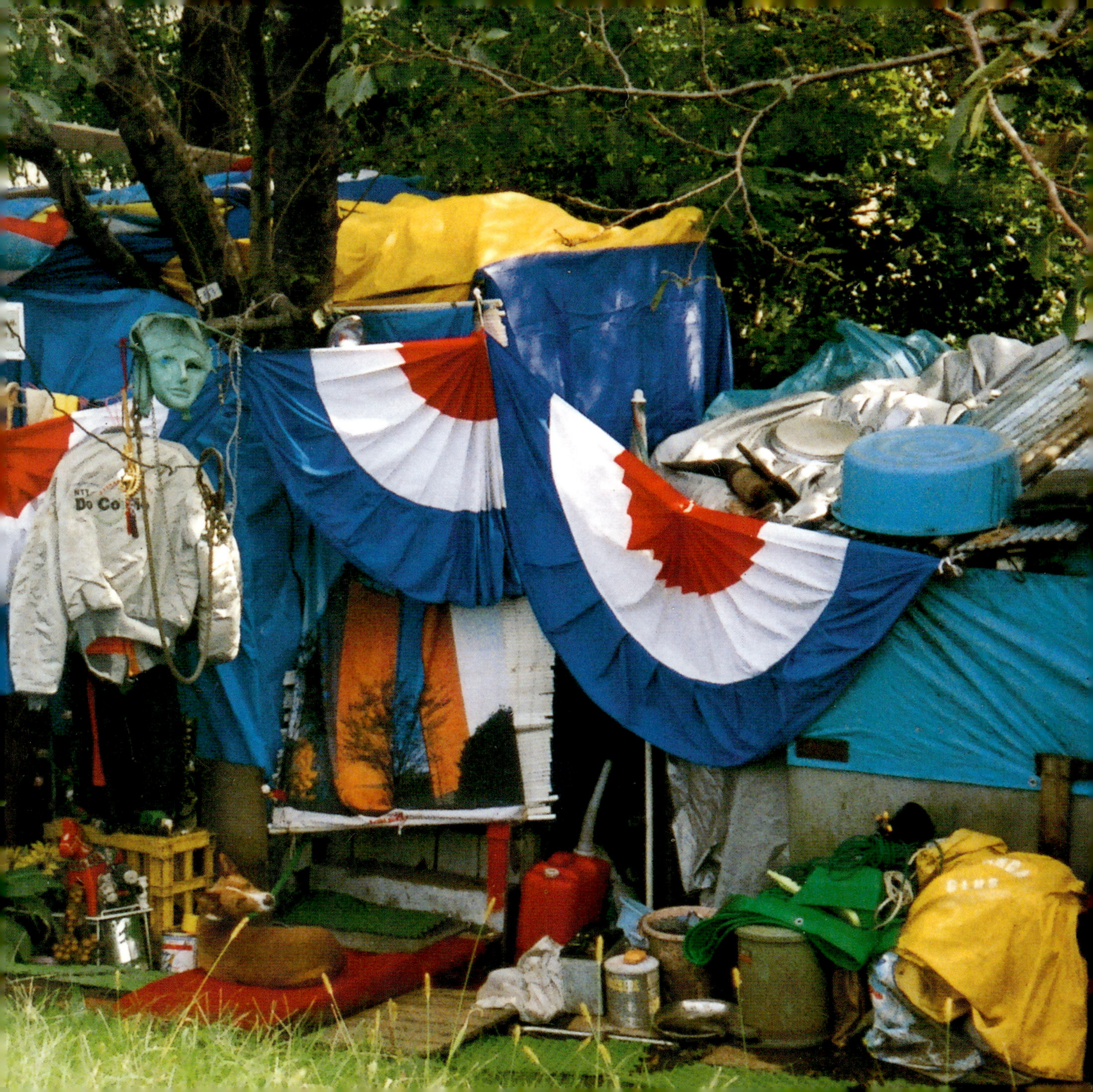

## A Neighborhood Association President's House
## 町内会長の家

多摩川河口から5キロほど上流にある。もはや普通の一戸建ての住まいである。屋根、柱、壁はすべて木材で作られている。窓にはアルミサッシが取り付けられている。ここに住んでいる50代の男性は1994年に、持っていた4万円と友人から借りた3万円の計7万円でこの家を作った。部屋は1畳ほどの物置きと4畳半ほどの和室が1つ。床にはカーペットが敷かれ、冬でもさほど寒くないという。丈夫な家構えのためか、よく近隣の住人たちが暖をとりに来るそうだ。そのうち、なにか困ったことがあったらこの男性の家に駆け込むようになった。"まるで町内会長だよ"と彼は言う。内壁は拾ってきたペンキで白く塗られており、狭い中でも自分の空間を演出し、快適に暮らしている。また、小銭を貯めては絵具を買い、少しずつだが絵を描き続けている。彼はわずか7万円でこの生活を手に入れたのである。

This house is located 5 kilometers from the mouth of the Tamagawa River. With a roof, pillars and walls all made of wood and a window with an aluminum sash, it is just like any ordinary house. A man in his fifties lives here. In 1994, with 40 thousand yen of his own and 30 thousand yen from a friend, he built the house. It consists of a storeroom of one mat in size and a four-and-a-half mat Japanese-style room. He says that the carpet keeps the room from getting very cold in the winter. Maybe because the house is so durable, neighbors often stop by to warm themselves. Over time, they also started seeking refuge at his house when they got into trouble. "I'm like a neighborhood association president," he says. Although space is limited, he controls it well in order to live comfortably. The inner walls are painted white with paint he found. Little by little he continues to paint pictures by saving change to buy the colors. For a mere 70 thousand yen he was able to achieve this life.

**A Morning Glory Wall**
朝顔の塀

物干ザオを組み合わせたものに朝顔のツルをからませている。住宅街の閉鎖的なコンクリート塀とはあまりにも対照的である。

Morning glories are trained up over the joined laundry pole, which is quite a contrast to the closed concrete wall of a residential district.

**A Signboard House**

看板の家

看板を壁がわりに利用して家を作っている。看板の裏面の木枠が家に表情を与えている。

This house was built using signboards as walls. The wooden frames of the back of the signboards give the house expression.

## An Ex-Cook's Kitchen
## 元板前さんのキッチン

多摩川河口そばにあるこの家は一見、普通のビニールシートハウスであるが、中に入ってみると部屋は本格的な作りになっている。4畳半1間で床にはゴザが敷いてあり、とても清潔感のある部屋である。住人は元板前の男性。部屋の一角を占める台所がそれを物語っている。ガスコンロに、包丁、フライパン、魚焼き器などが完備されている。調味料もそろっているため大抵の料理ならここで作ることができる。電気の設備も万全である。電気はバッテリーを利用していて、切れると近くの自転車屋で充電してもらうそうだ。

At first glance, this house near the mouth of the Tamagawa River looks like a typical blue plastic sheet house. One look inside, however, reveals a normal room of four-and-a-half mats in size. There is a rush mat spread out over the floor and the room is very clean. Its male inhabitant is an ex-cook and the kitchen that occupies one corner of the room tells that story. The kitchen is equipped with a gas range, kitchen knives, a frying pan, a fish grill, etc. And the full set of spices would allow for the preparation of almost any dish. Electricity is also available. When the battery he uses runs out, he takes it to a nearby bicycle shop to get recharged.

ご購読ありがとうございました。
今後の資料とさせていただきますので
アンケートにご協力をお願いいたします。

# voice

お買い上げの書名

ご購入書店
　　　　　　　　　　　　市・区・町・村　　　　　　　　　　書店

本書をお求めになった動機は何ですか。
　□新聞・雑誌などの書評記事を見て（媒体名　　　　　　　　　　　　）
　□新聞・雑誌などの広告を見て
　□友人からすすめられて
　□店頭で見て
　□ホームページを見て
　□著者のファンだから
　□その他（　　　　　　　　　　　　　　　　　　　　　　　　　　）
最近購入された本は何ですか。（書名　　　　　　　　　　　　　　　）

本書についてのご感想をお聞かせ下されば、うれしく思います。
小社へのご意見・ご要望などもお書き下さい。

ご協力ありがとうございました。

読者ハガキ

おそれ入りますが、切手をお貼り下さい。

## 151-0051
### 東京都渋谷区千駄ヶ谷3-56-6

(株)リトルモア 行

# Little More

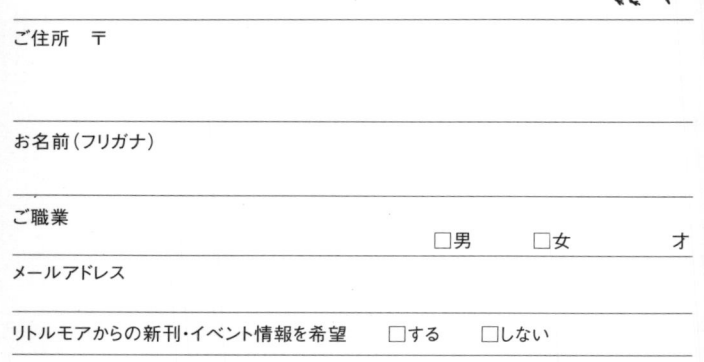

---

ご住所 〒

---

お名前(フリガナ)

---

ご職業
　　　　　　　　　　　　□男　　□女　　　　オ

メールアドレス

---

リトルモアからの新刊・イベント情報を希望　　□する　　□しない

※ご記入いただきました個人情報は、所定の目的以外には使用しません。

---

小社の本は全国どこの書店からもお取り寄せが可能です。

[Little More WEB オンラインストア]でもすべての書籍がご購入頂けます。

# http://www.littlemore.co.jp/

クレジットカード、代金引換がご利用になれます。
税込1,500円以上のお買い上げで送料(300円)が無料になります。
但し、代金引換をご利用の場合、別途、代引手数料がかかります。

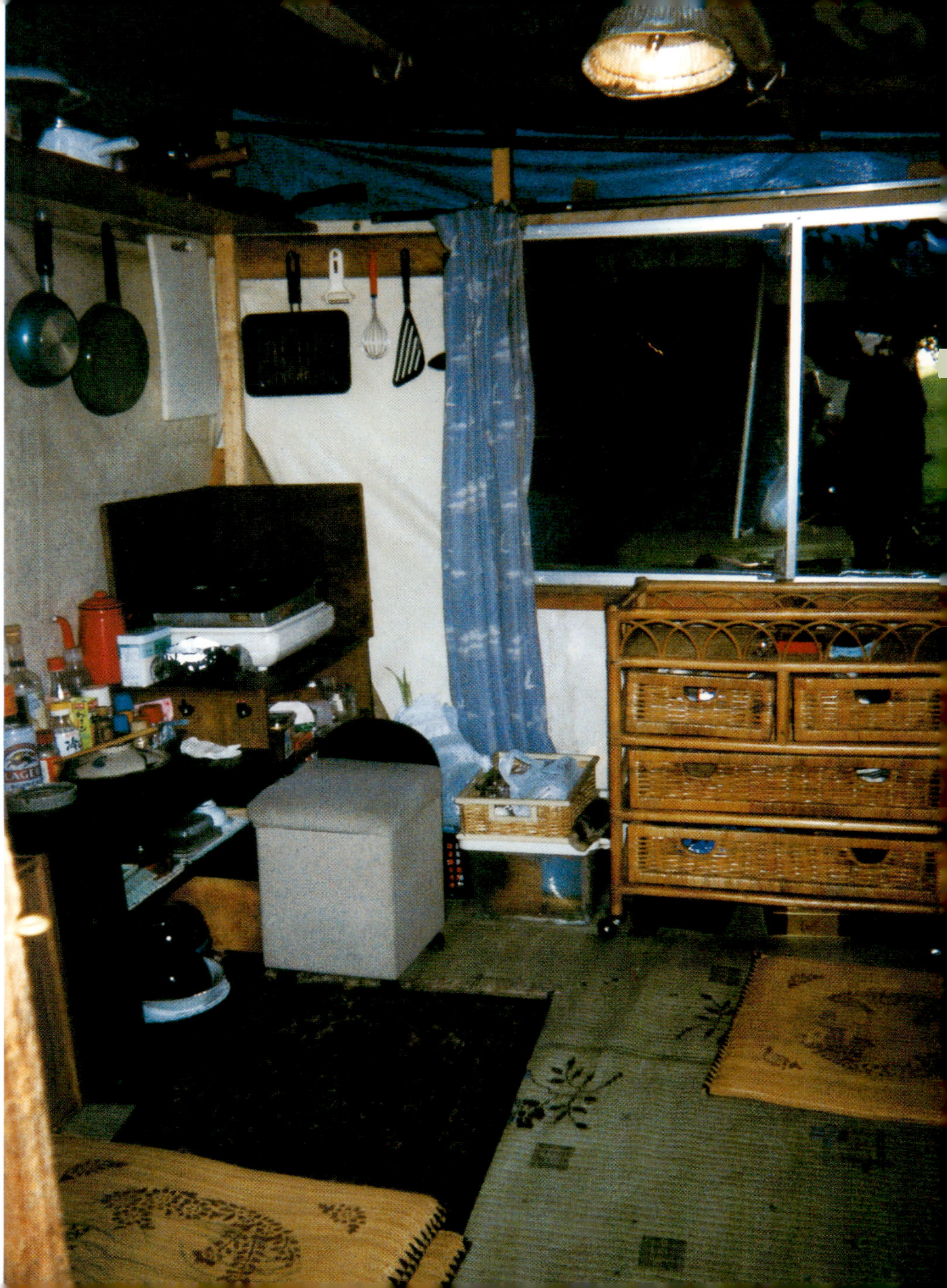

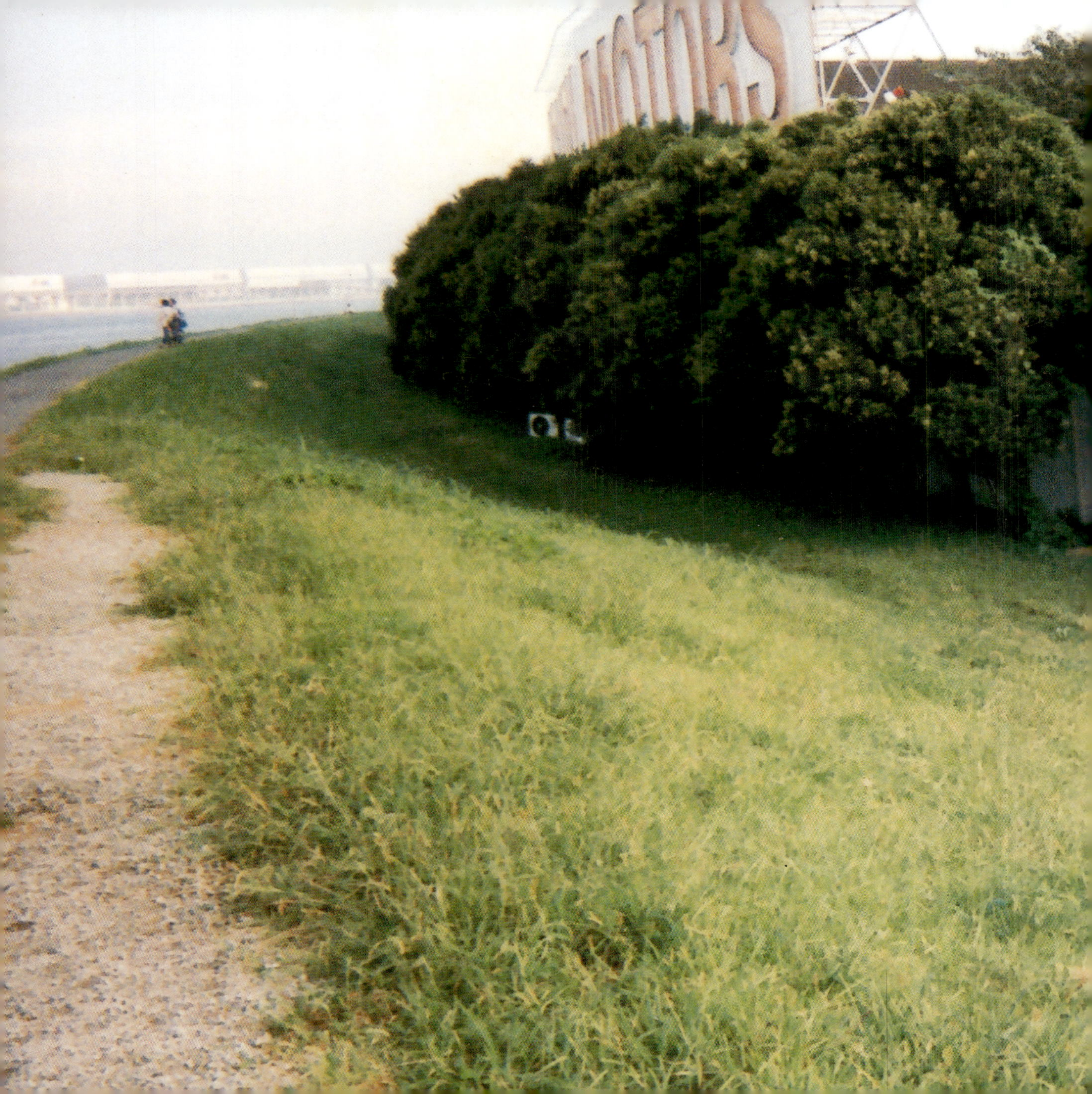
MOTORS

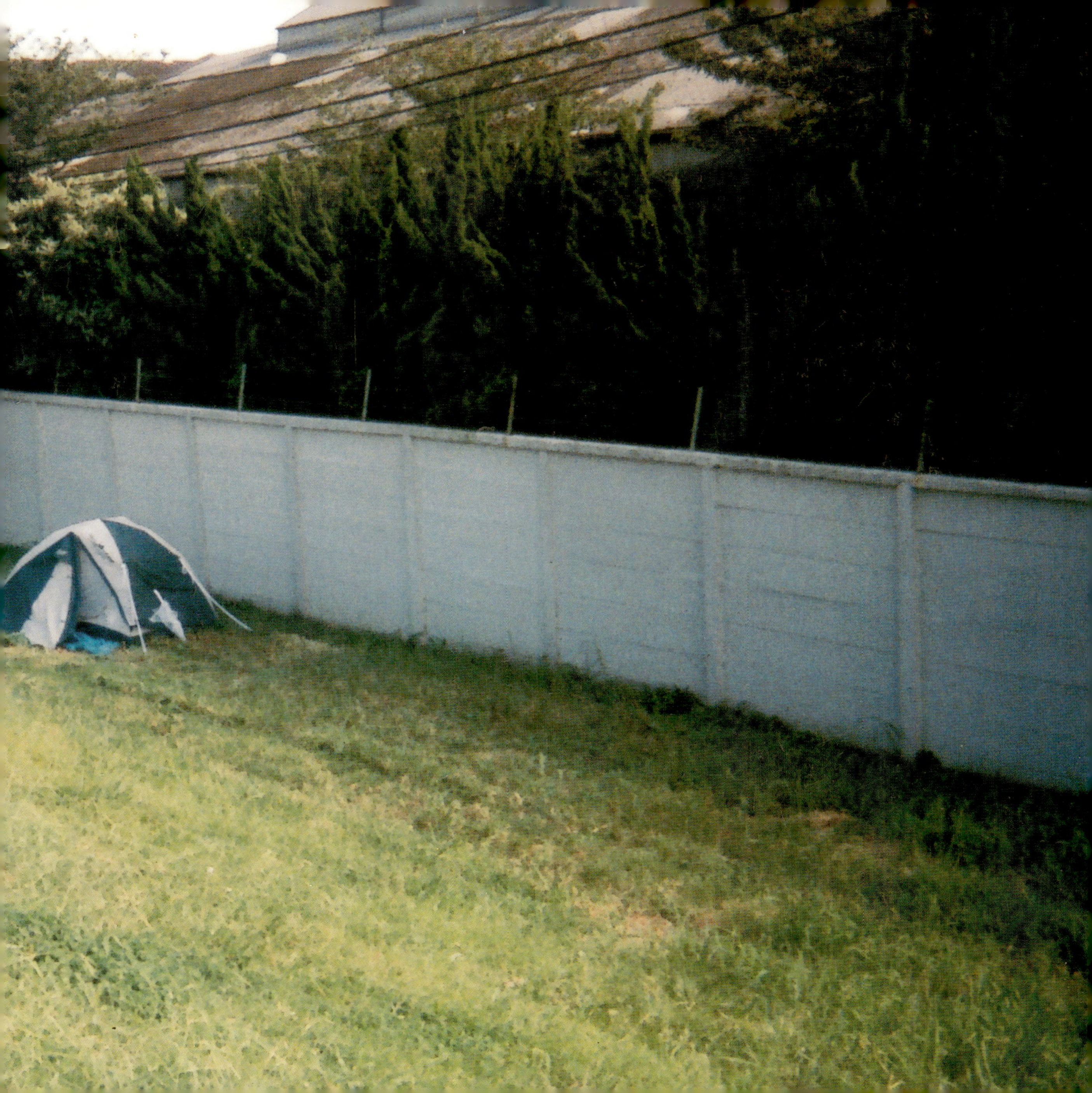

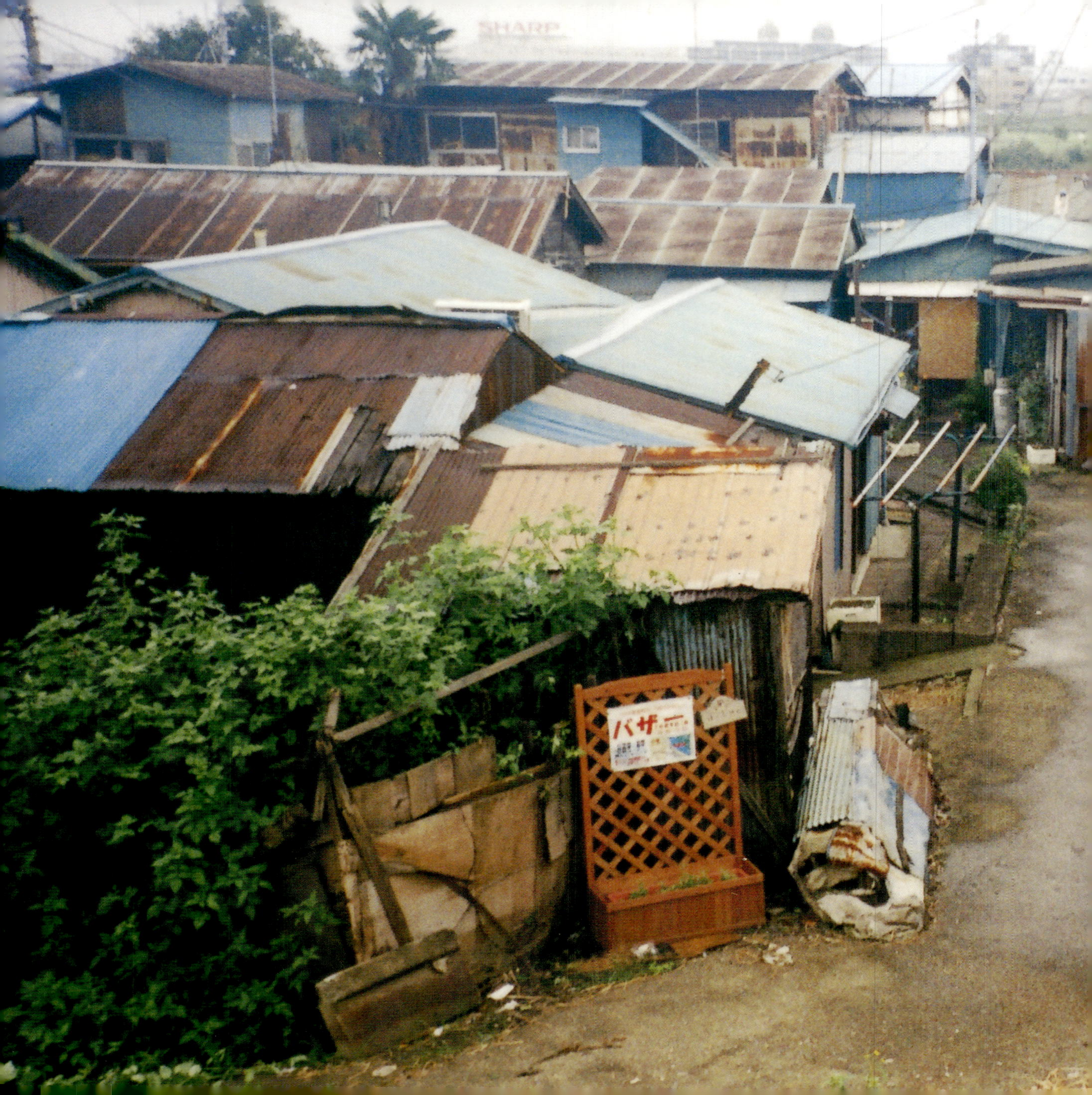
SHARP
バザー

### Asia Along the Tamagawa
多摩川のアジア

多摩川のすぐ横にあるこの住居群には、韓国、中国、その他さまざまな国籍の人々が生活している。密集した家々の間をぬって狭い路地が通っている。話を聞いた女性は1965年からここに住み続けているそうだ。

People of a variety of nationalities, including Korean and Chinese, live in this cluster of houses on the Tamagawa River. Narrow alleys snake through the densely built-up houses. A woman I spoke to said she has lived here since 1965.

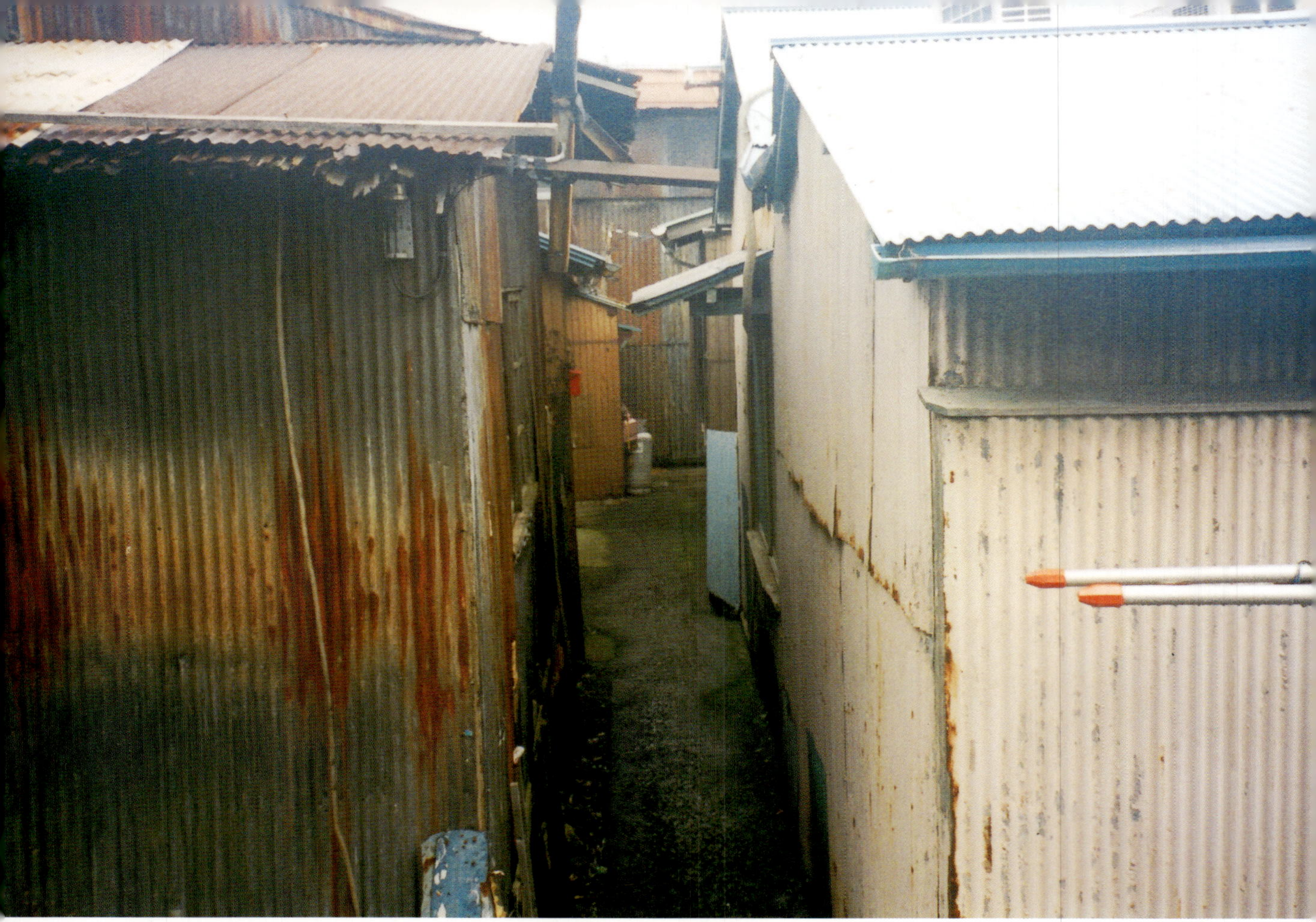

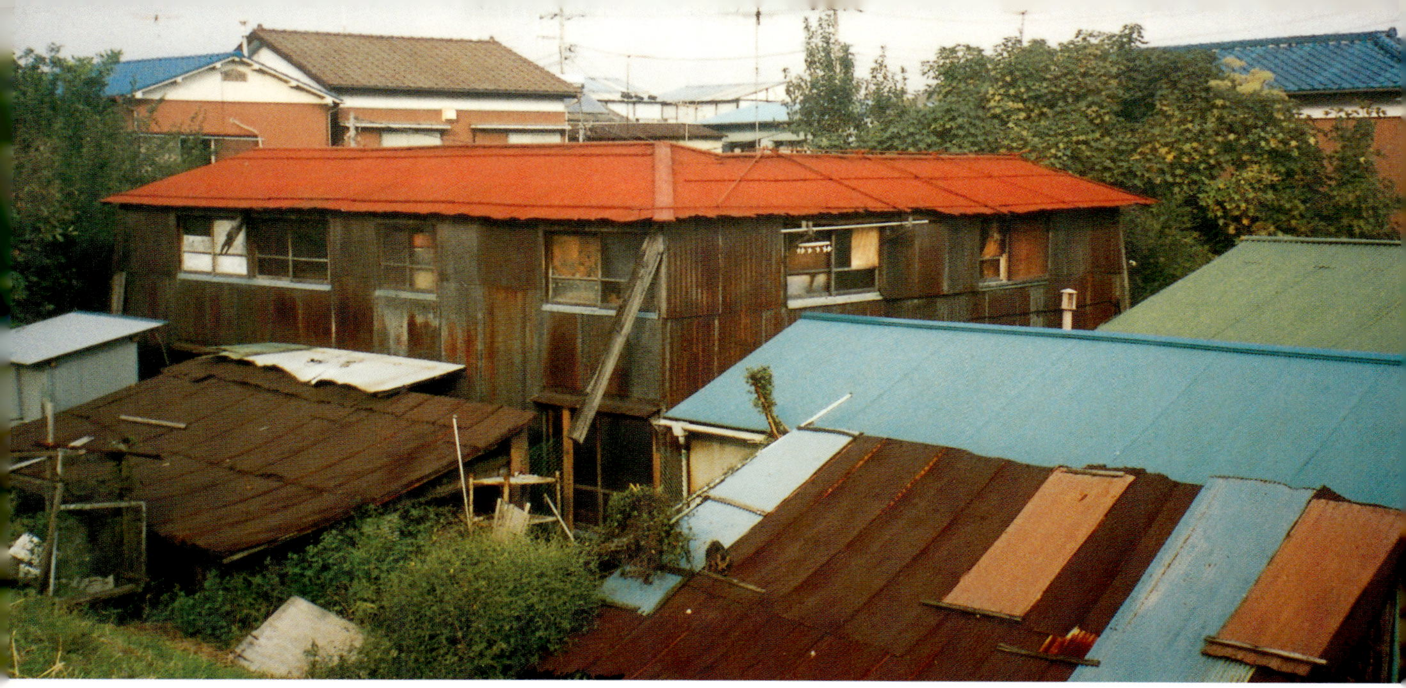

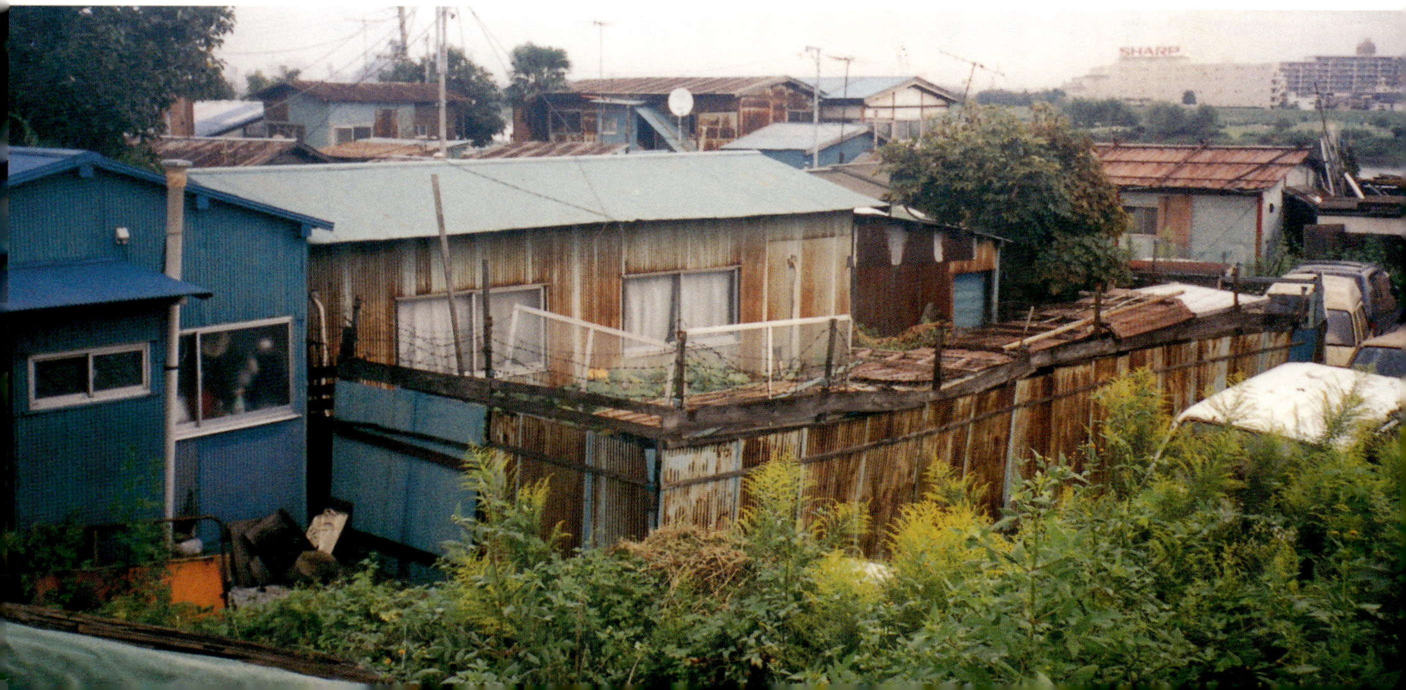
SHARP

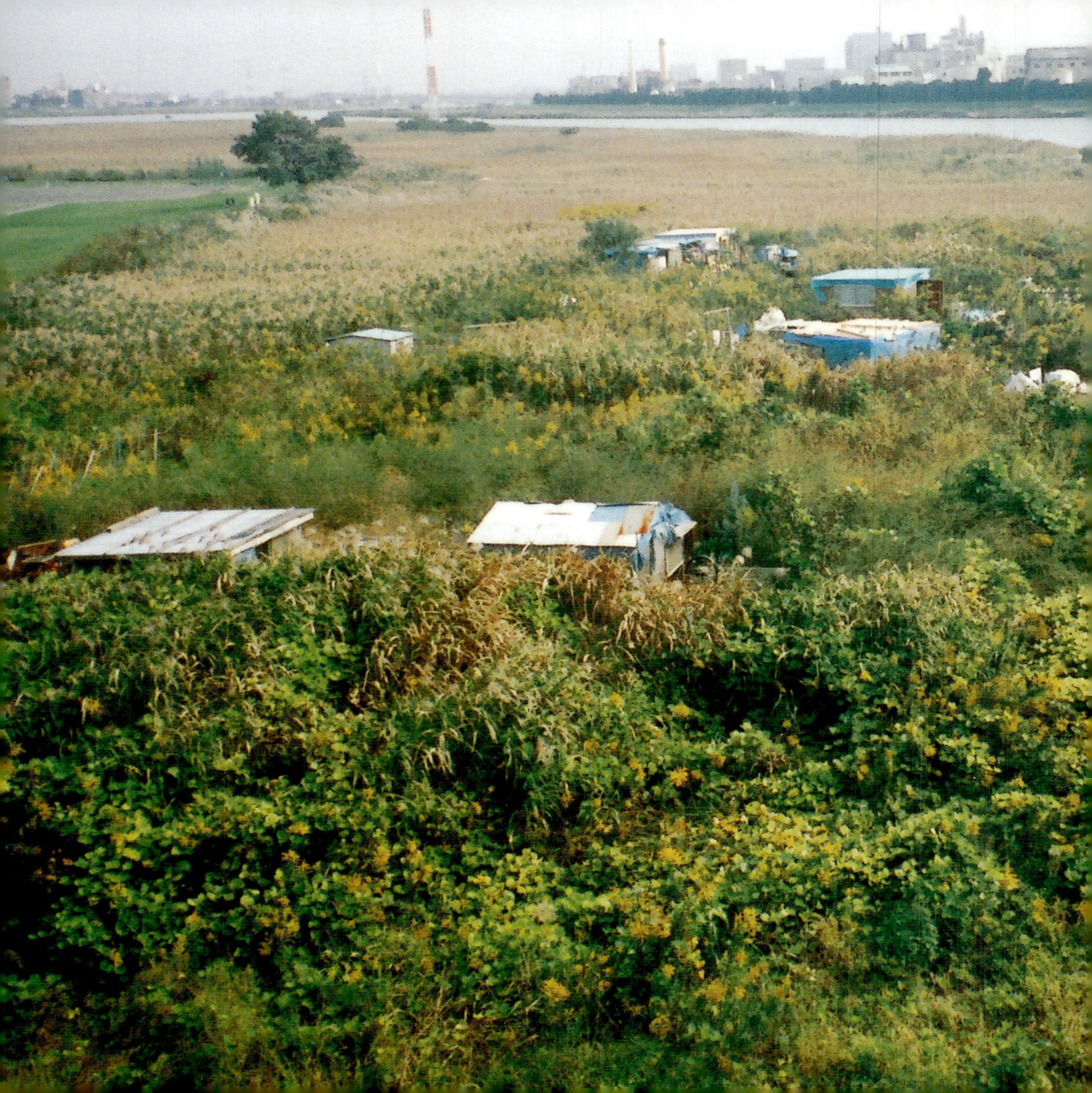

## The Garden City
## 田園都市

六郷橋下の住居群。彼らは河原を少しずつ開拓しながら家を建てている。中には畑を作っている者も見られる。

This is a group of houses near the Rokugobashi Bridge. As the inhabitants build their houses, little by little they are reclaiming the dry riverbed. Some of them work the fields.

## An Agricultural Researcher's House
### 農業研究員の家

前頁の住居群の中で一番初めに建った家である。60代の元大工の男性が数匹の猫と住んでいる。解体された家の一部を再利用して建てている。農業研究の名目で土地を使用しているという。畑では茄子、スイカを栽培している。隣には庭つき一戸建の猫の家がある。

This is the first built house among the houses of previous page. An ex-carpenter in his sixties lives here with a number of cats. The house was built by reusing part of a house that was torn down. The man says he uses the land for agricultural research. Eggplant and watermelon are grown in the field. Next door is a cat house with a garden.

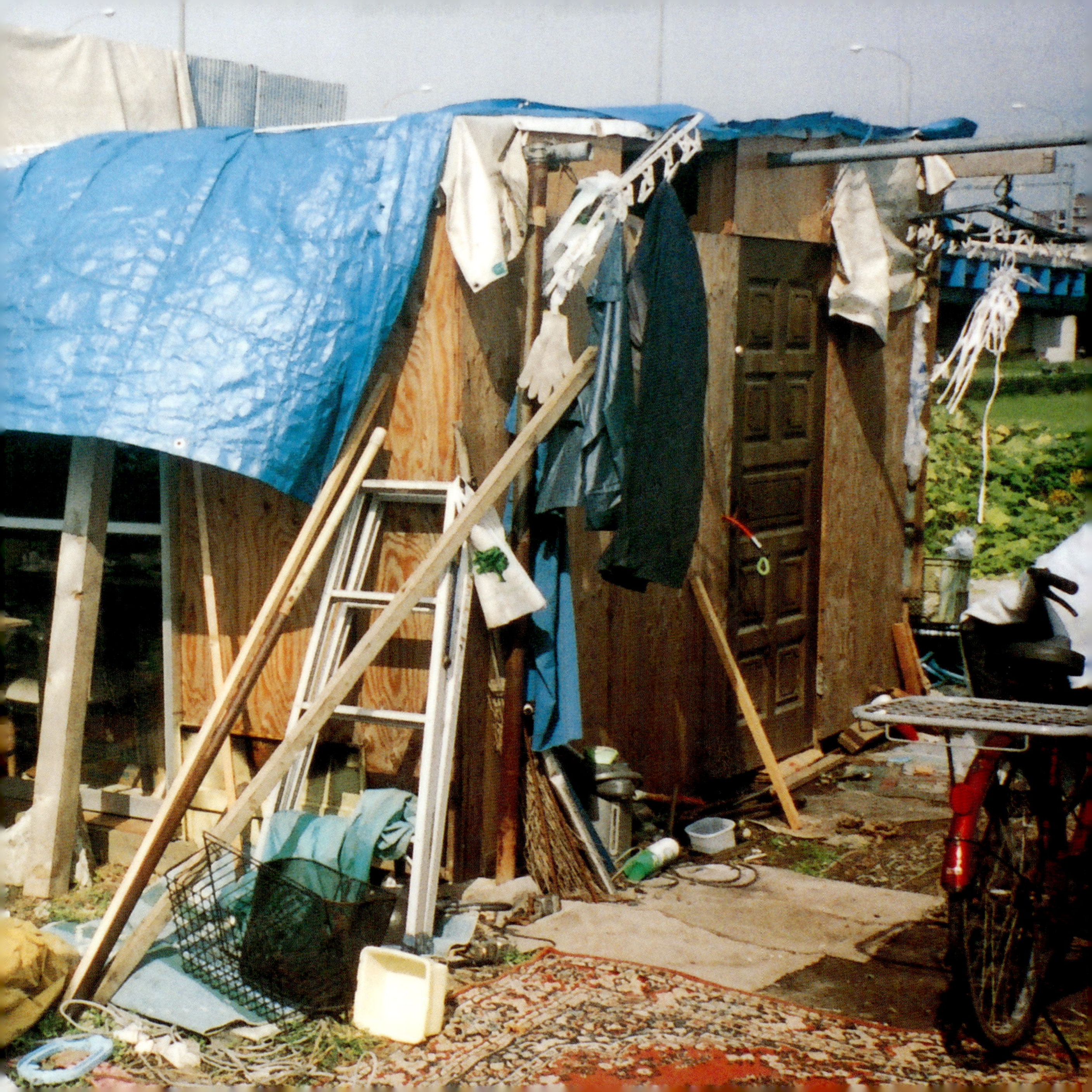

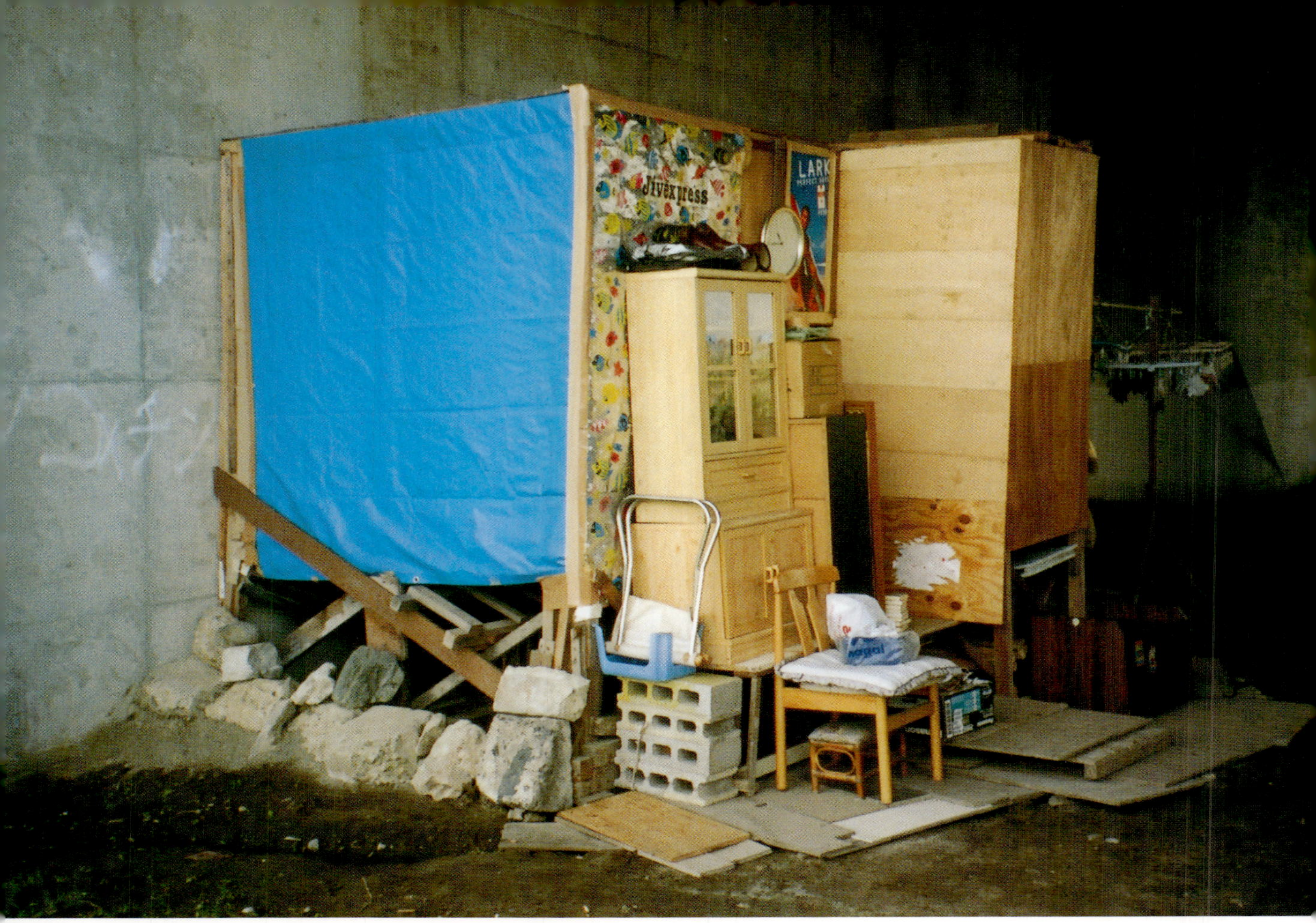
Jivexpress
LARK

**A Living-Room Out on the Road**

表に出てきたリビングルーム

六郷橋下の住居。橋を屋根として利用している。それによって、家具を外に置くことができ、室内に広い寝室を得ることに成功している。

This house is located under the Rokugobashi Bridge. Since the bridge is used as a roof, furniture can be placed outside the house so the dweller has a larger bedroom inside the house.

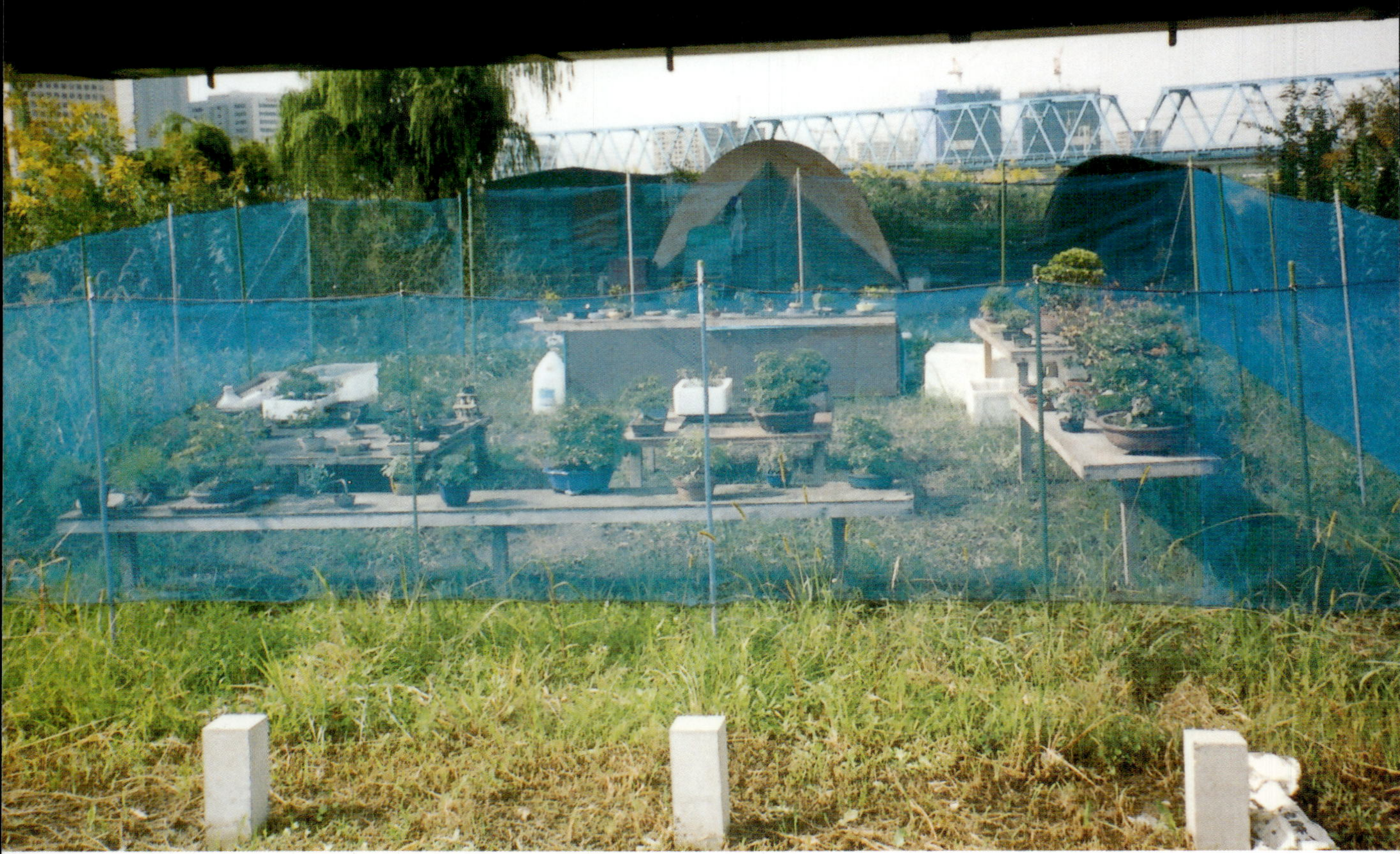

拾ってきた銀杏の実をきれいに袋詰めし産地直売している。価格は1パック500円から最高級極上品Lサイズの3000円までさまざま。

Ginkgo nuts are picked up, packed and sold directly by the pickers. Prices vary from one bag for five hundred yen to three thousand yen for the large sized, highest quality nuts.

公園の階段を利用して、豪華なテラスを作っている。

The stairs of a park are used to create a gorgeous terrace.

## Ornaments of Mickey Mouse and Bear

ミッキーマウスと熊の置物

熊の置物、ミッキーマウスの時計、銀杏の木で作った柵、柵に伸びる朝顔のツル、入り口には犬小屋のドア、部屋の中には天皇皇后両陛下の写真……その他さまざまなものがこの家を装飾している。

Bear figurines, a Mickey Mouse clock, a fence made with a ginkgo tree and morning glory vines reaching toward it, the door to a dog house at the entrance, photographs of the imperial couple inside the house... These and a variety of other items decorate this house.

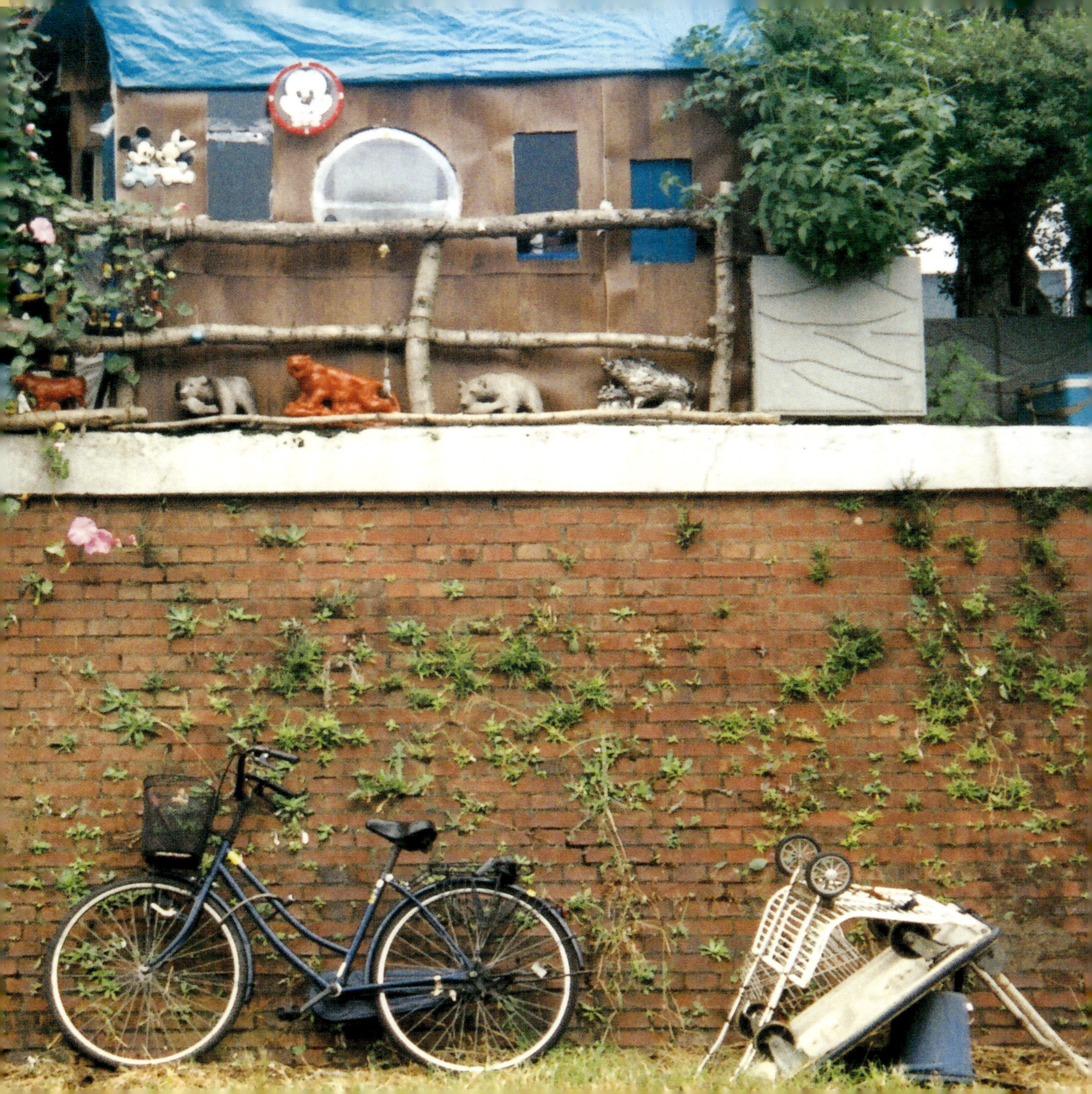

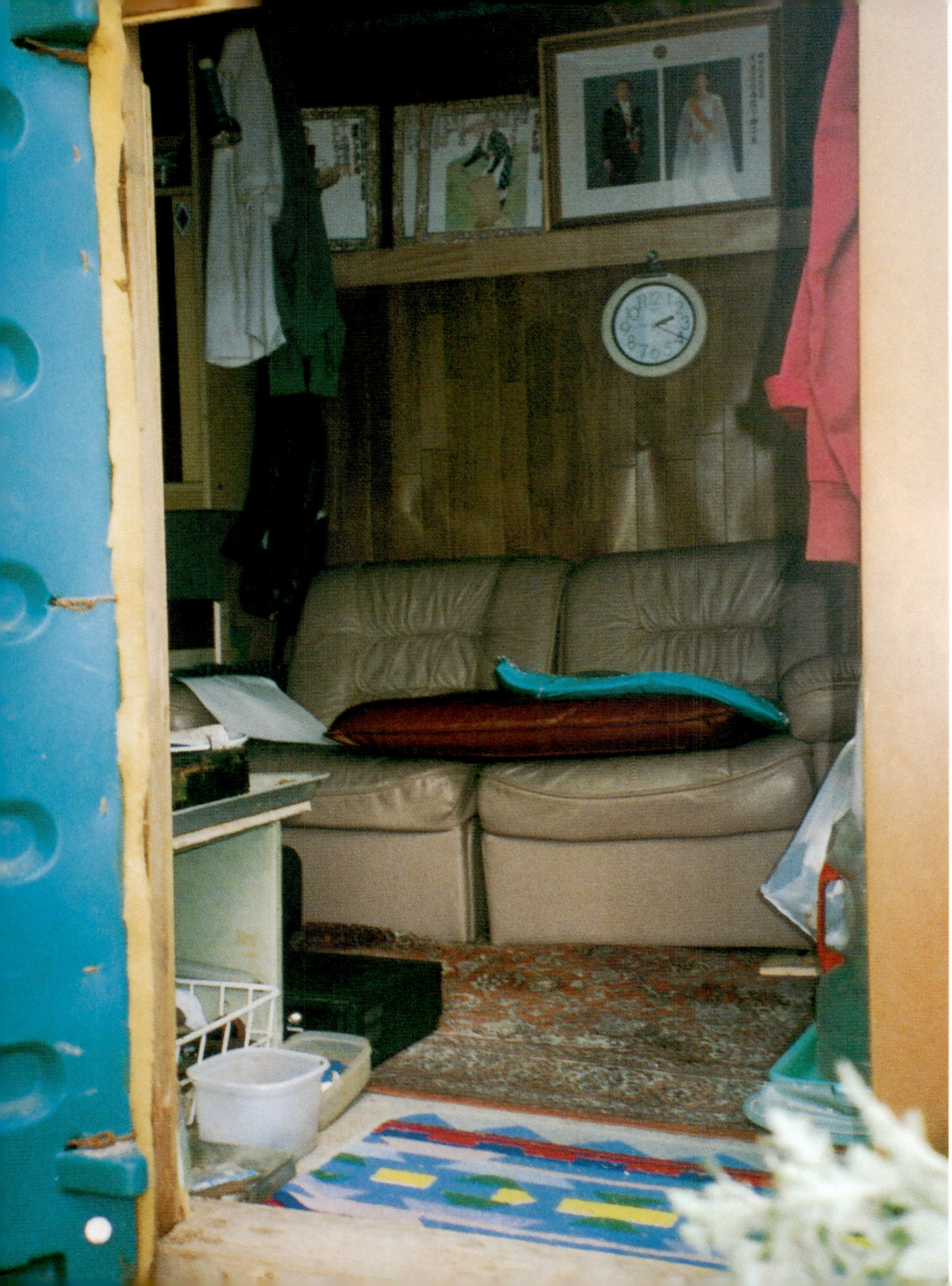
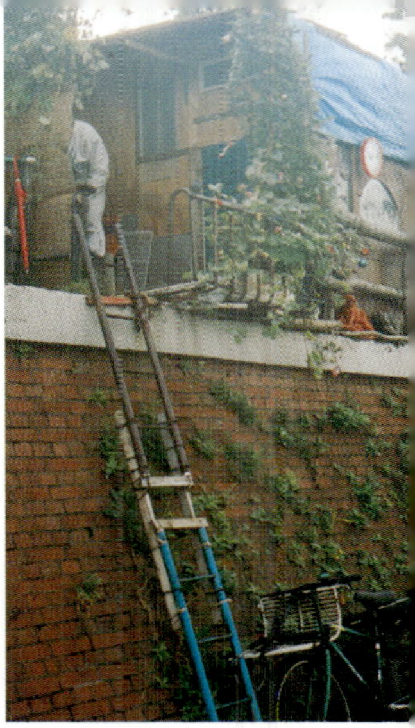

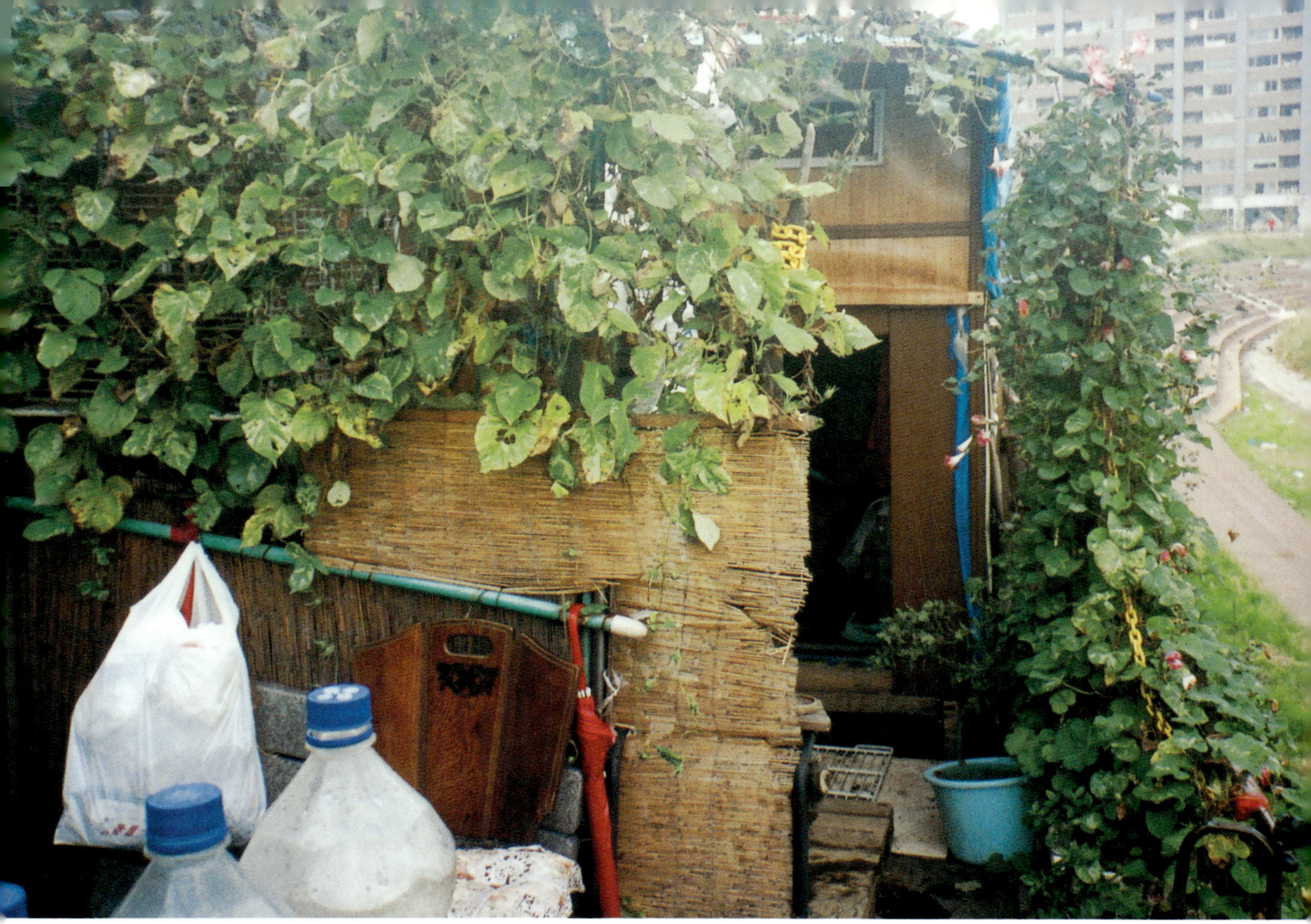

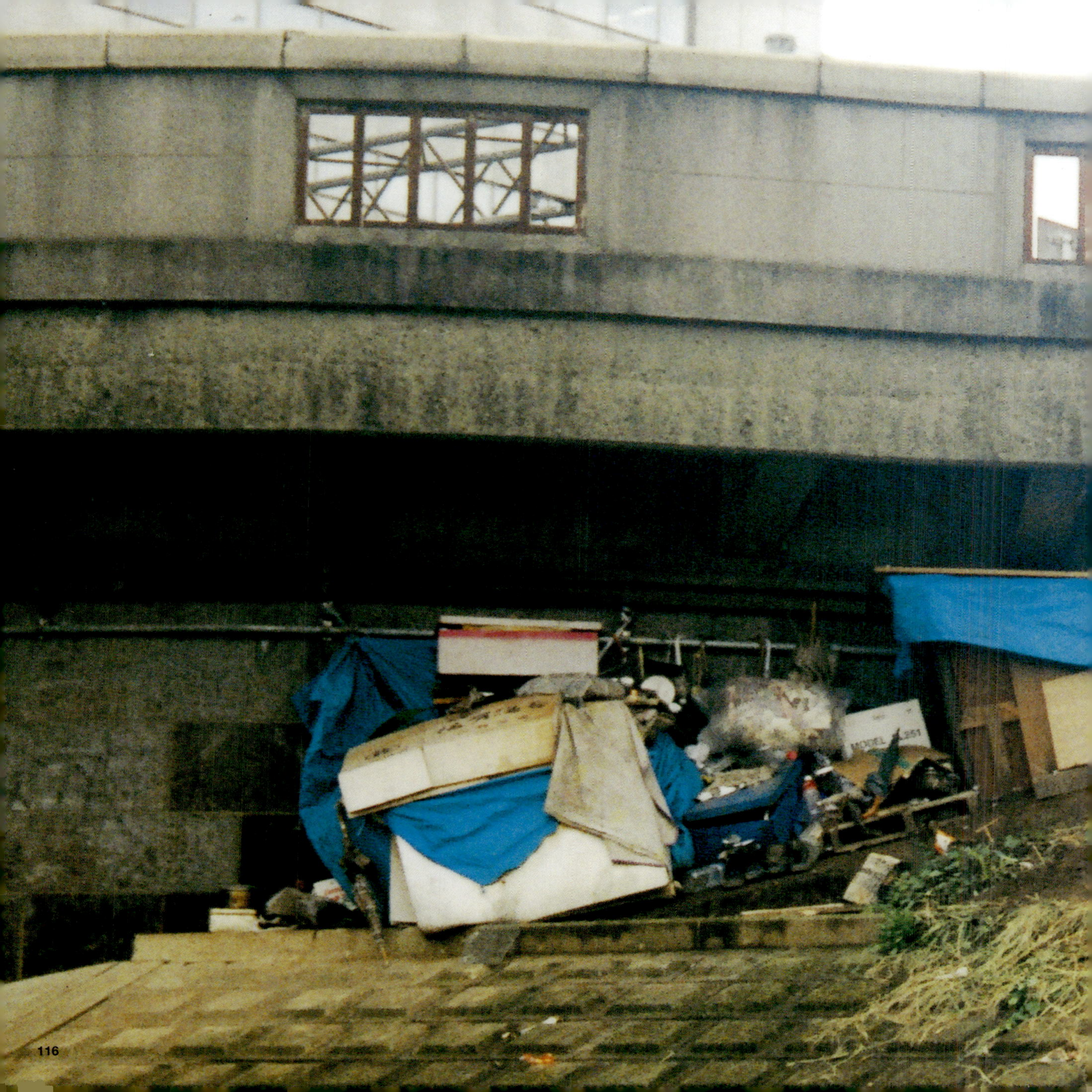
MODEL

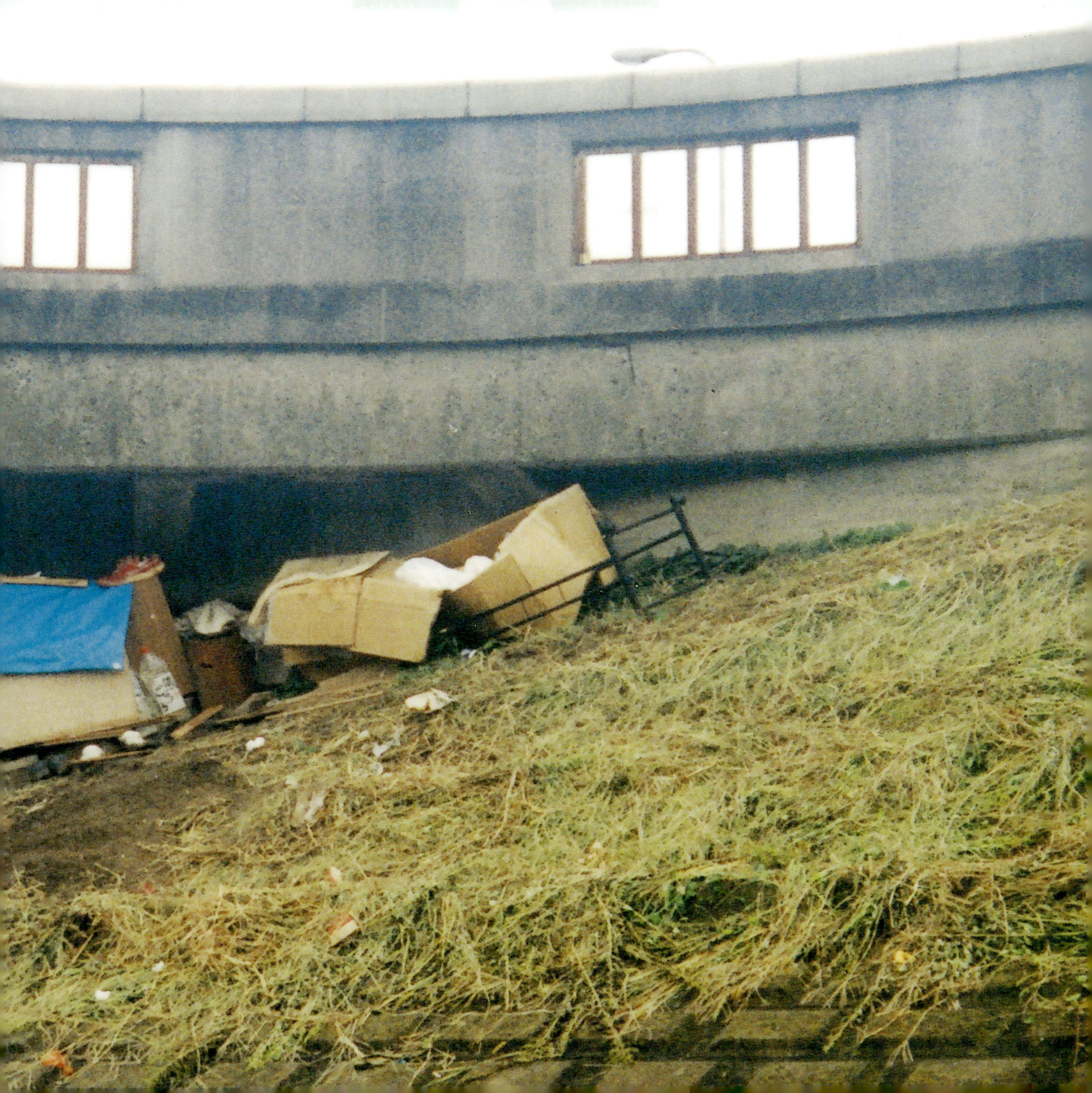

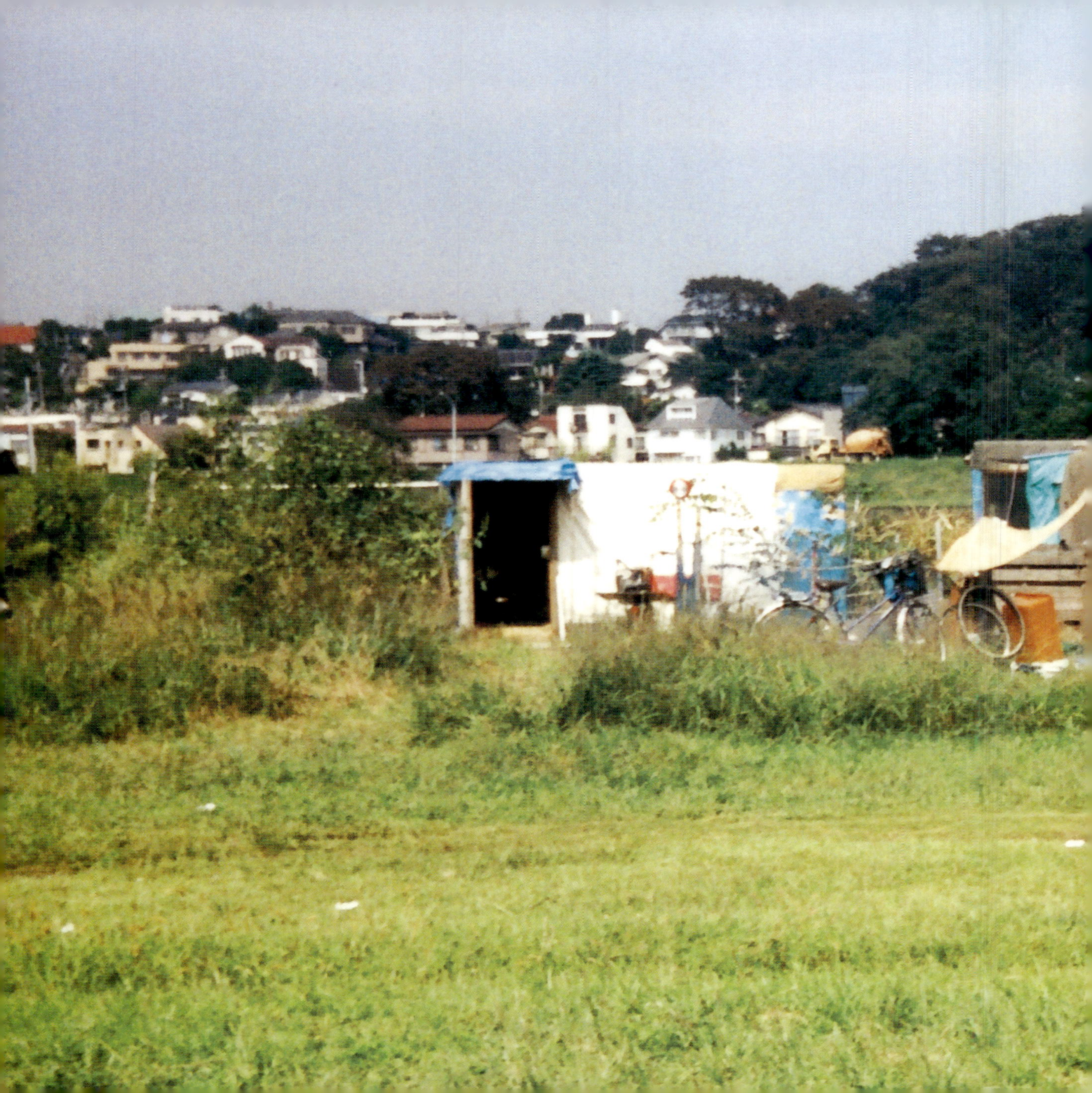

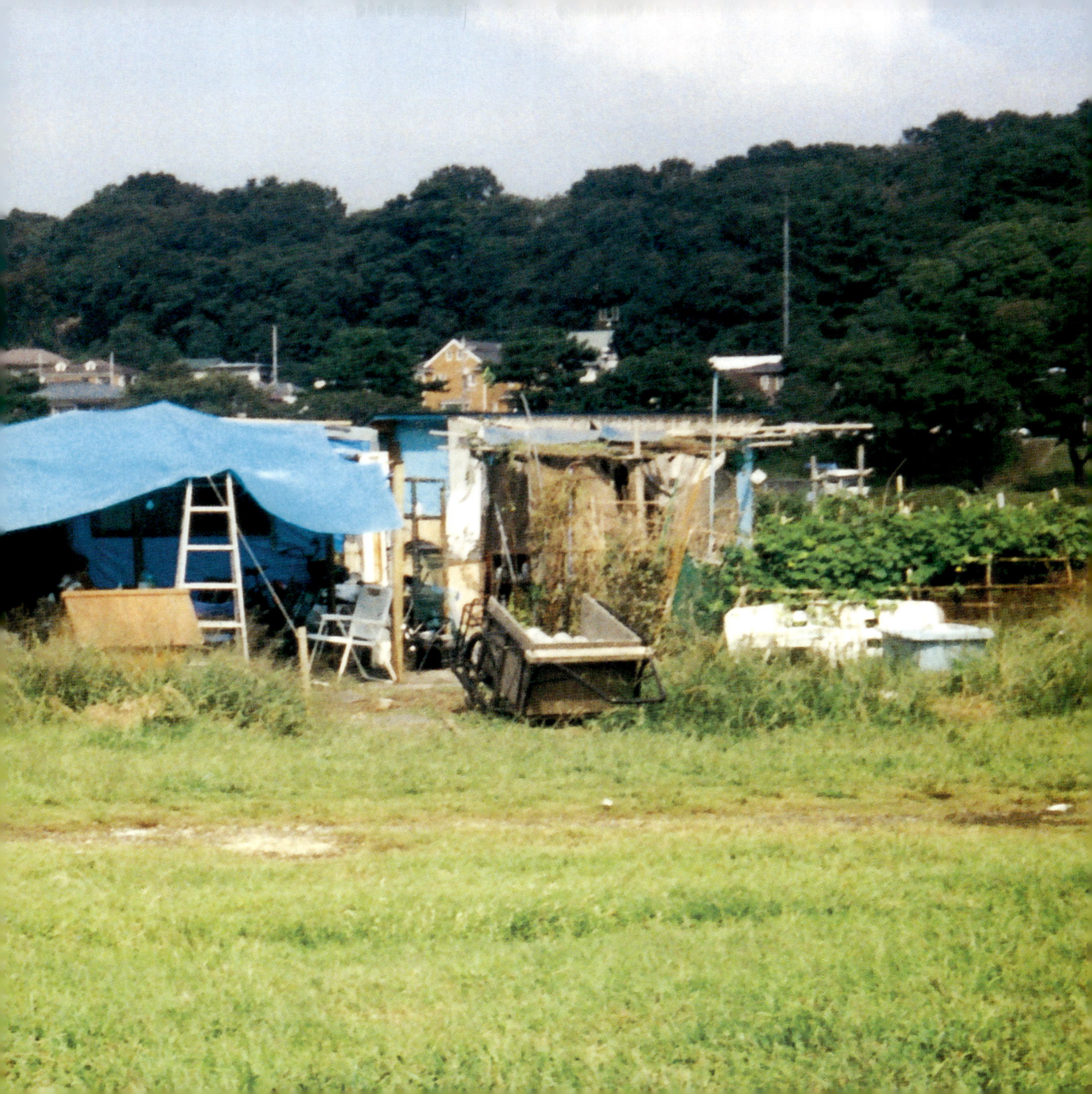

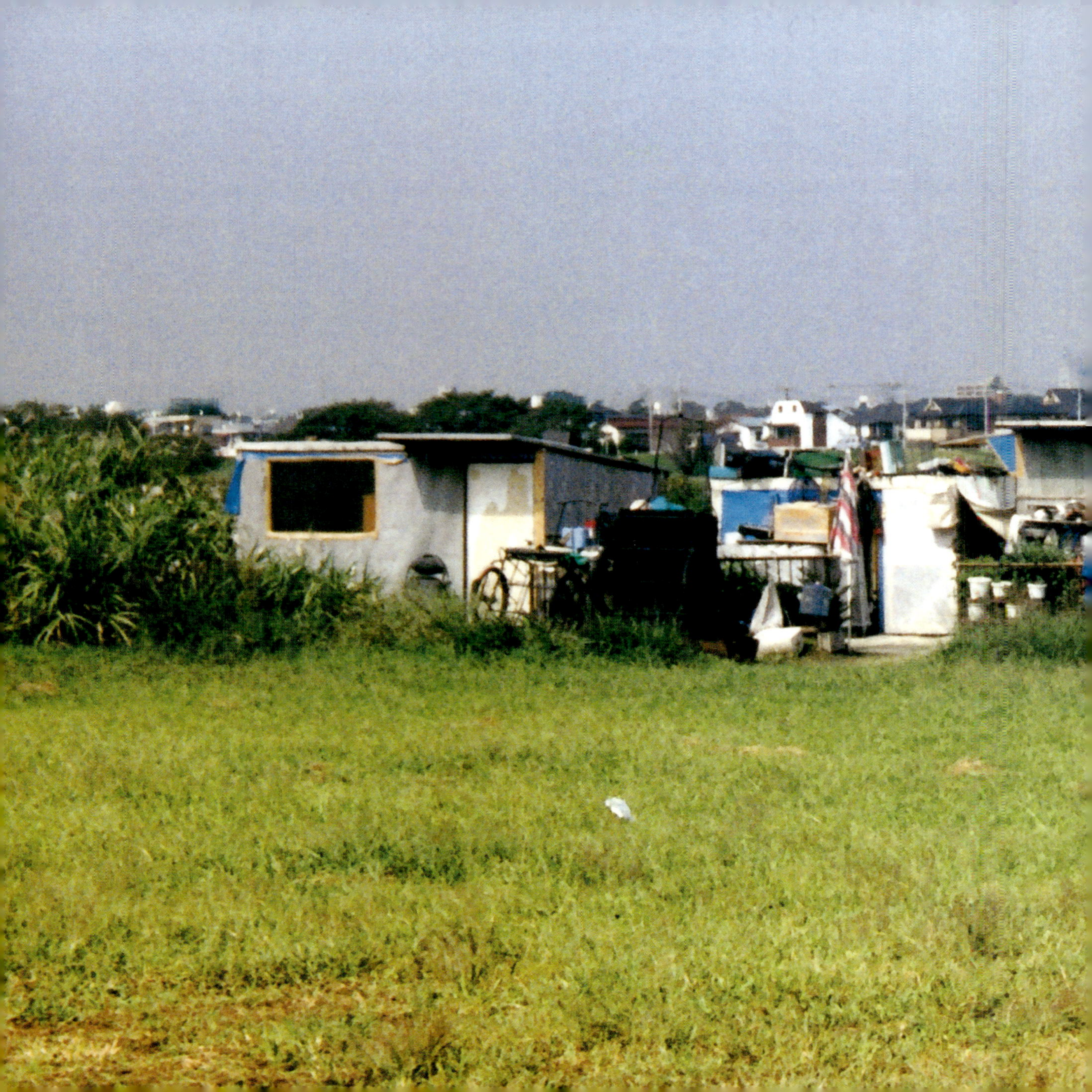

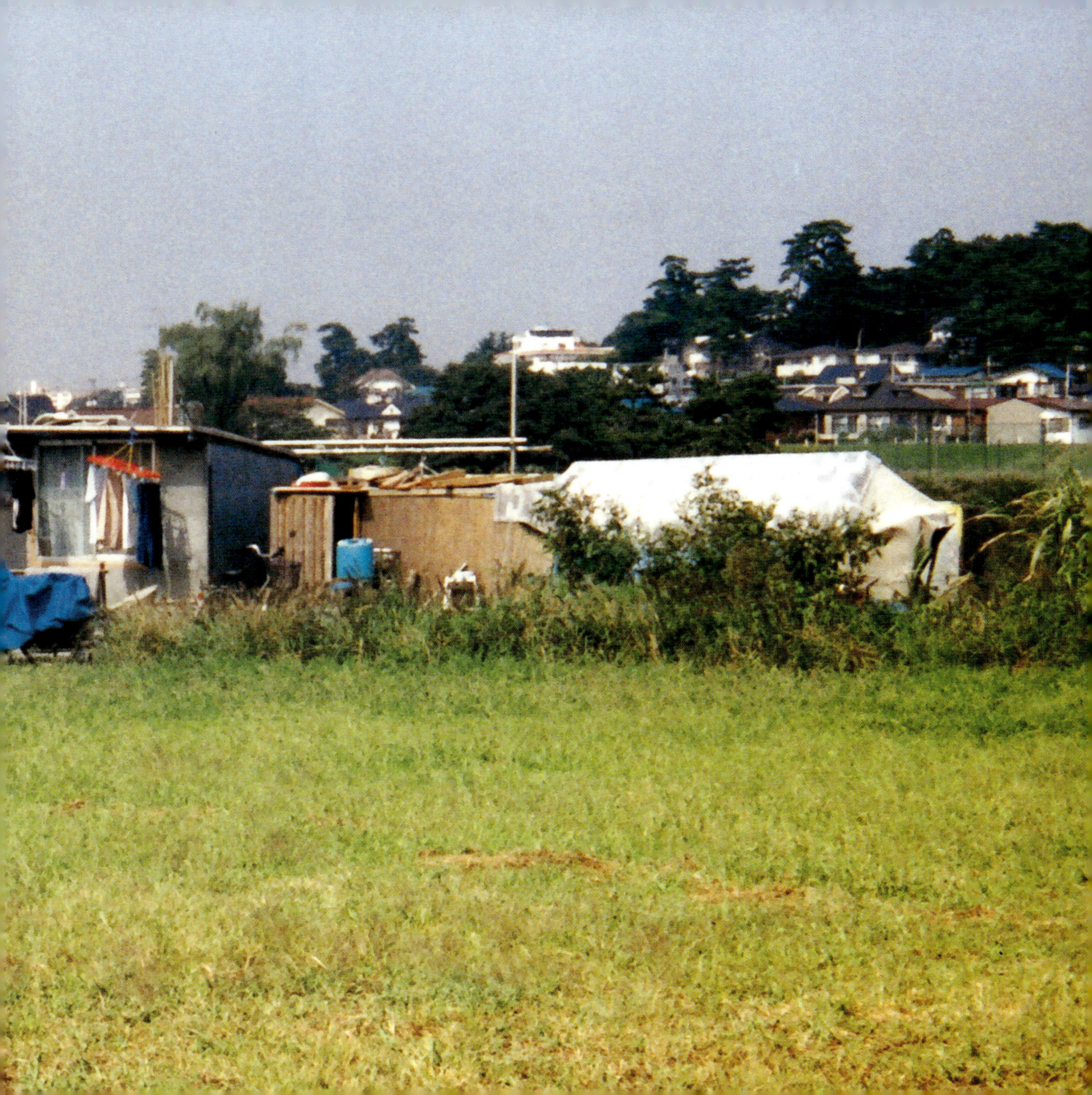

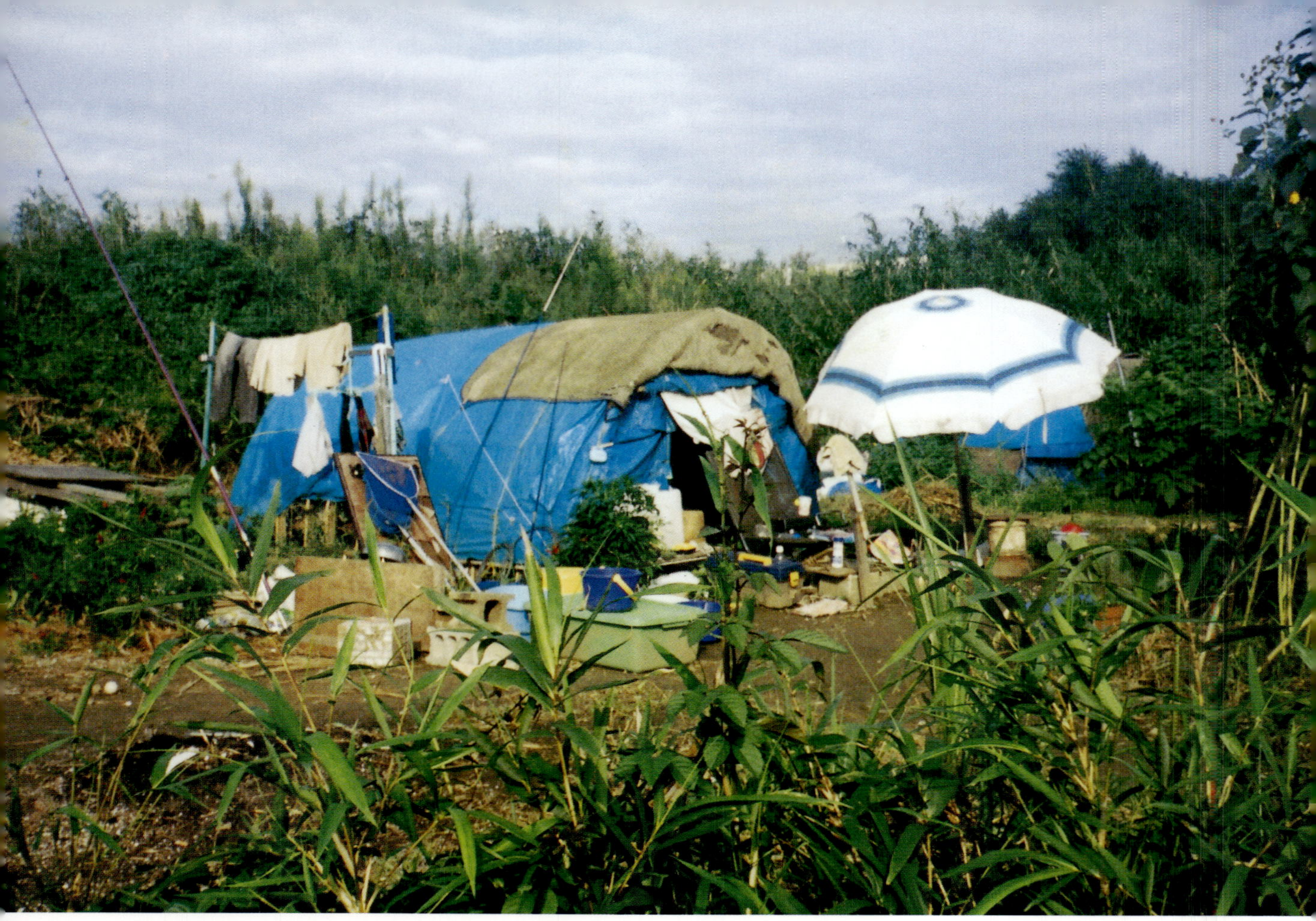

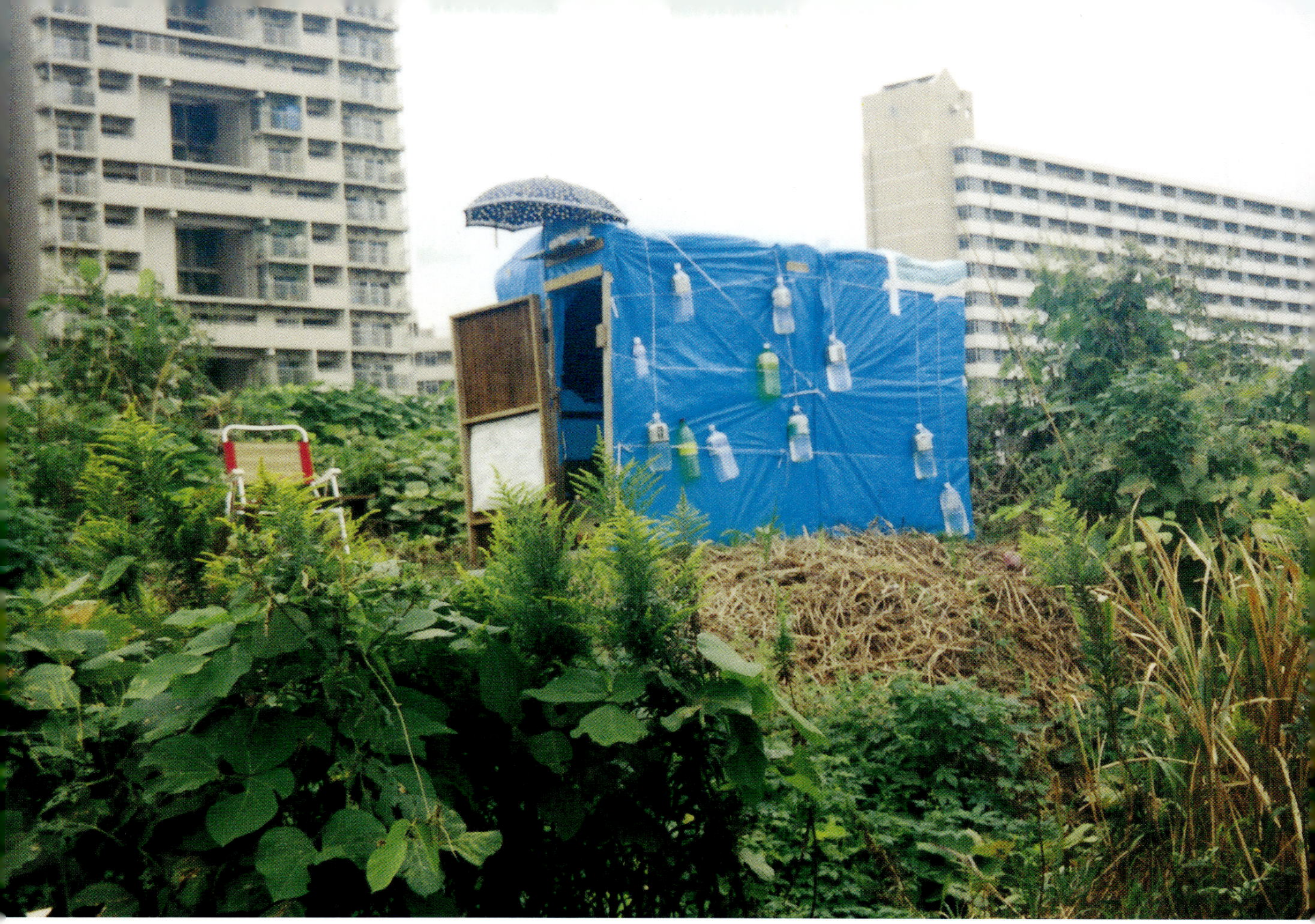

## Animal Paths by the Tamagawa
## 多摩川のケモノ道

多摩川にある住居は草むらの奥深くにひっそりと建っていることが多い。草むらが幾度となく踏みつけられることによって、その住人しか通ることのない道ができる。

Most houses built beside the Tamagawa River are nestled deep in the grass. Treaded again and again, a path used only by the inhabitants is made.

'00 10 05

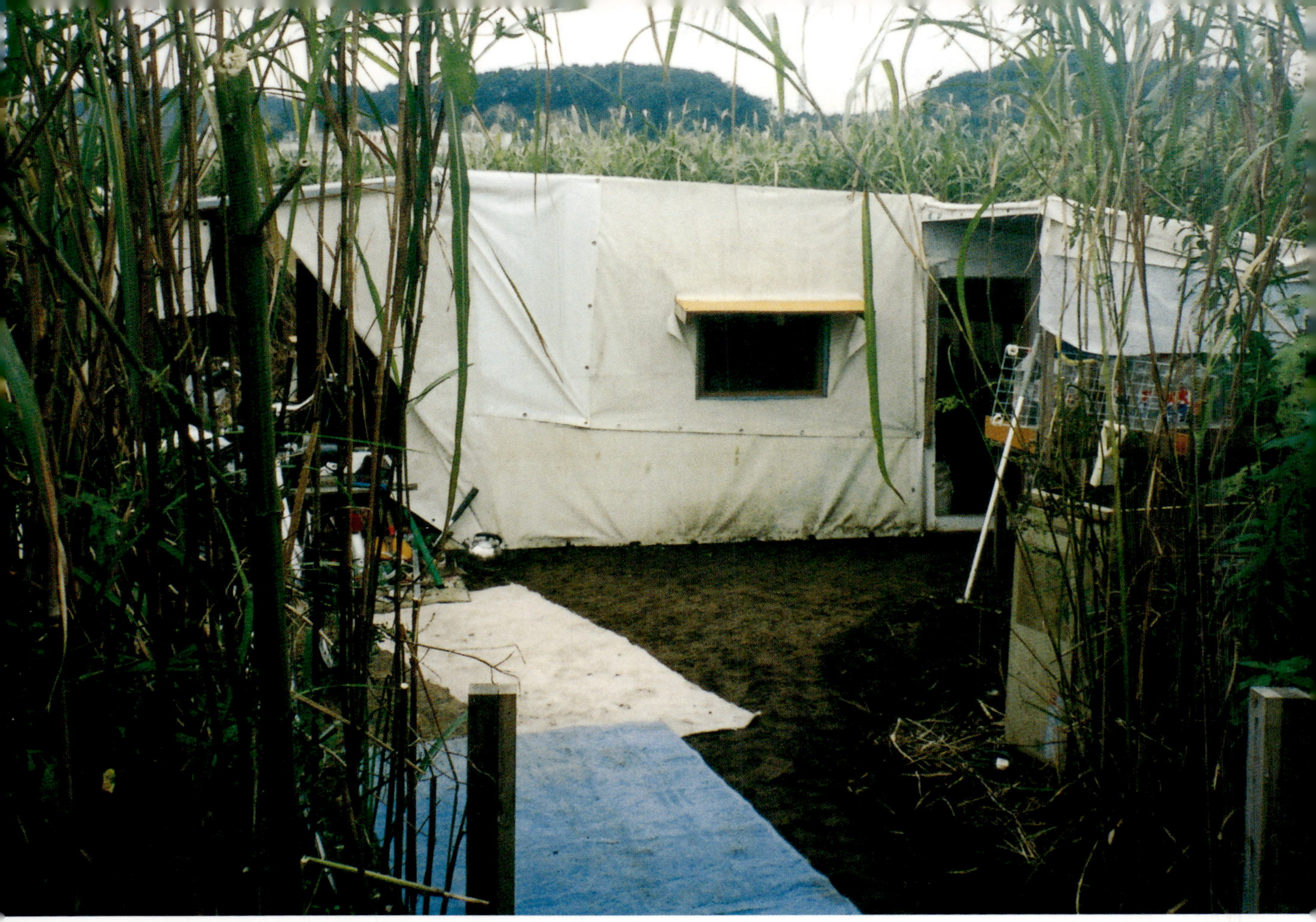

**The Tamagawa Electronics Store**

多摩川の電器屋

前頁の道を歩き続けて辿り着いた家。部屋は台所と居間に分けられている。住んでいるのは50代の男性で、彼は元電気関係の職人だった。ここでは電化製品を拾ってきて自分で直したり、知人に売ったりしている。また隣人たちの壊れた電化製品の修理もする。

This house was found by following the paths of the previous page. It is divided into a kitchen and a living room. Its inhabitant is an ex-electrician in his fifties. Here he fixes broken electrical appliances he finds and sells them to acquaintances. He also repairs the broken appliances of his neighbors.

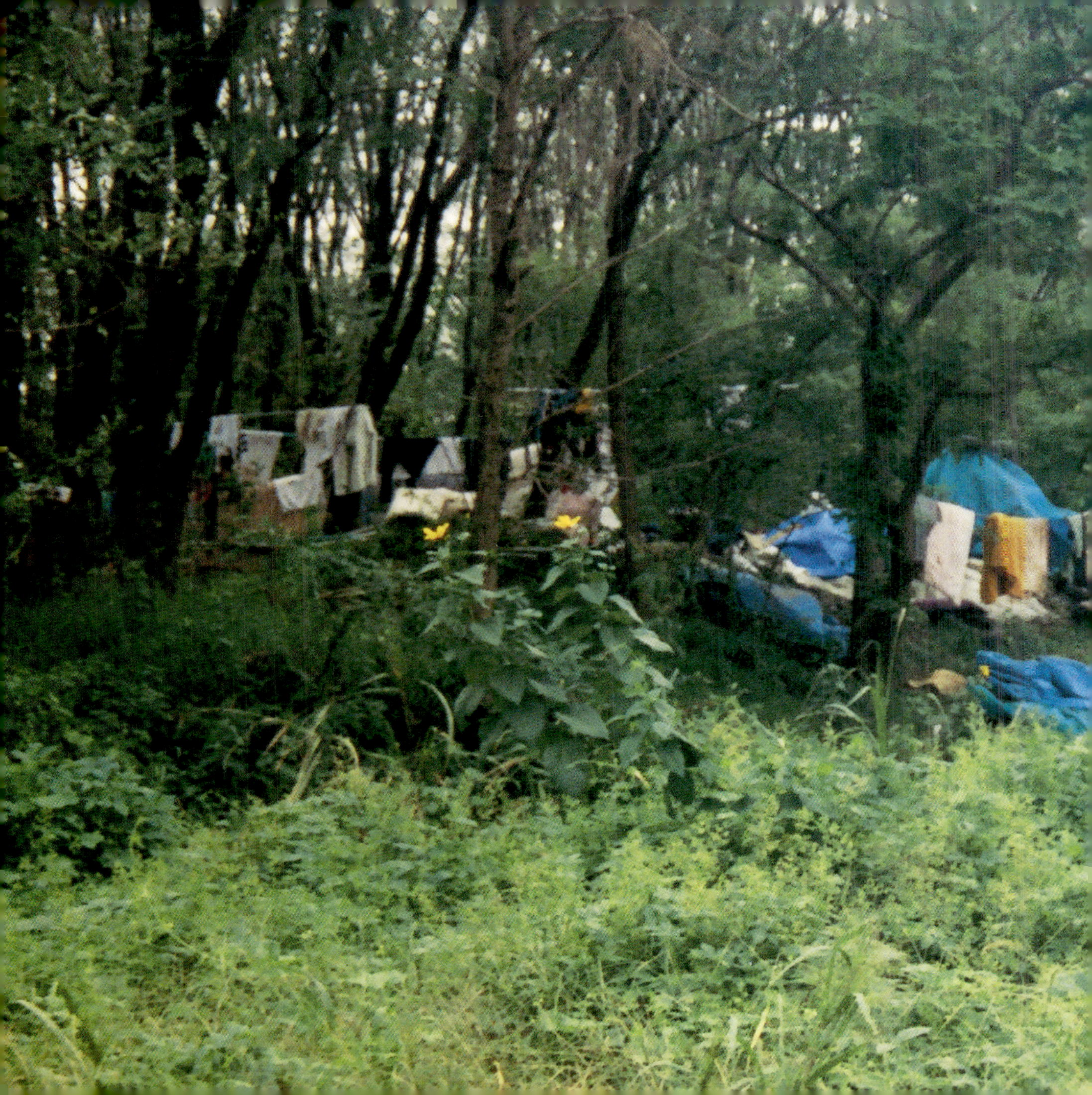

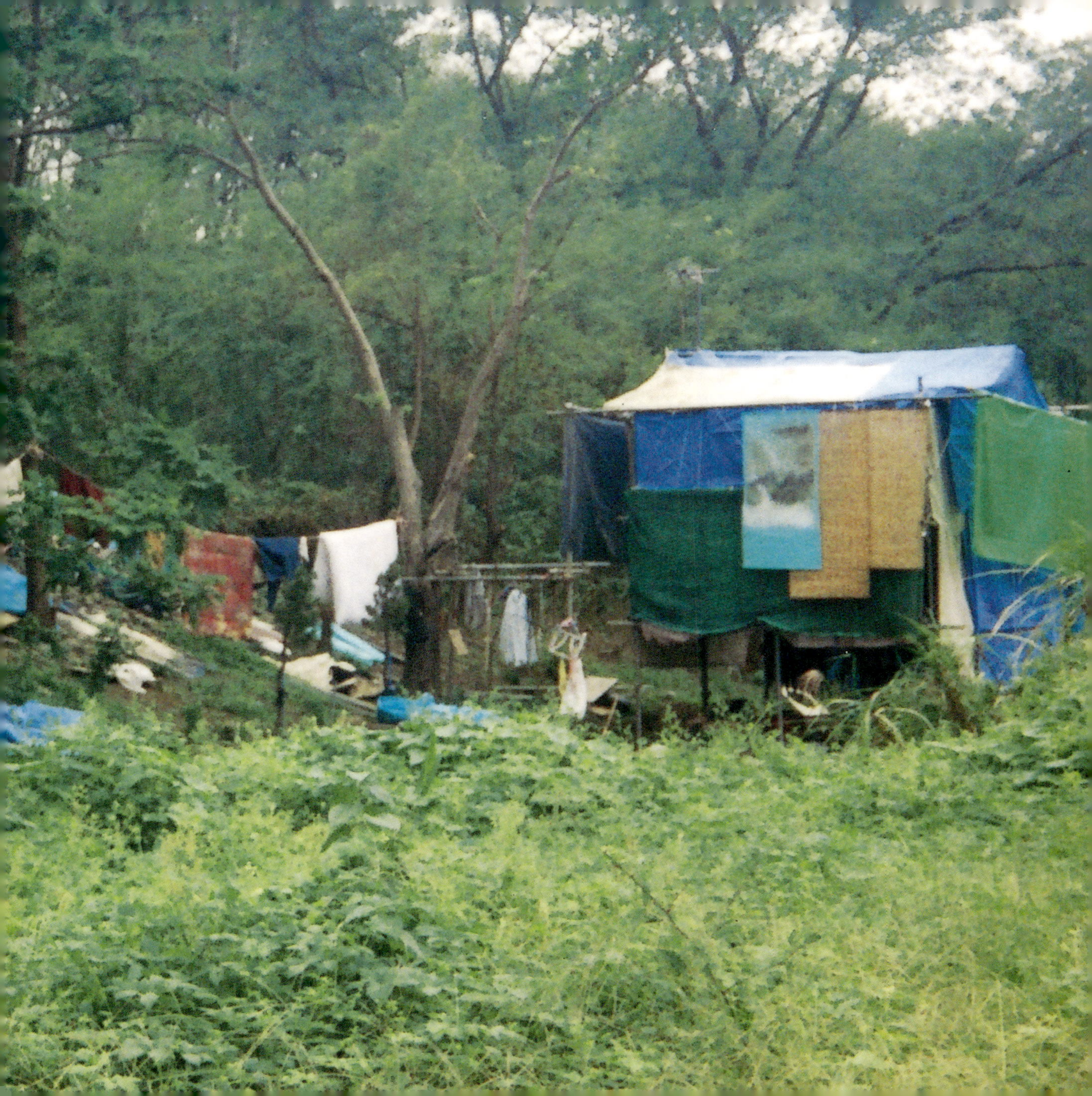

**A Clay Pipe House**
土管の家

立川市にある土管住居である。直径150cmほどの土管が地面に突き刺さっていて、その中に男性と猫が住んでいる。

This is a clay pipe house in Tachikawa city. The pipe is about 1.5 meters in diameter and sticks into the ground. A man and his cat live in the pipe.

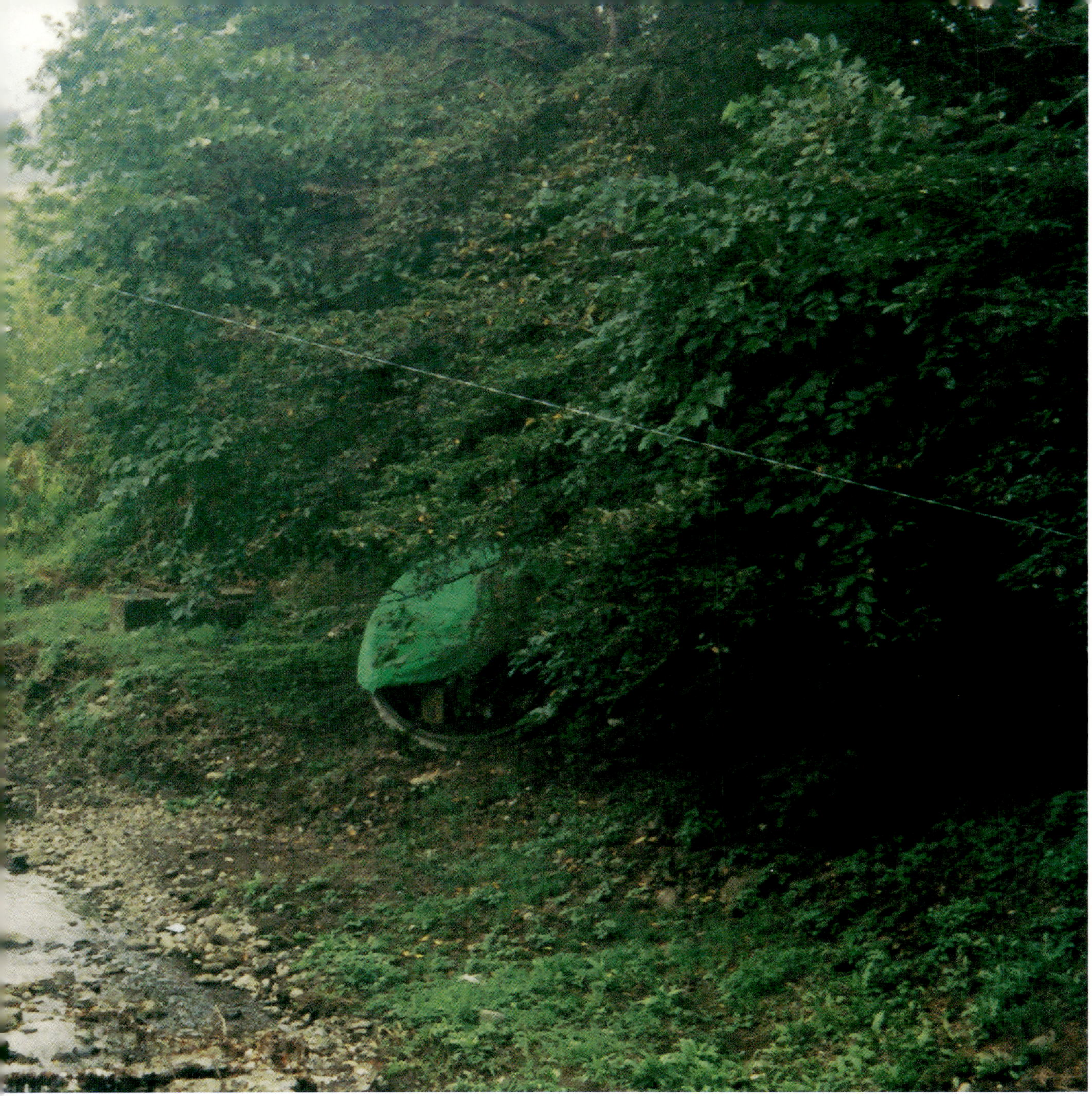

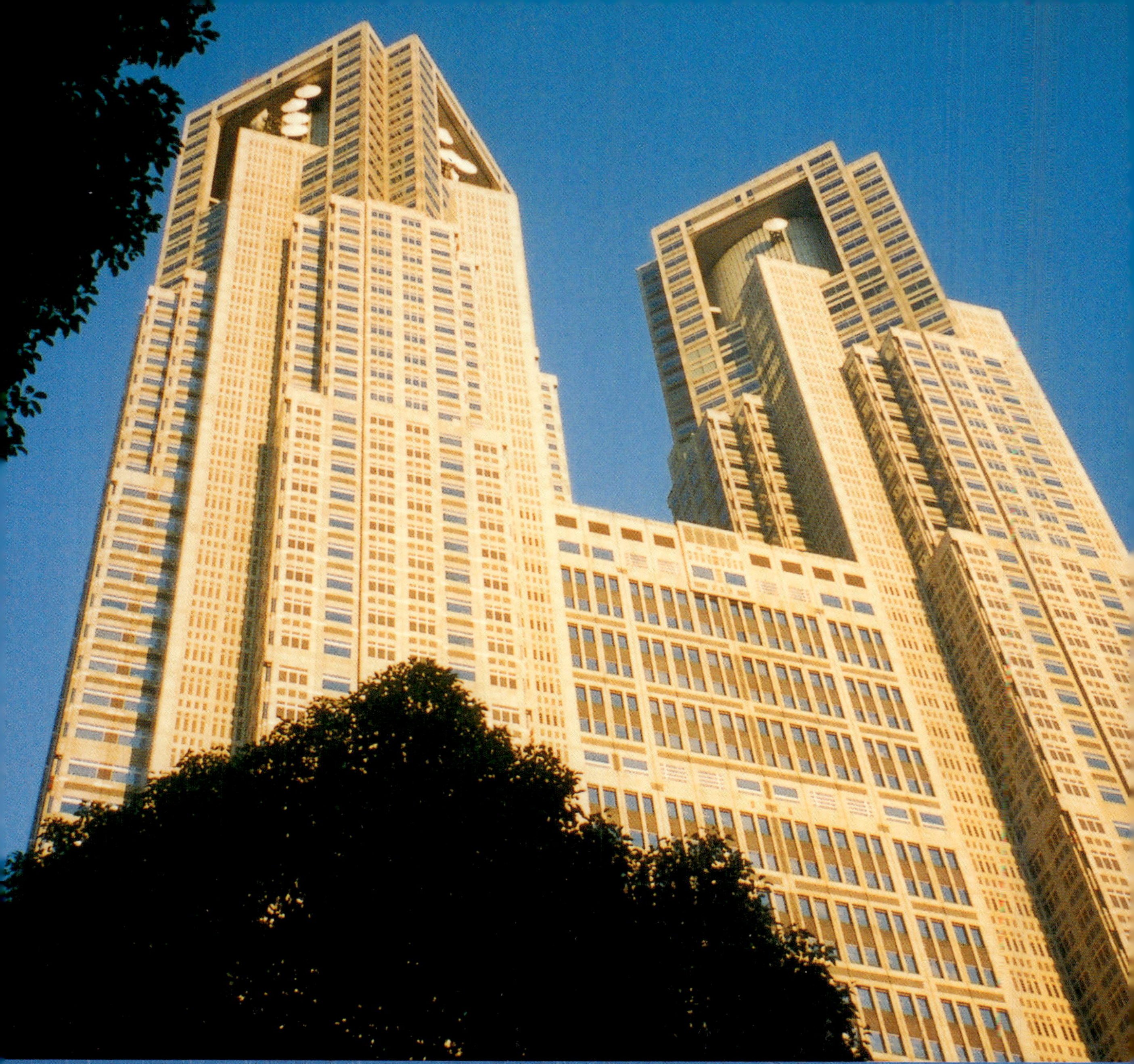

**Shinjuku Chuo Park**
新宿中央公園

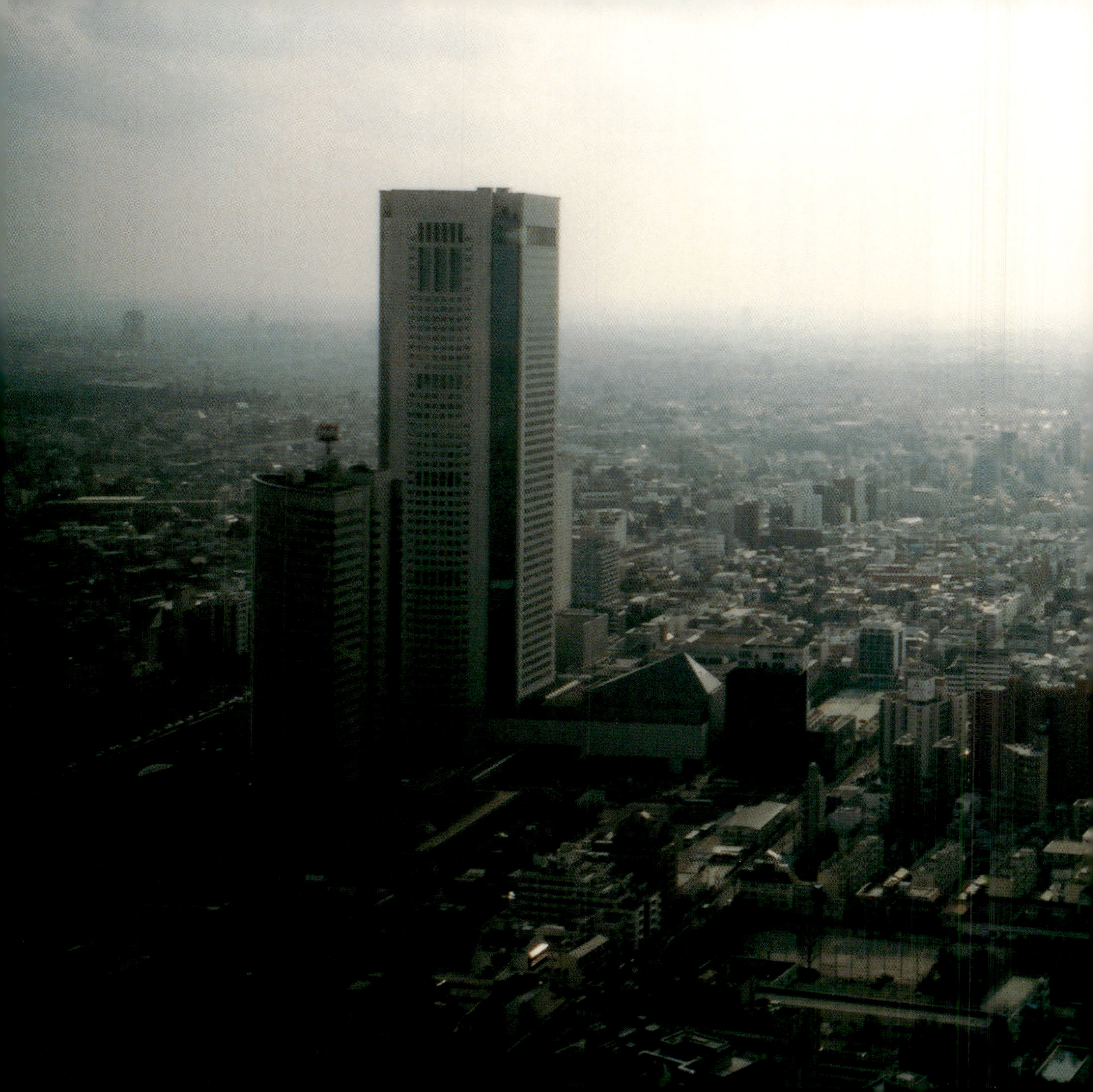

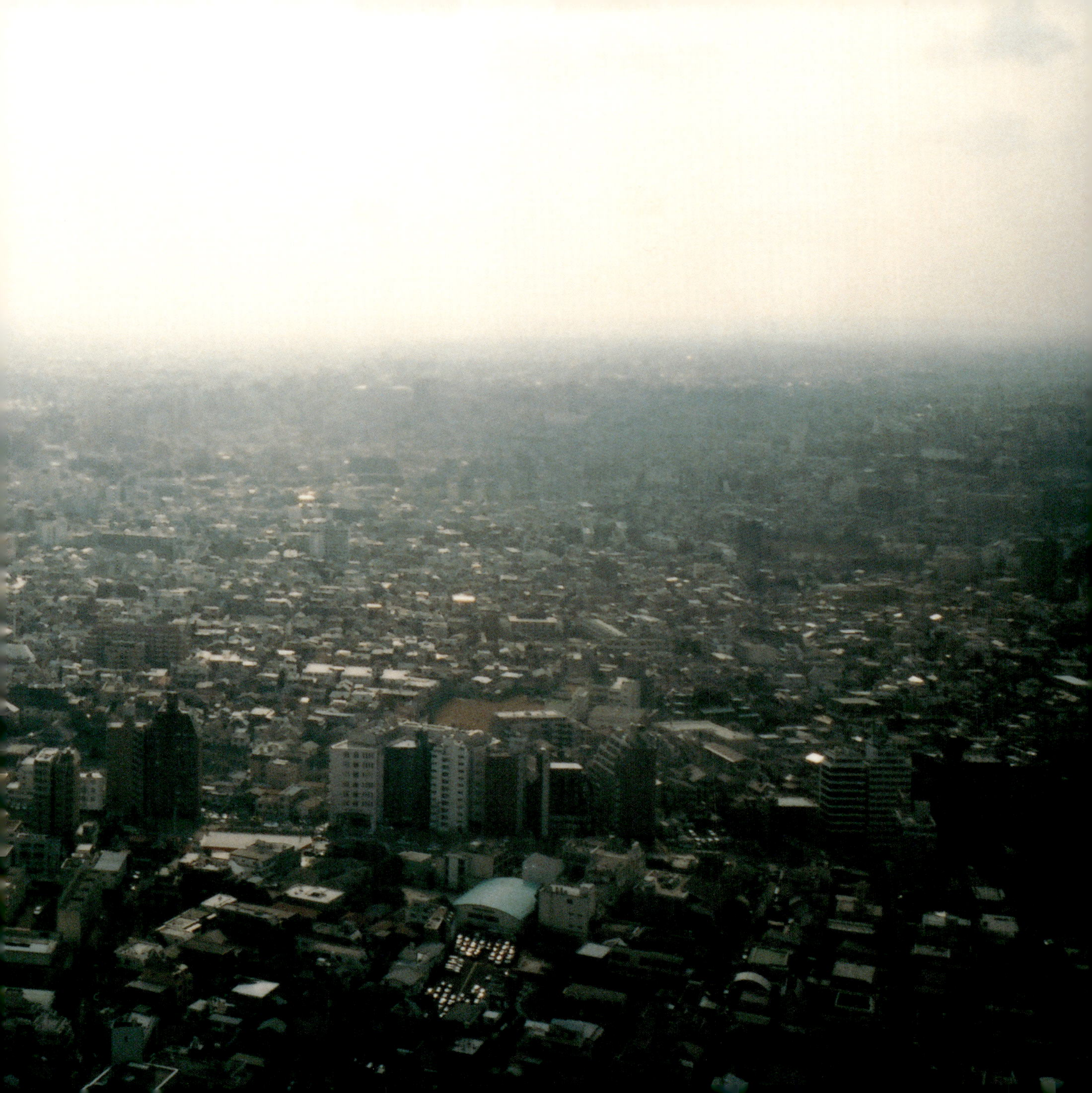

新宿中央公園の案内図。ここには約100軒ほどの家がある。そして家を持たない無数の野宿者が生活している。

This is an information map of Shinjuku Chuo Park. There are about a hundred houses in the park, where countless people live.

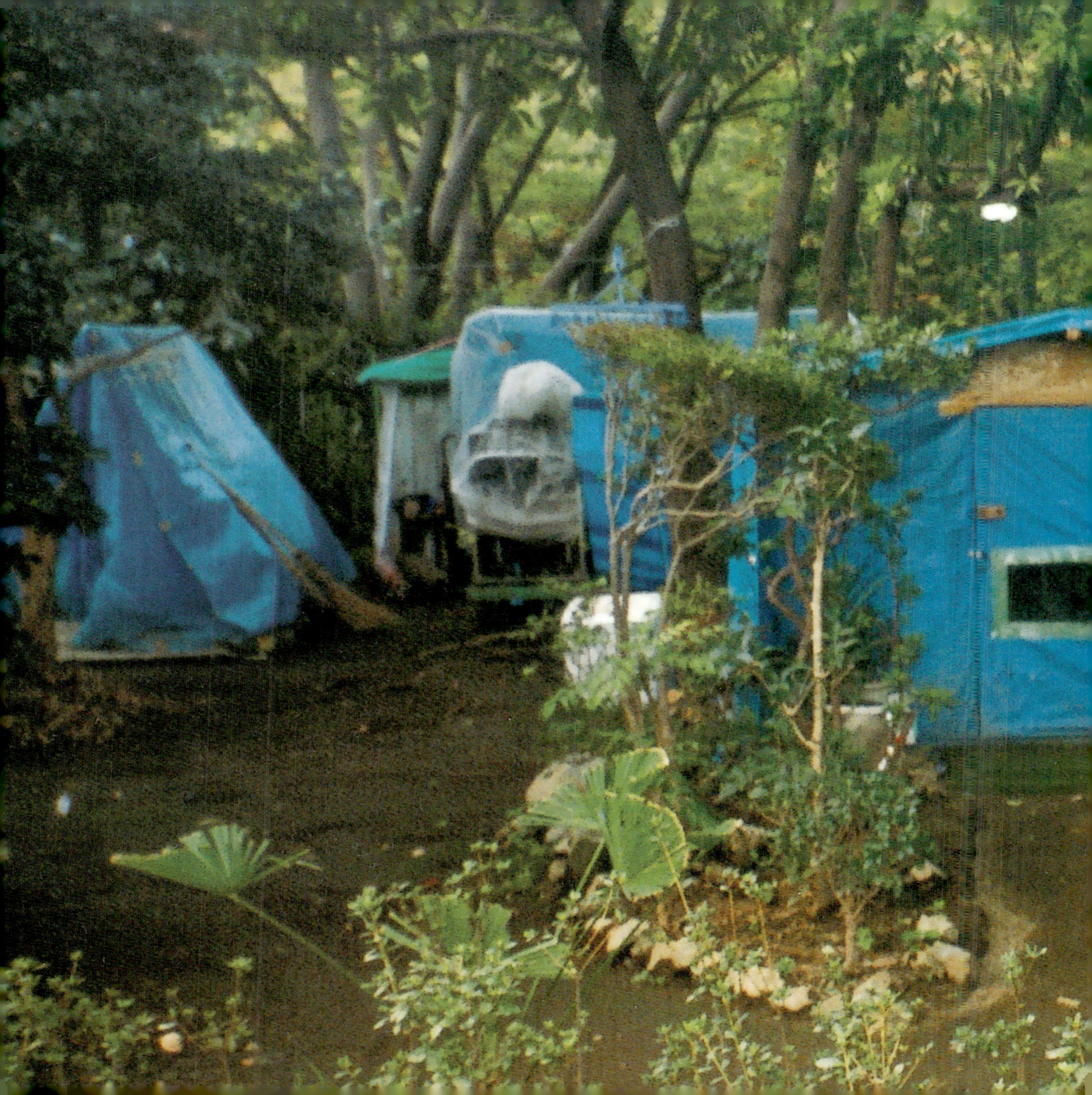

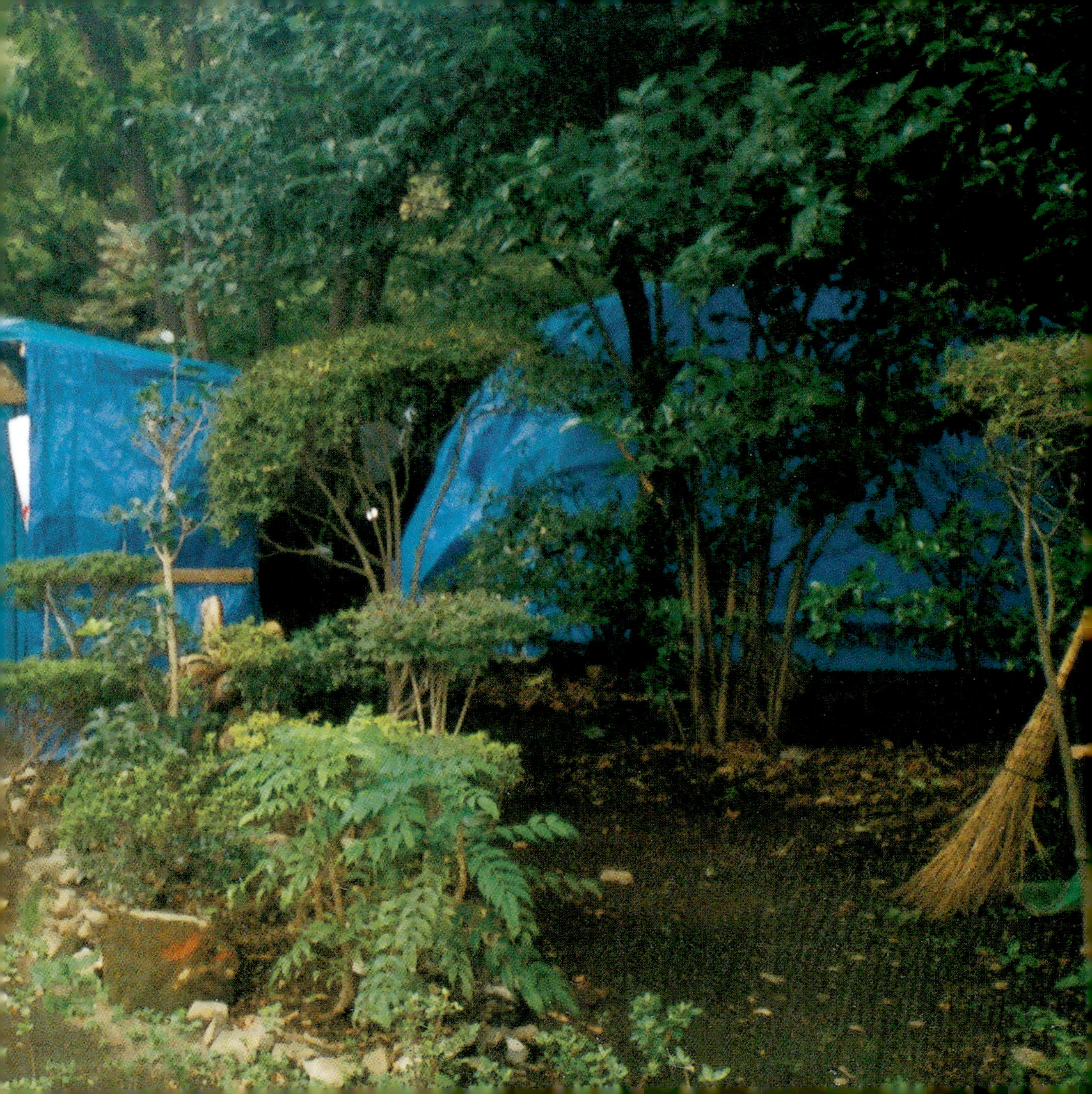

## Shinjuku Nest
新宿の巣

70代の男性が住む家。入り口は非常に狭く、部屋の中に入ると広くなっている作り。おそらく外からの危険を避けるためであろう。外から内部はほとんど見えないようになっている。木材を柱とし、その周りをダンボールで囲って壁とし、ビニールシートを張って屋根にしている。部屋の中には手前が寝床、奥には食事をするスペースがある。

A man in his seventies lives in this house. The entrance is very narrow, but the inside is spacious. This is probably to avert any danger from the outside. The inside of the house is almost completely invisible from the outside. The house is made of timber pillars with cardboard walls around them and a blue plastic sheet as a roof. Inside the room there is a bed in the front and a dining space in the rear.

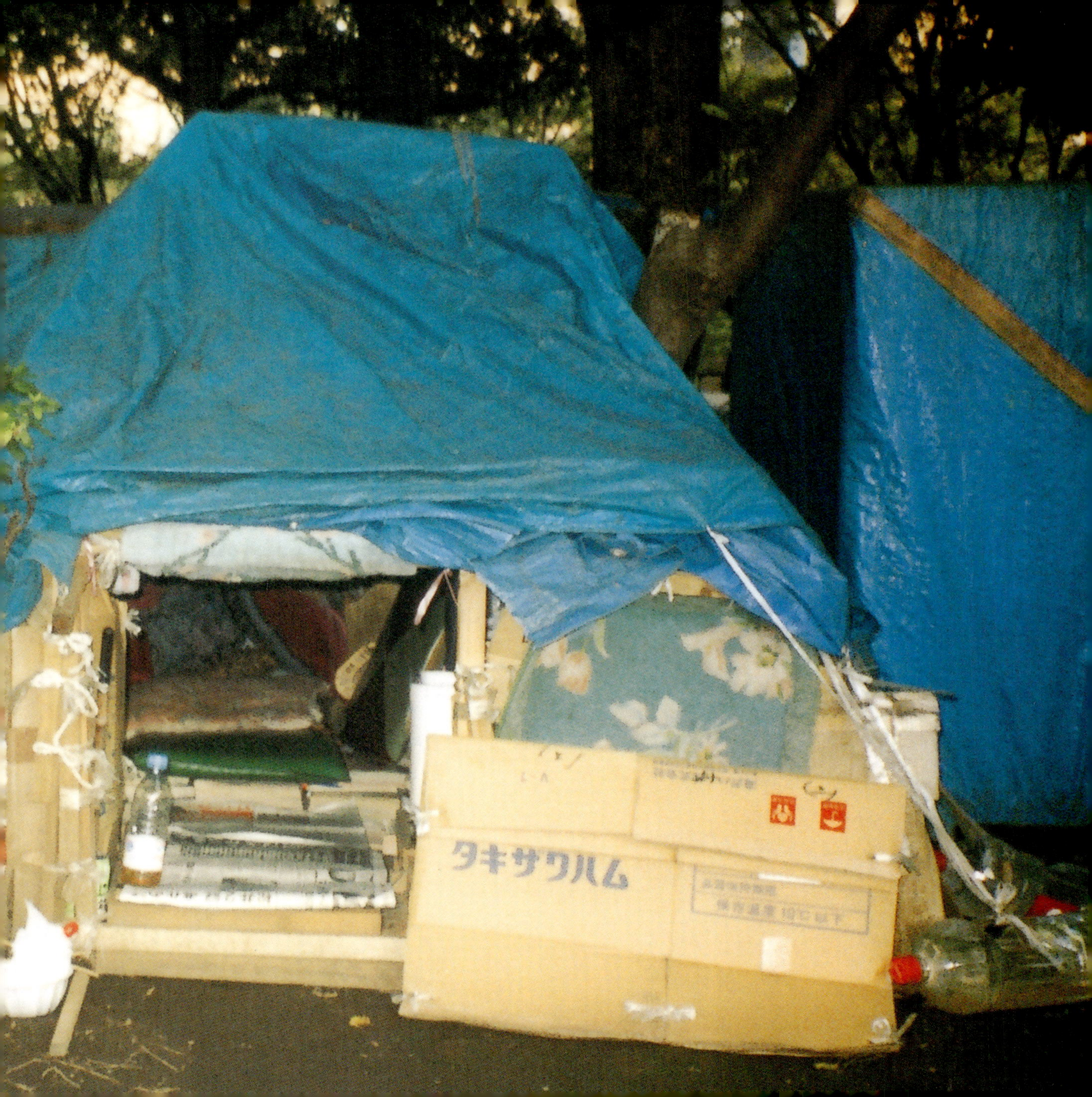
タキサワハム

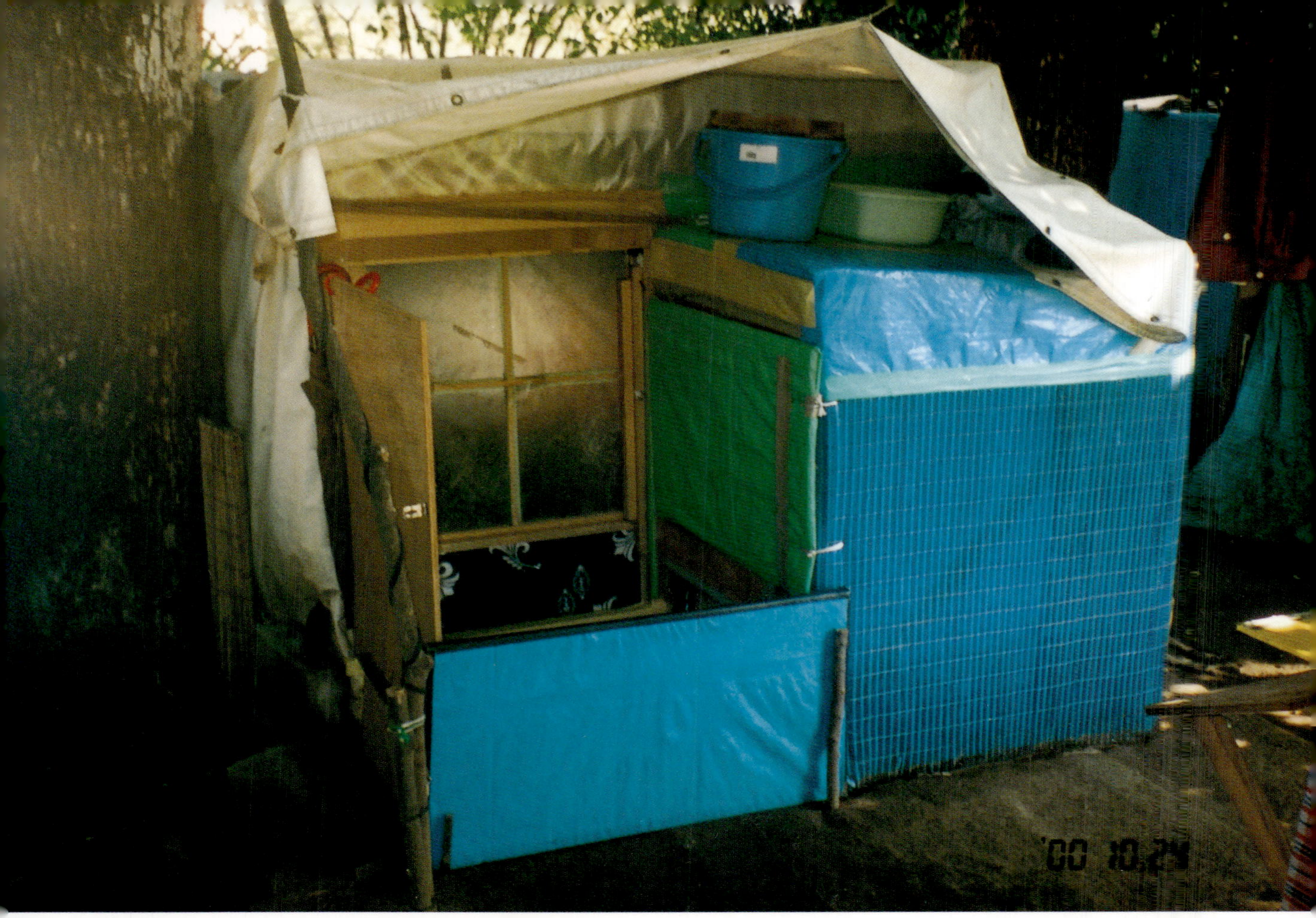
'00 10.24

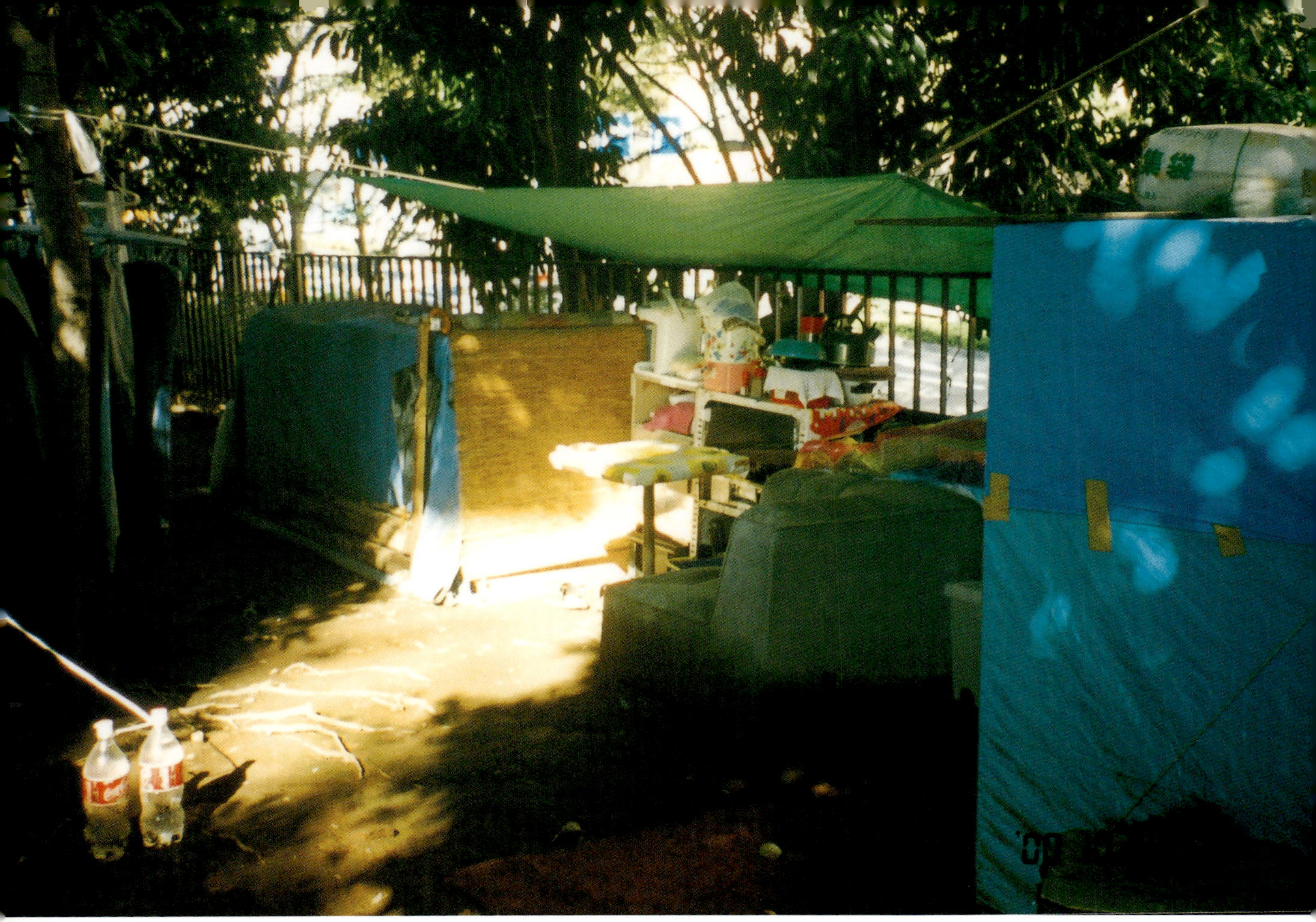

**Shinjuku Chuo Park Village**

新宿中央公園村

新宿中央公園の中には数箇所の住居群が存在し、それぞれが1つのコミュニティとして機能している。

In Shinjuku Chuo Park there are several clusters of houses. Each functions as a community.

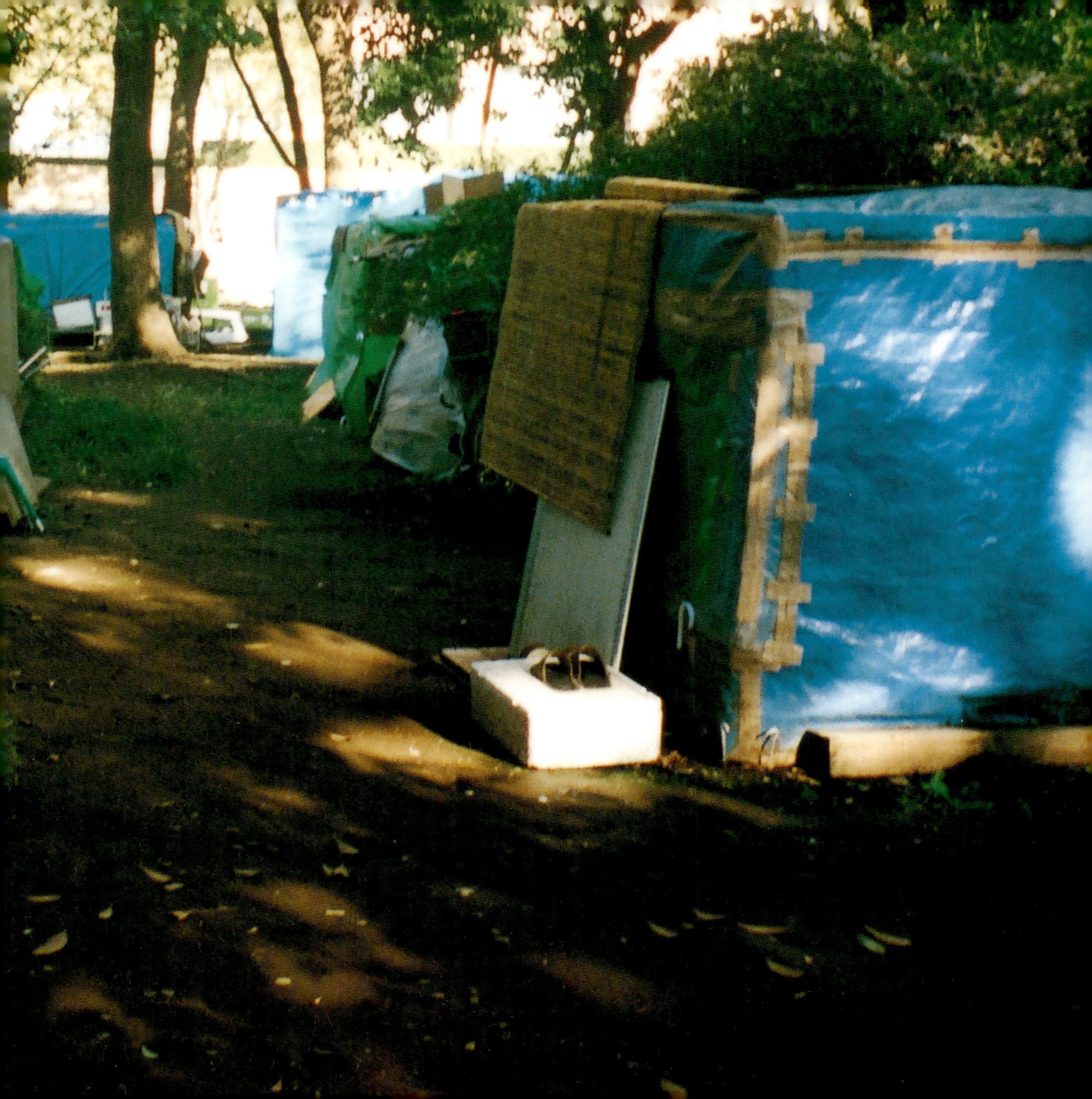

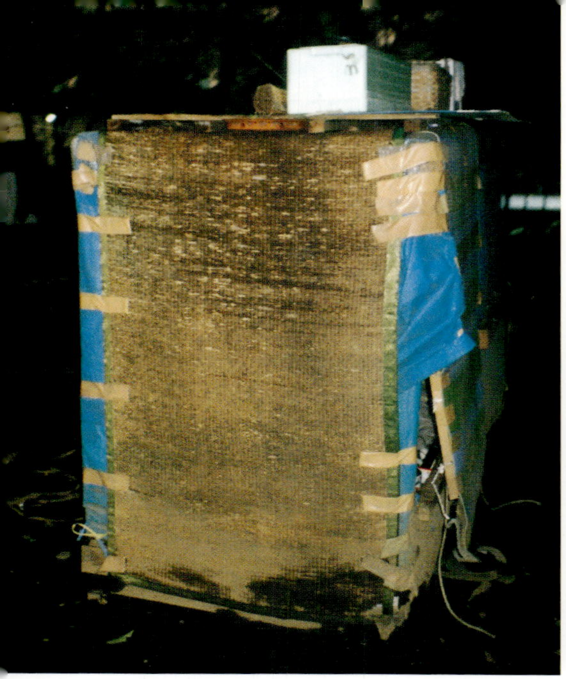
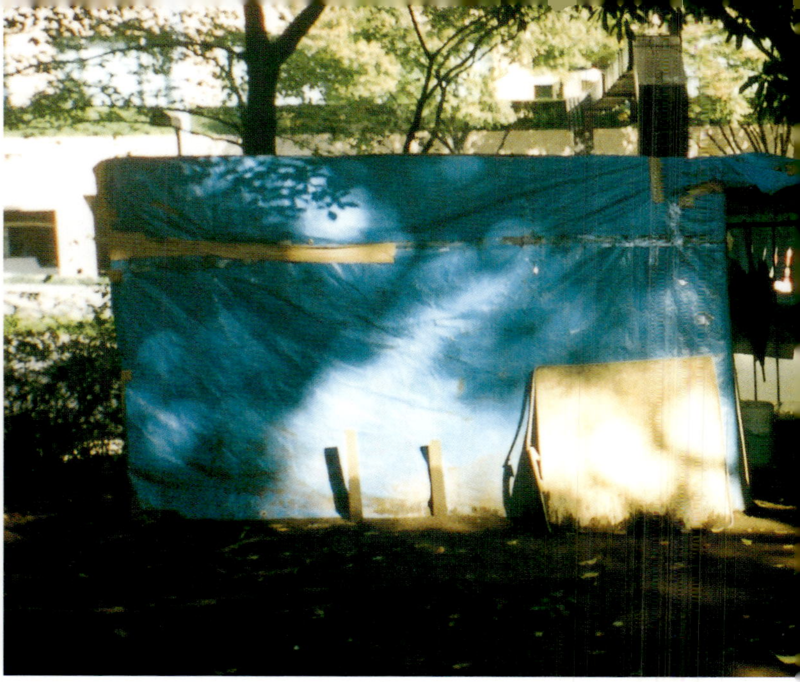
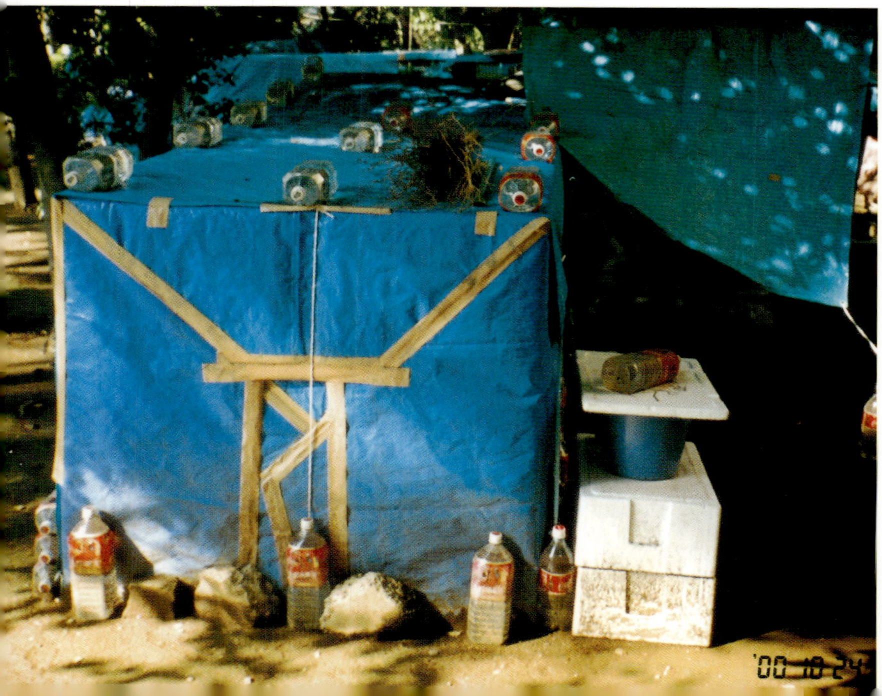
'00 10 24
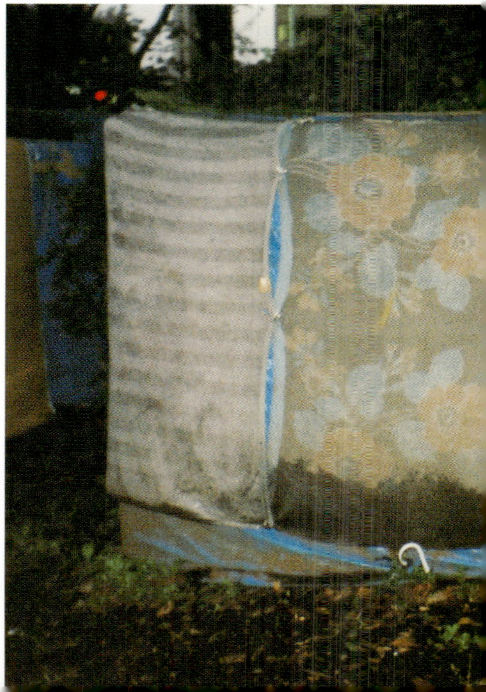

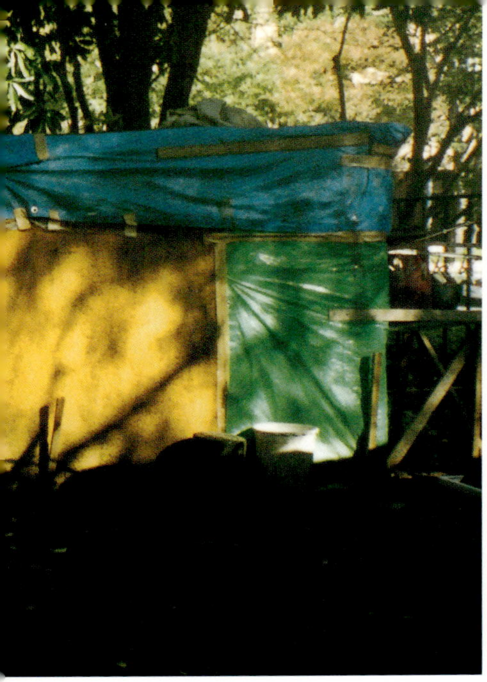
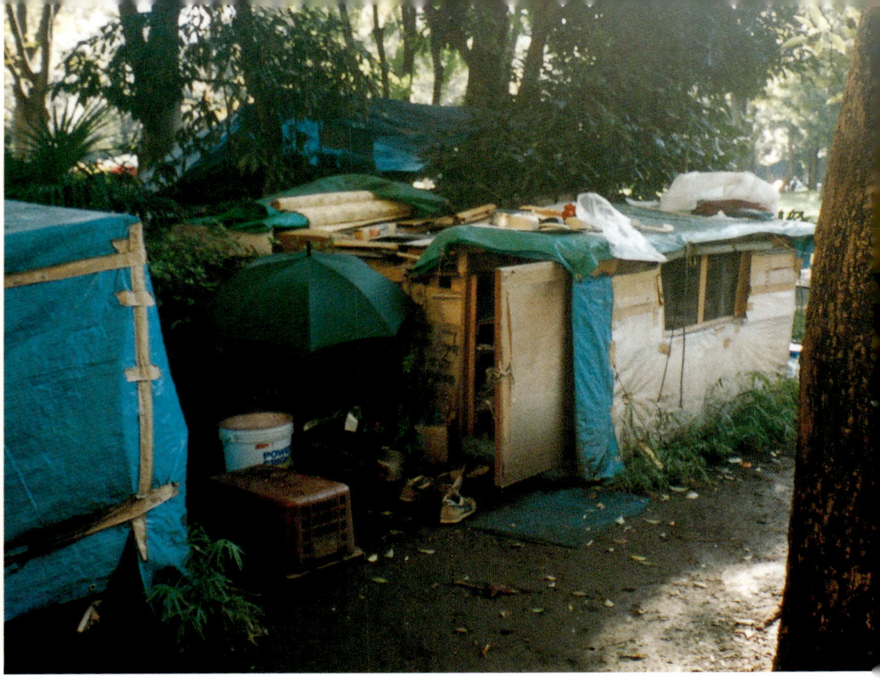
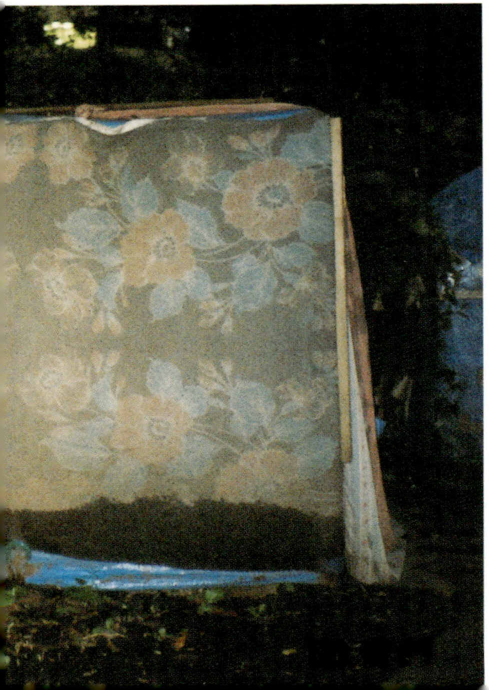
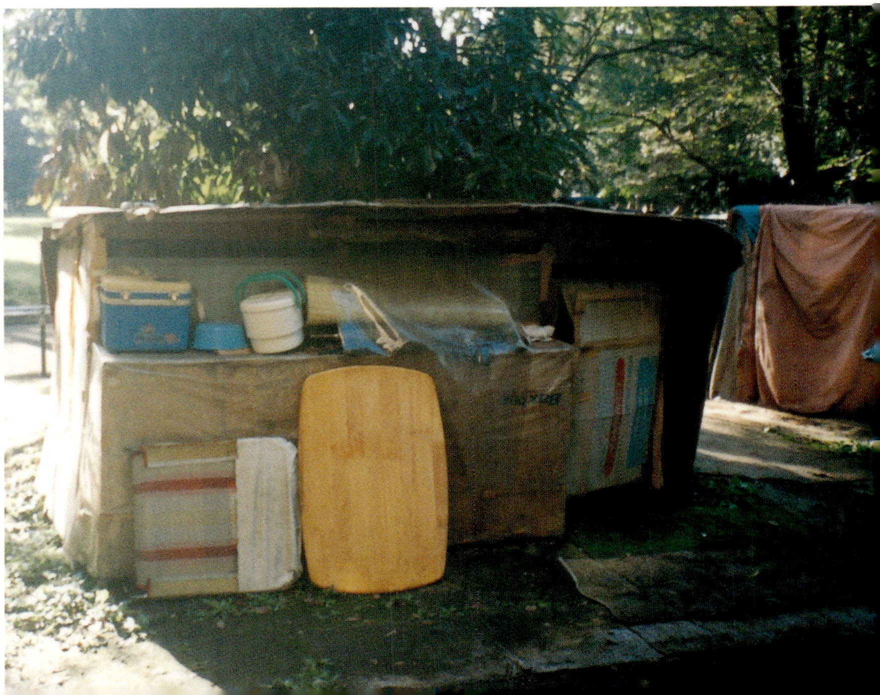

**Strange Objects in Shinjuku West**

新宿西口の奇妙な物体

新宿駅西口と都庁を結ぶ通路に奇妙な物体が並んでいる。実はこれは、この場所にダンボールハウスを建てられないように東京都が設置した障害物なのである。かつてここにあった住居群は、あとかたもなく消えてしまっている。

Strange objects line the passage between the West Gate of Shinjuku Station and the Tokyo Metropolitan Government Office. As it turns out, all of these objects were installed by the City of Tokyo to prevent cardboard houses from being built in the area. The cluster of houses that once existed here has completely disappeared.

'00 10 24

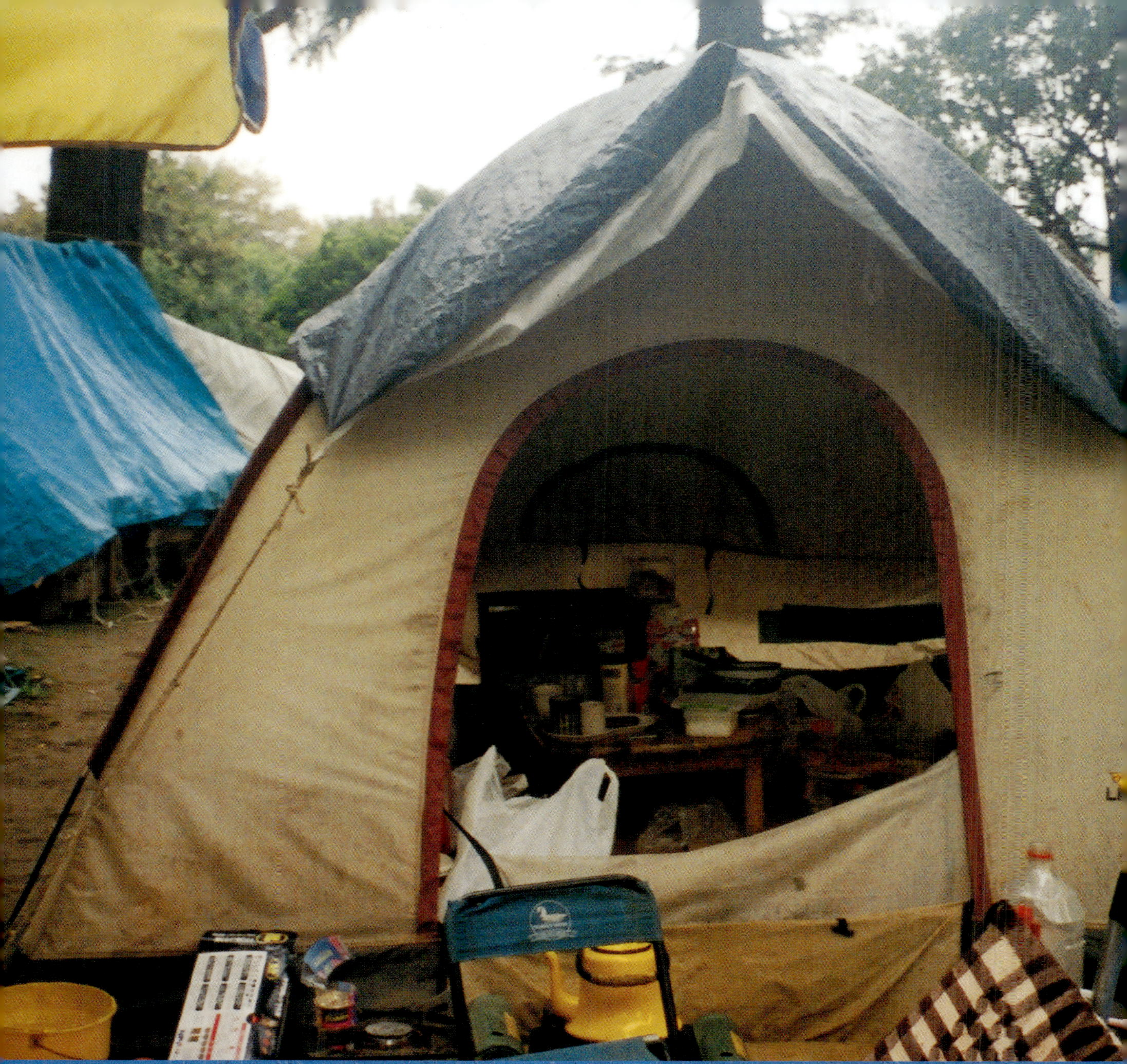

**Toyama Park**

戸山公園

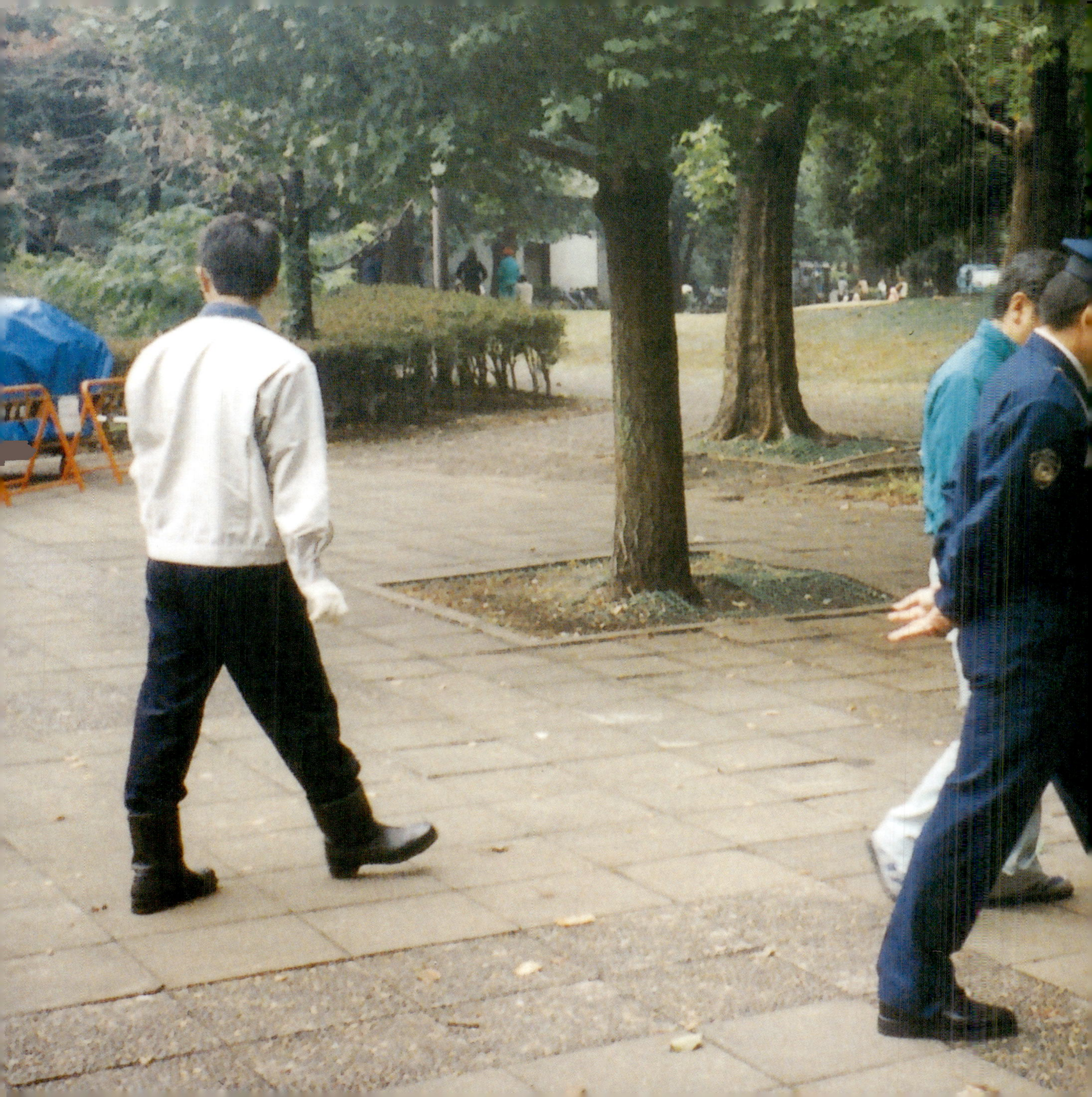

**Total Removal**
全面撤去

戸山公園に建つ住居群は20日に1度、全面撤去される。そのためここの住人は家を解体し、家財道具一式とともに公園の隅に一時待機する。

Houses in Toyama Park are removed every twenty days. Each time inhabitants temporarily take down their houses and stand by in the corner of park with all of their belongings.

153

**A House with Swaying Artificial Flowers**

造花が揺れる家

60代の男性が住むこの家の周りには、たくさんの造花が飾られている。鉄筋のビニールシートを掛けただけの簡単な作り。彼は家の中で毎日、理想の女性の絵を描いている。

A lot of artificial flowers adorn this house, where a man in his sixties lives. The structure of the house is simple— a vinyl sheet placed over reinforced steel rods. His days are spent in the house drawing images of the ideal woman.

撤去前

Before Removal

撤去後

After Removal

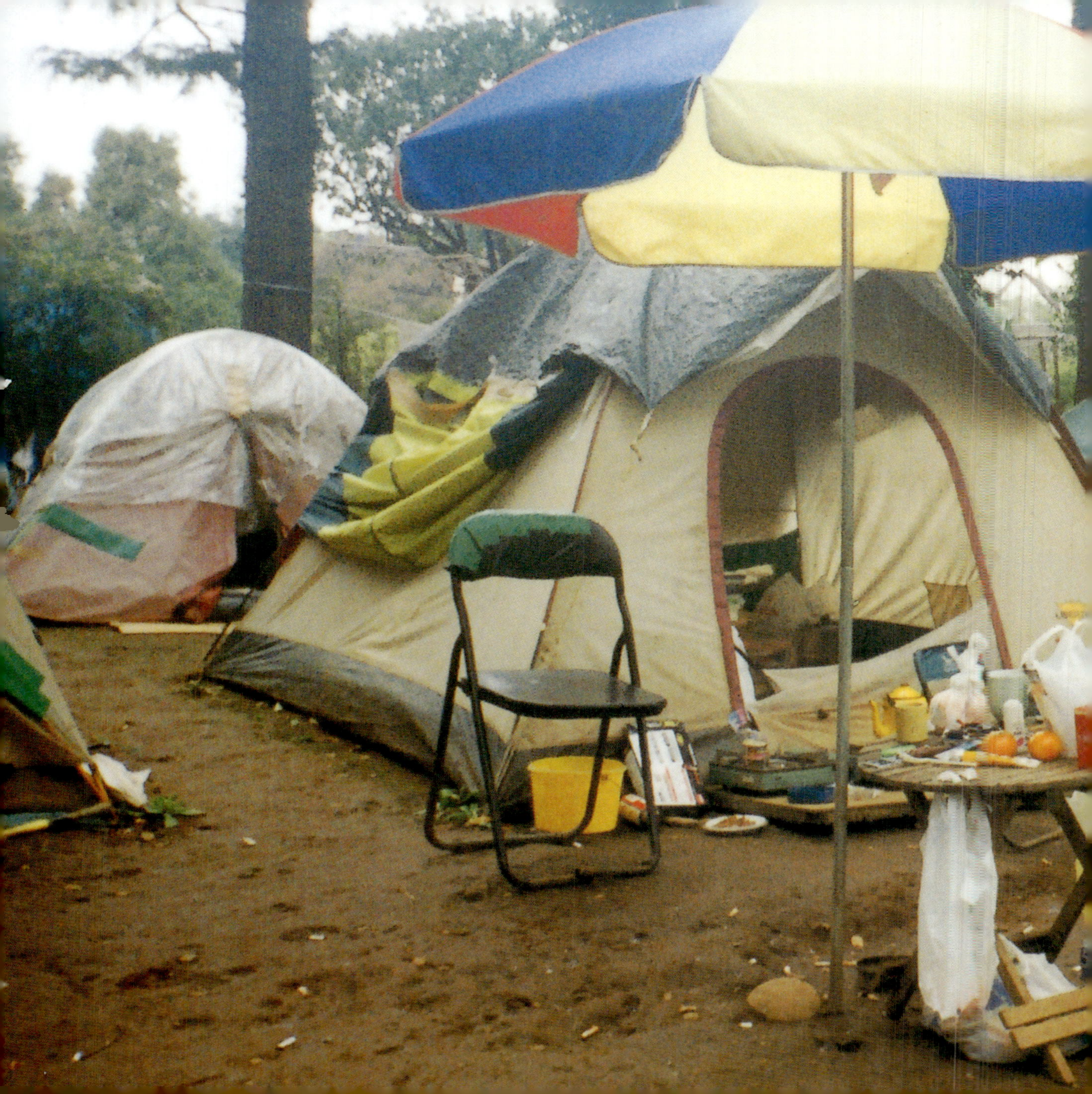

**Toyama Campground**

戸山キャンプ場

戸山公園には、日雇いの仕事で収入を得ている人も少なくない。彼らの多くはテントを購入し生活している。撤去が頻繁に行われるため、家をその度に建てなおすより、断然楽だからだ。

Many people in Toyama Park are day laborers. Many of them purchase tents. This is much easier than having to rebuild every time their houses are removed from the park.

**A Room for Dining, Studying and Sleeping**

食卓兼書斎兼寝室

狭い空間の中で、すべてのことができるように、家具や布団の配置など、こだわりが随所に見られる。人間にとって本当に必要な部屋の広さはどれぐらいなのだろうか。

In order to be able to do everything in the small space, the inhabitant of this house is particular about the arrangement of his furniture and bedding. How much space does a human being really need?

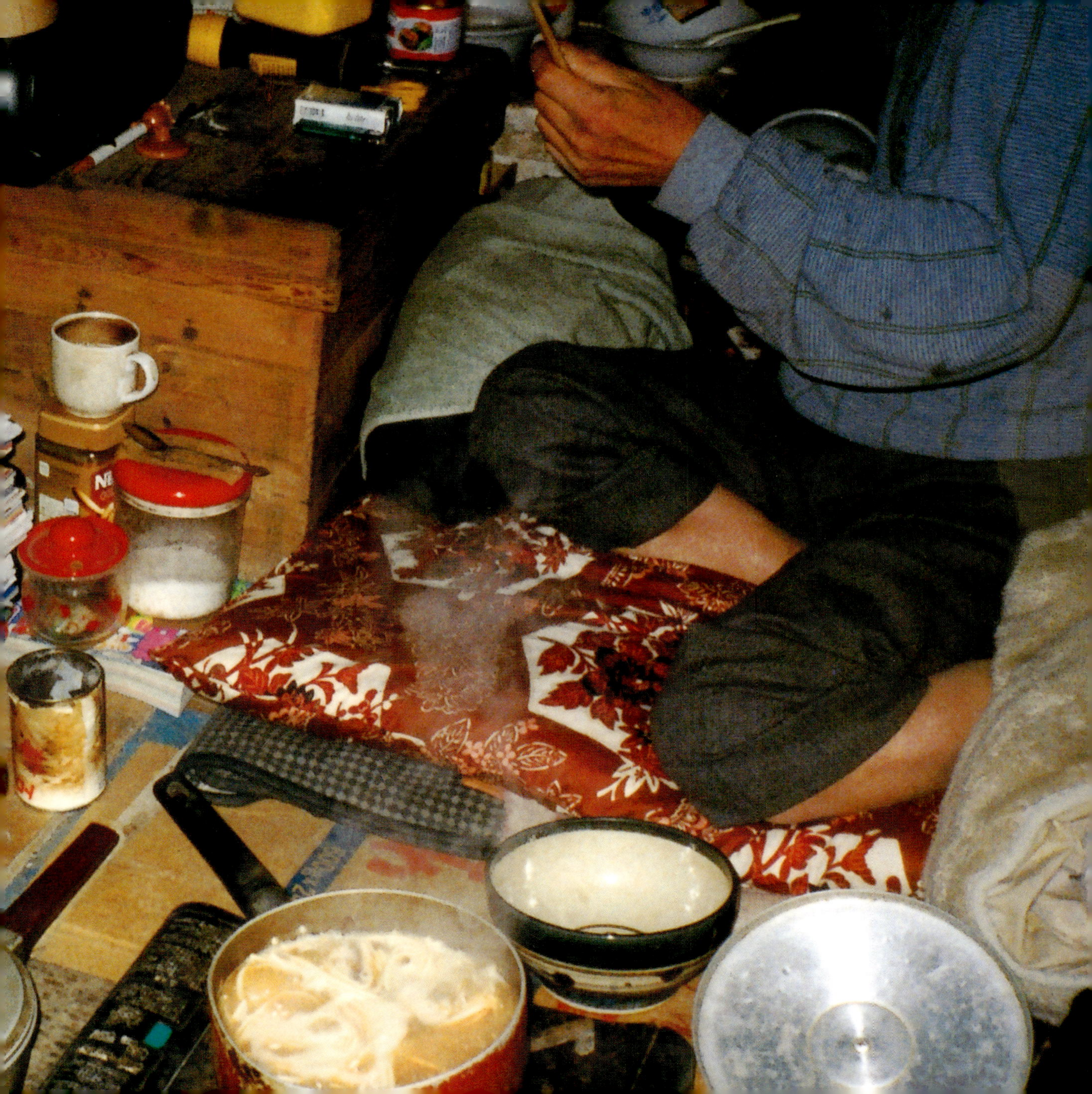

作りかけのダンボールハウス。まず、きれいに雑誌を並べ、その上にダンボールを重ねていく。あとはダンボールで囲いを取り付けたら出来上がり。ここは橋の下なので屋根は必要ない。彼の仕事は古雑誌売りである。

A cardboard house in the making. First, magazines are neatly arranged and then cardboard is piled on top of them. Finally, cardboard walls are put up and the house is done. Since this one is located under a bridge, there is no need for a roof. He sells used magazines for a living.

ダンボールを少しずつ重ね合わせながら並べ、穴の開いた部分に紐を通し、結ぶと出来上がり。

Put cardboard side by side to overlap a little bit, run strings through the holes to bind them together and it's finished.

壁H 1484

40
1444

```
           85
       30 ┌─────┐        3095
          │     │
       40 └──┬──┘ 55      3190
          30 │  │
             └──┘         3250
                 2058 2138
             ┌──┐                    220
          40 │30│
             │  │ 40
          32 └──┴────┐
                     │
                  70
```

20|40

40
1888

壁H 1928

倍

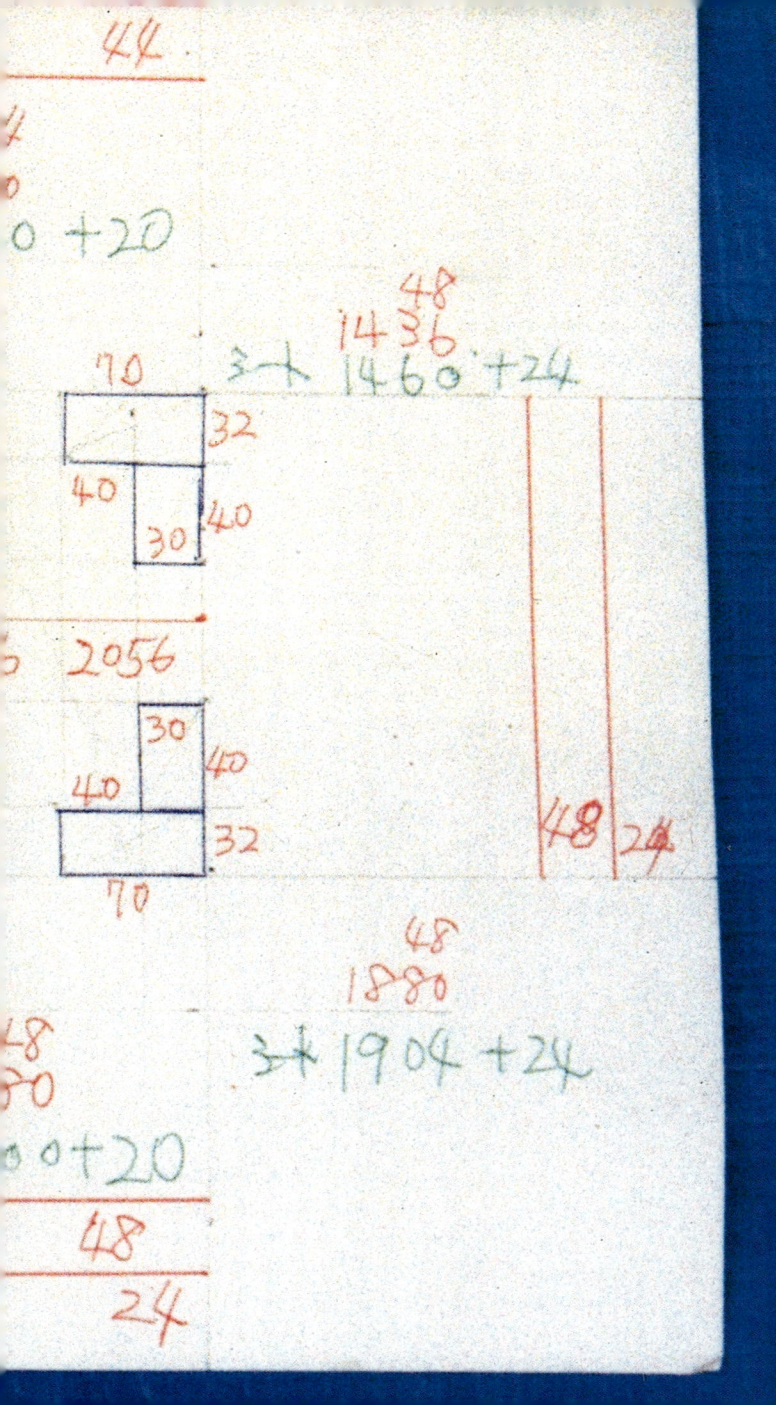

**An Architectural Plan for a Vinyl Sheet House**

ビニールシートハウスの設計図

かなり精密な図面になっている。柱は木材で作り、それにビニールシートをかぶせる。この図面は、鳶職人の住居。

This is quite a detailed plan—wood pillars with vinyl sheets spread over them. The plan is for the house of a steeplejack.

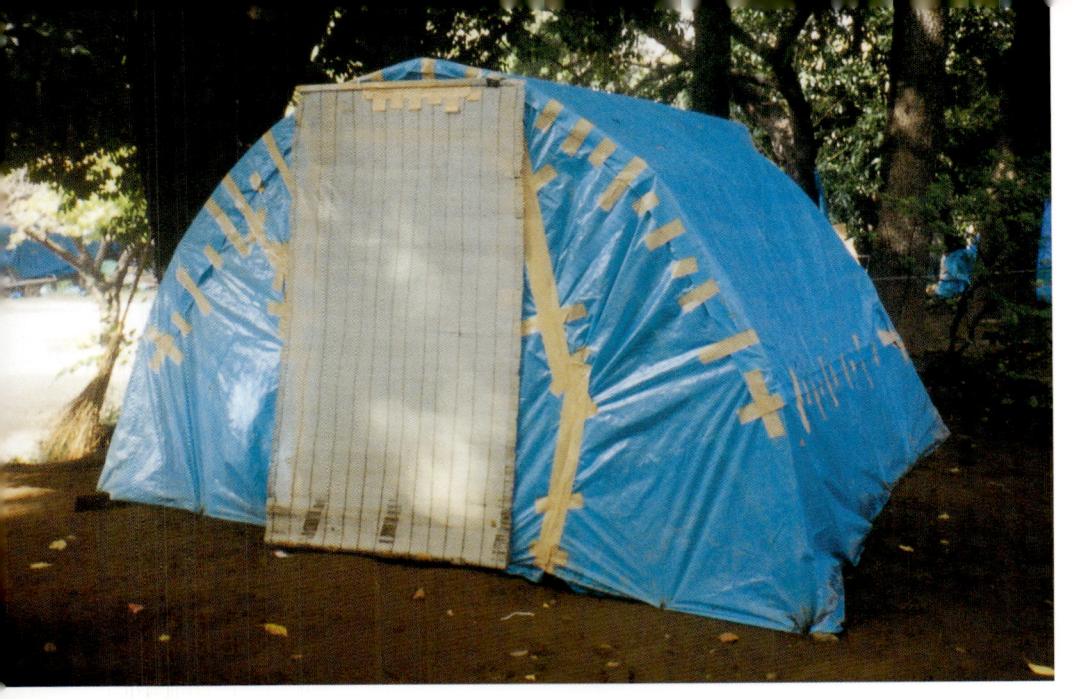

工事用の鉄筋でアーチを形作った家。玄関を開けると中にはテントが入っている。この形態のものは他にも見られた。

An arched house using reinforcing bars for construction. Opening the front door reveals a tent inside. This type of house is seen elsewhere.

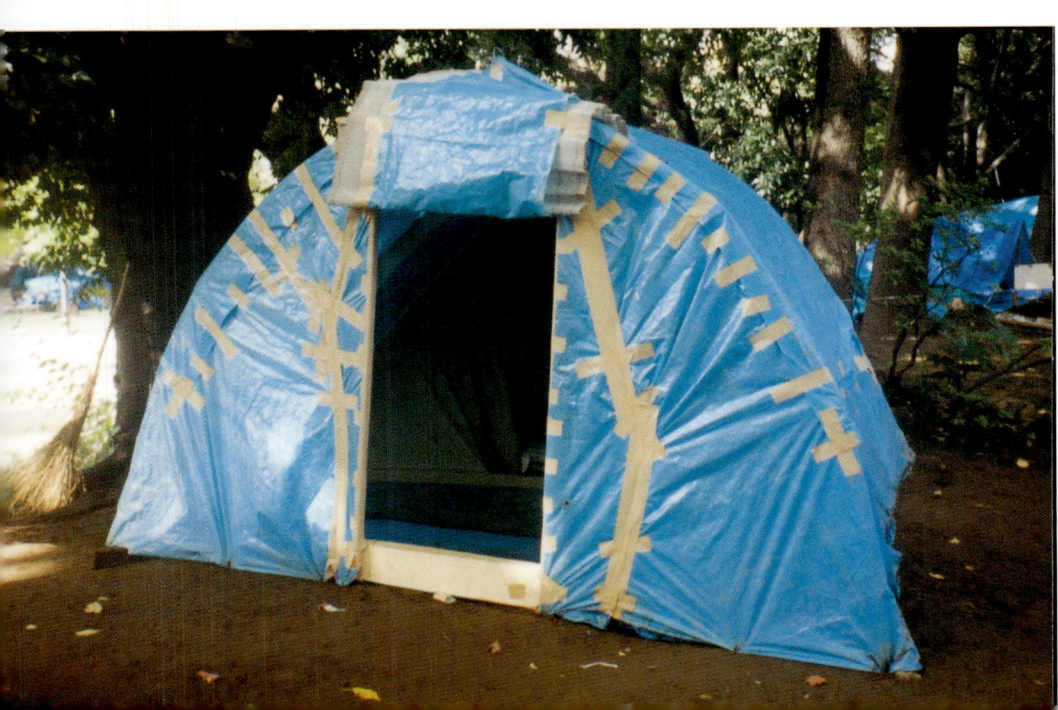

立入禁止

# Unique Pillars

変柱

通常は下の写真のように市販の角材で柱を組むのだが、上の写真では、なんと既存の植木を柱として利用している。

In most cases, as in the picture below, pillars are made with commercial square timbers. But the picture above shows living trees being used as pillars.

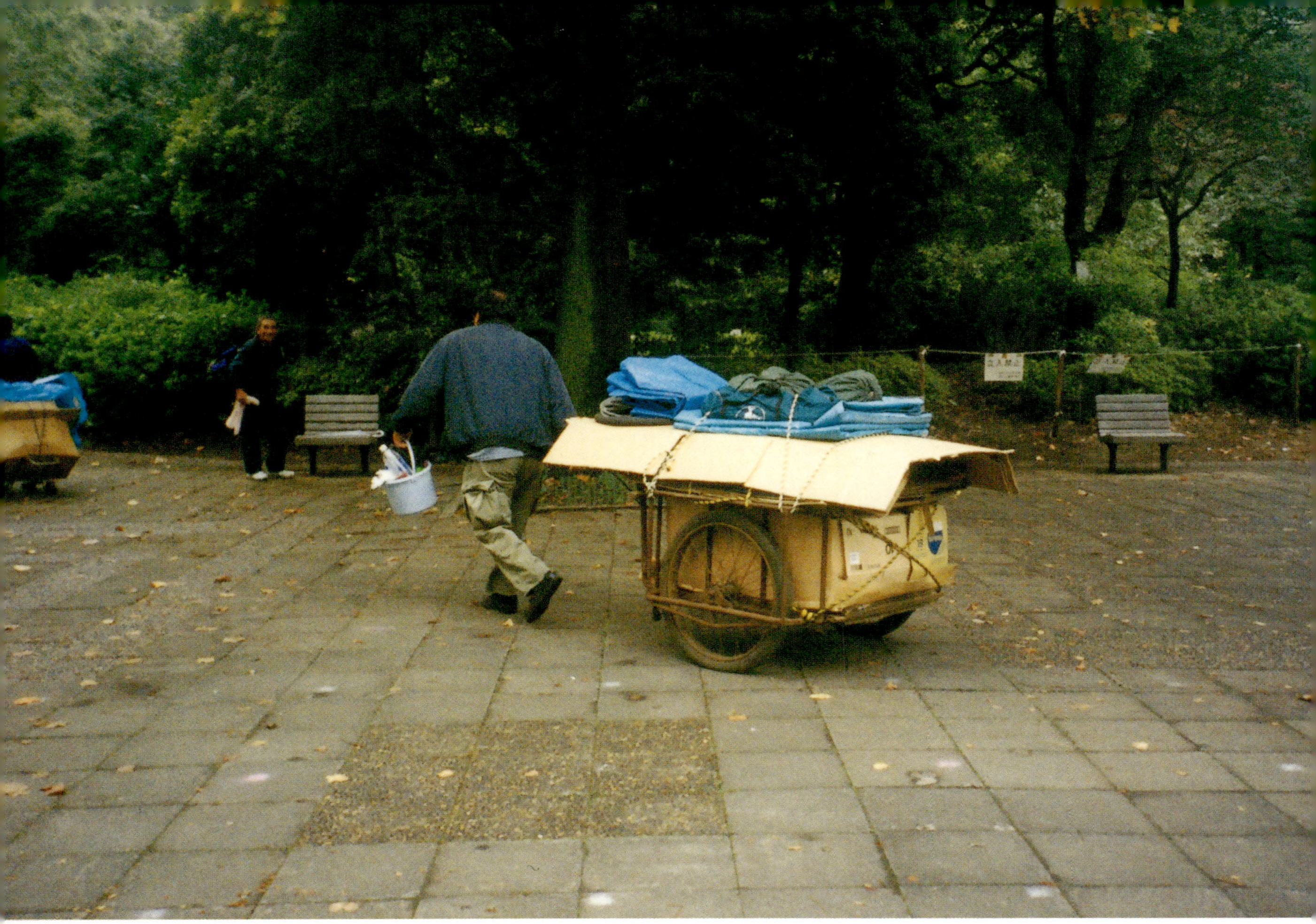

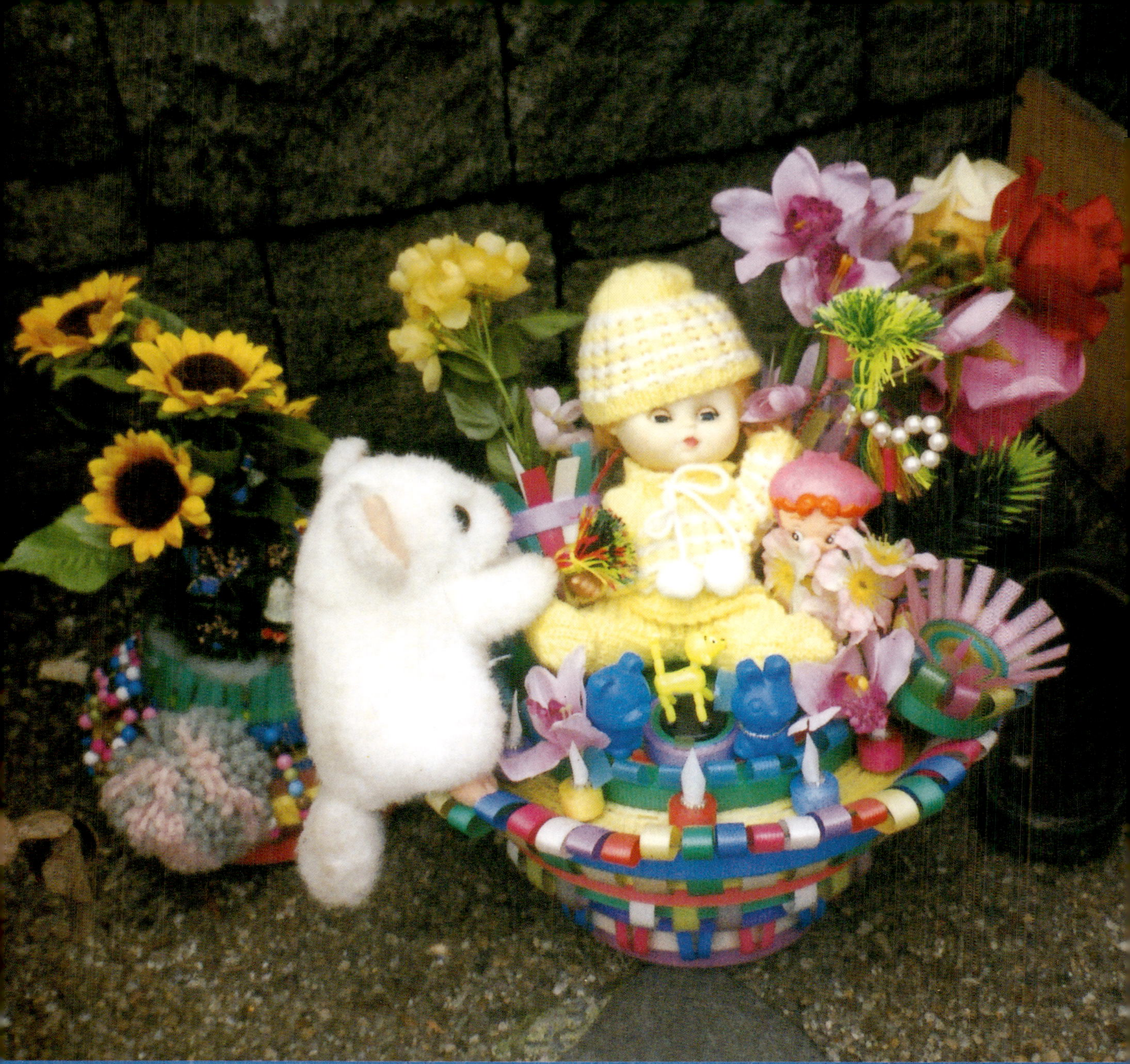

# The Sumidagawa
# 隅田川

## Simplified Houses
## 単純化する家

隅田川沿いの遊歩道には数多くのビニールシートハウスが林立する。それらは極度に単純化させられ、装飾もほとんど見られない。窓もなく、ビニールシートで囲まれた、ただの箱のようなものまである。月に1度全面撤去が行われるため、解体しやすく、組み立てが容易な形態に落ち着いたのであろう。

There is a line of vinyl sheet houses along the sidewalk running along the Sumidagawa River. They are extremely simple, with no decoration. There is even a windowless box-shaped house covered with a vinyl sheet. Because these houses are all completely removed once a month, the structures are easy to dismantle and put back up.

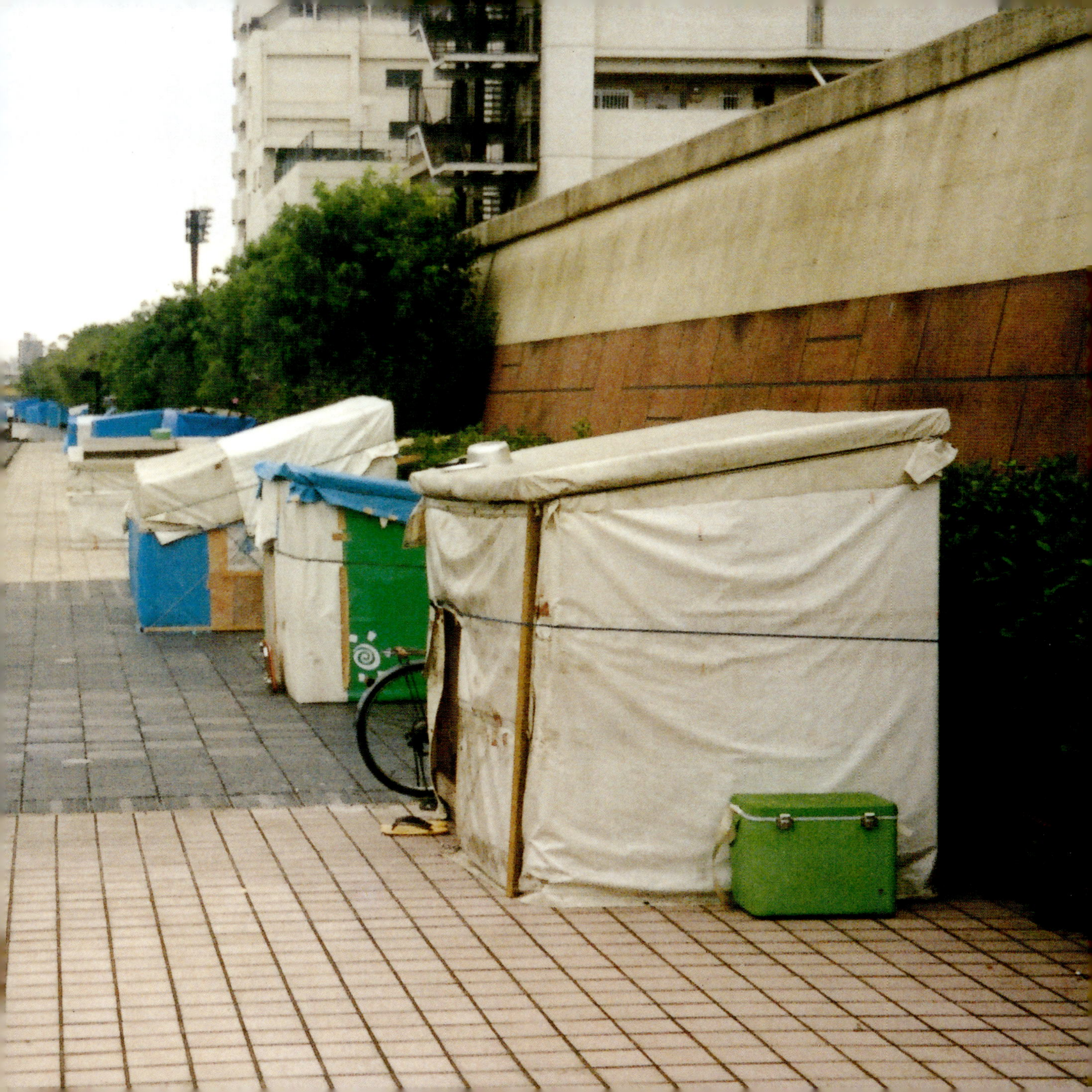

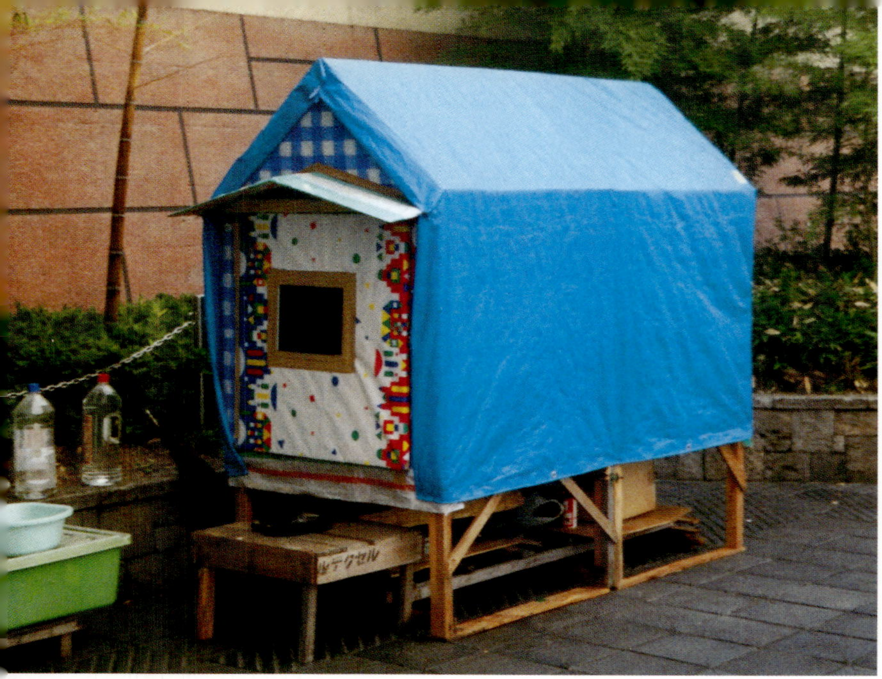

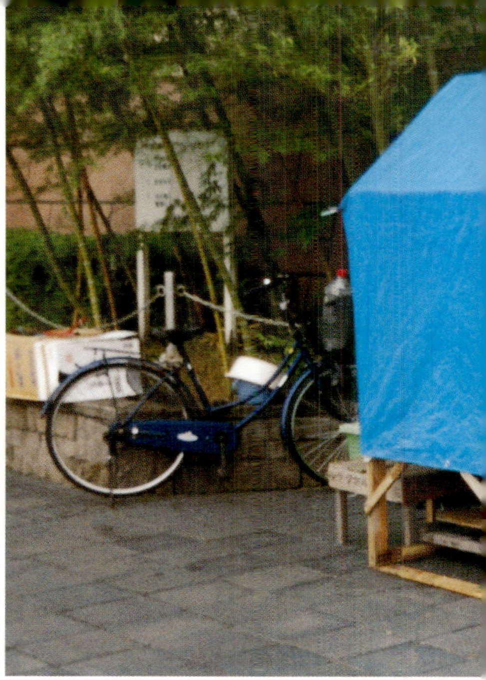

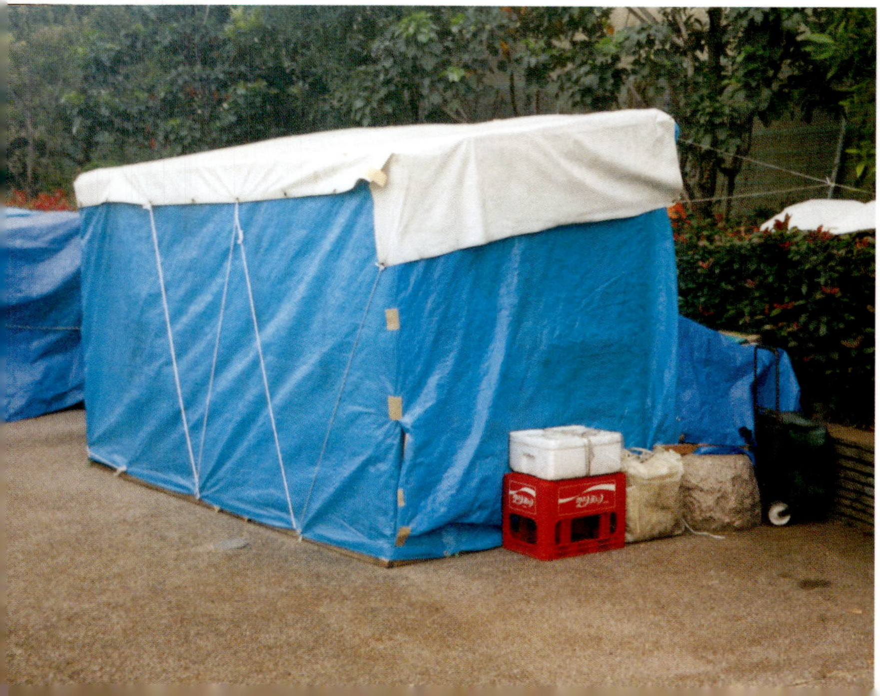

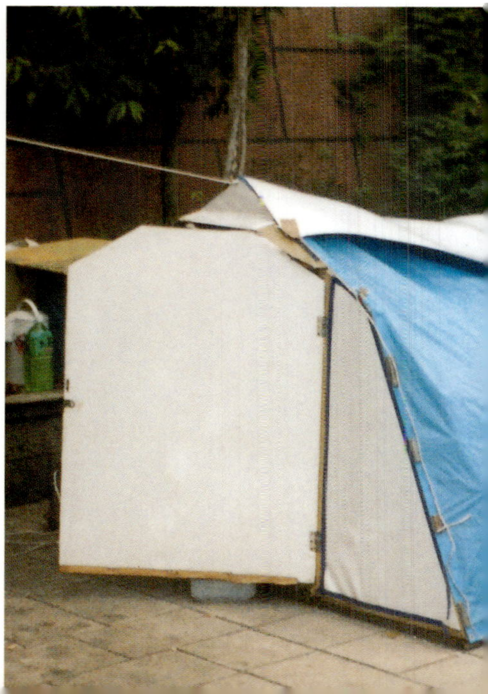

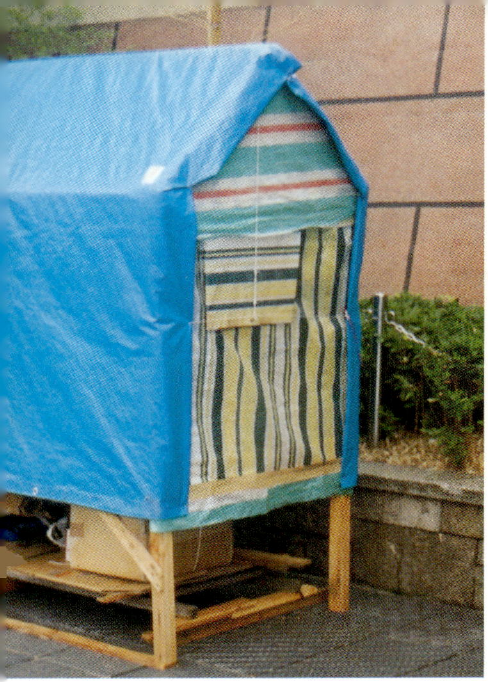
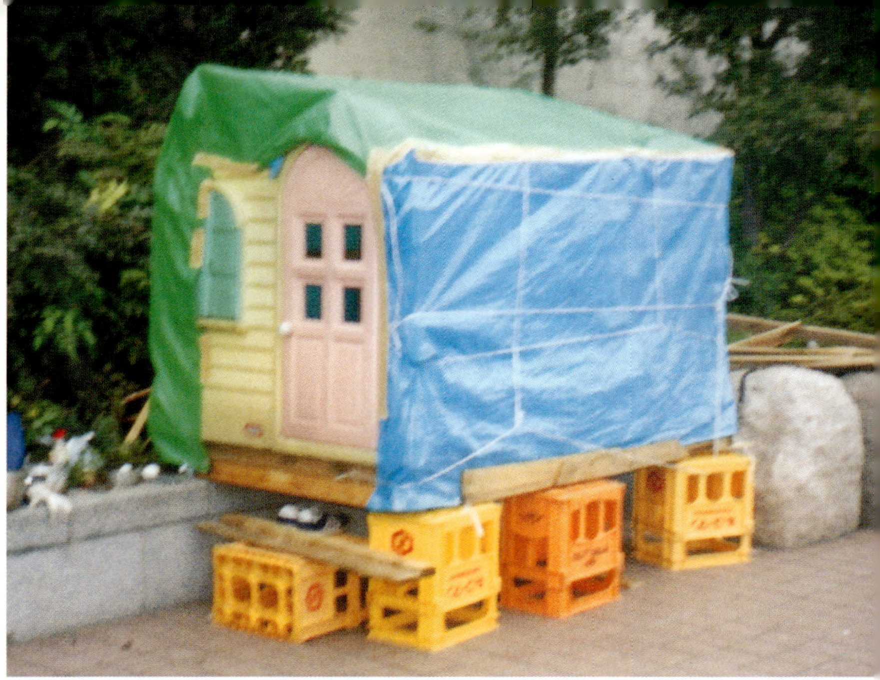
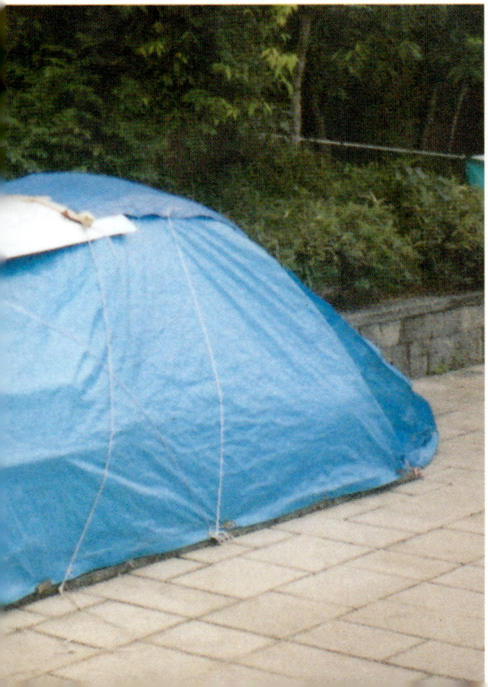
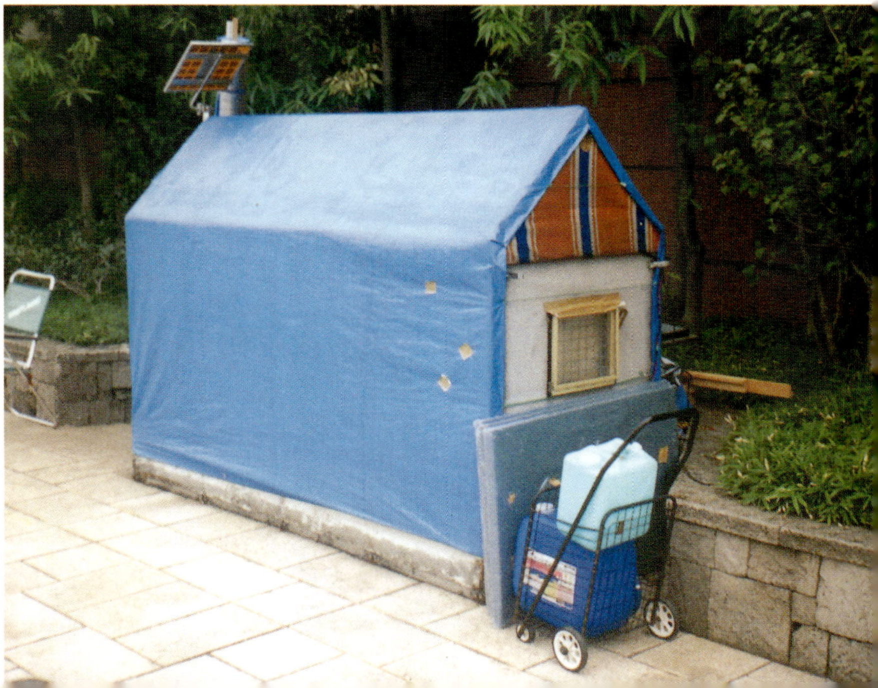

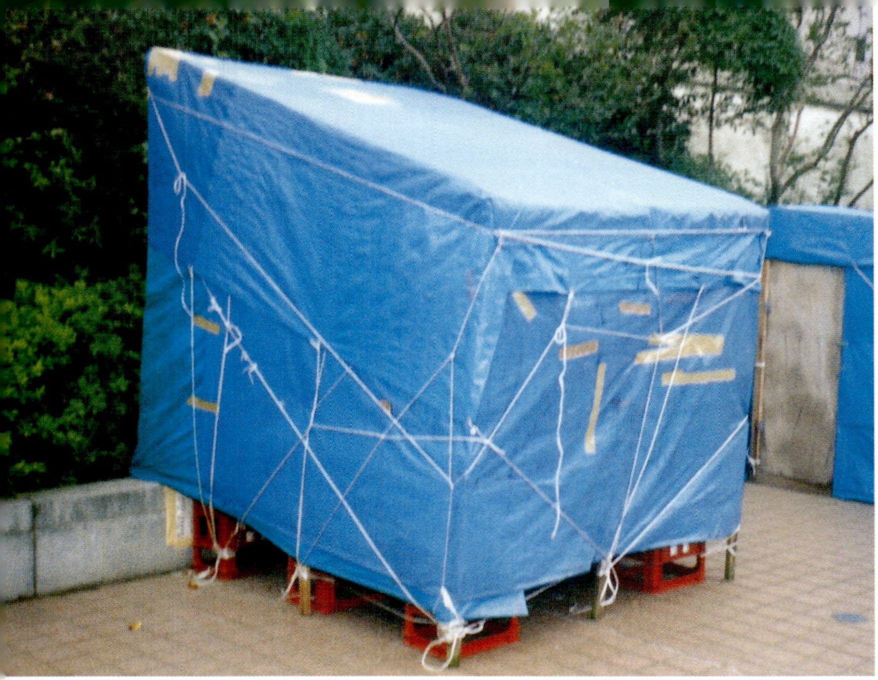
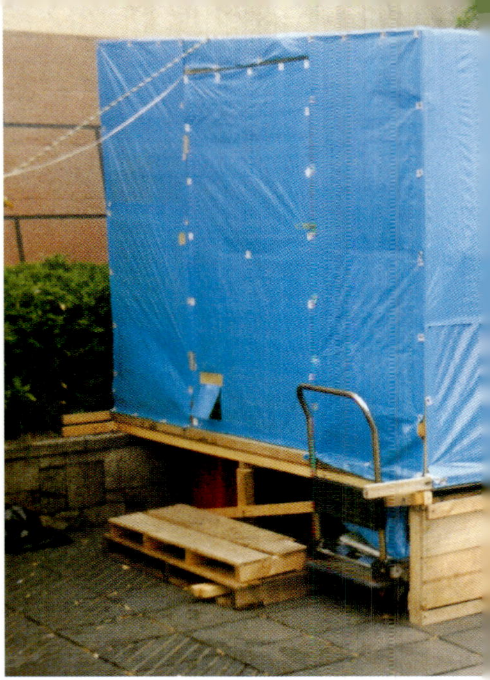
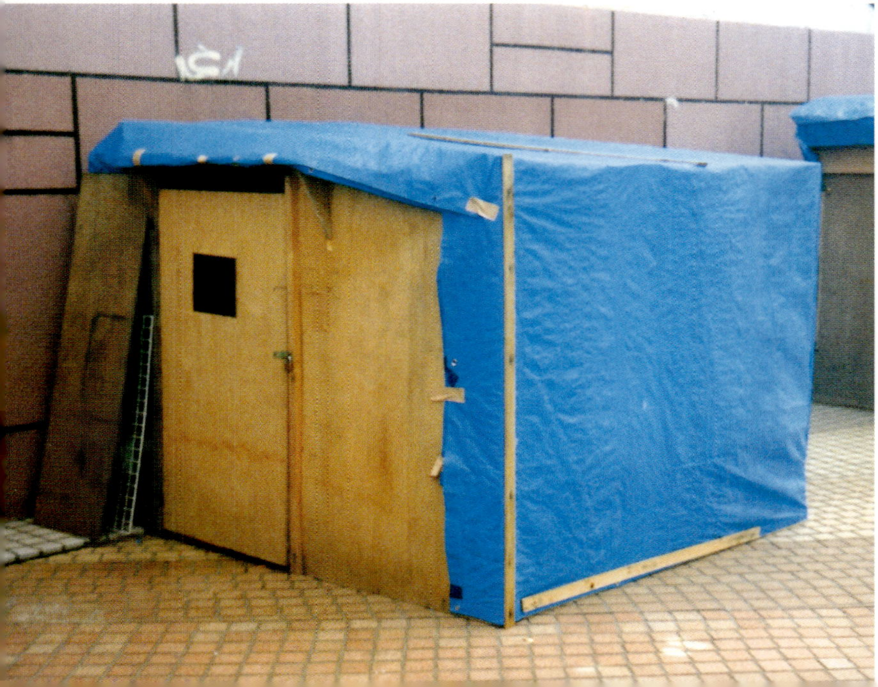
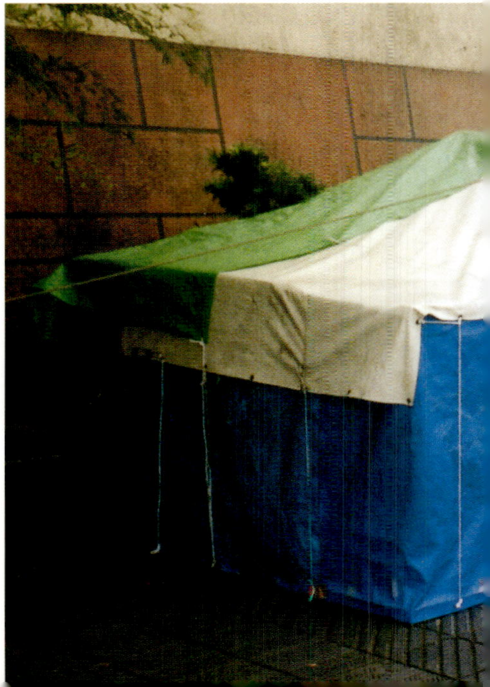

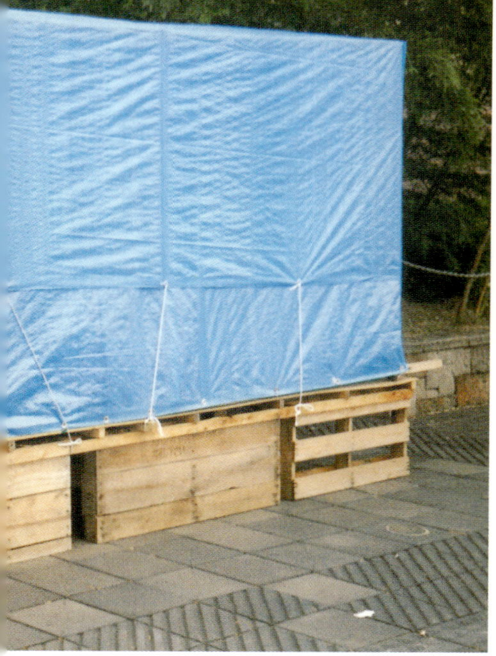
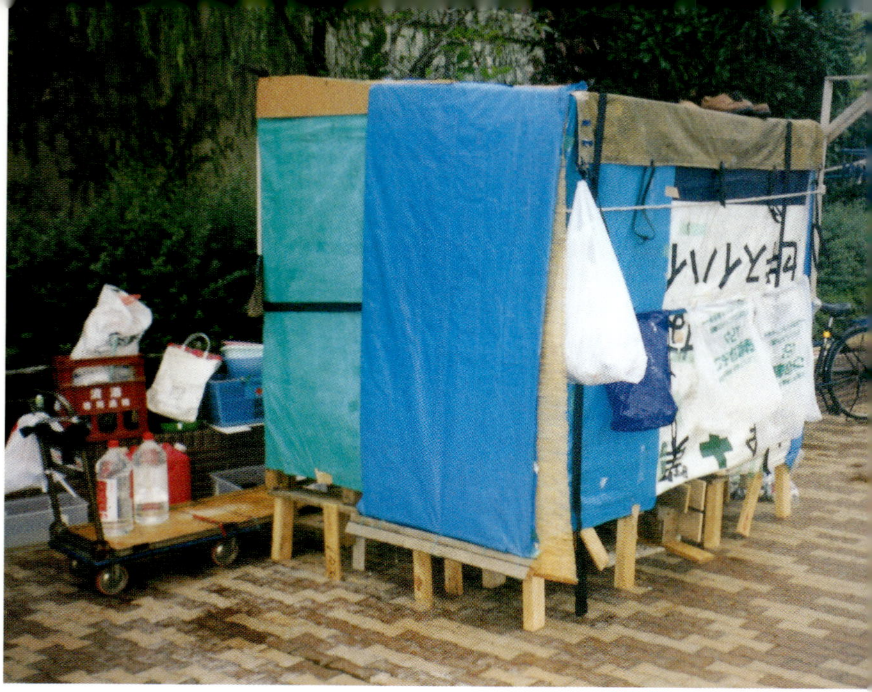
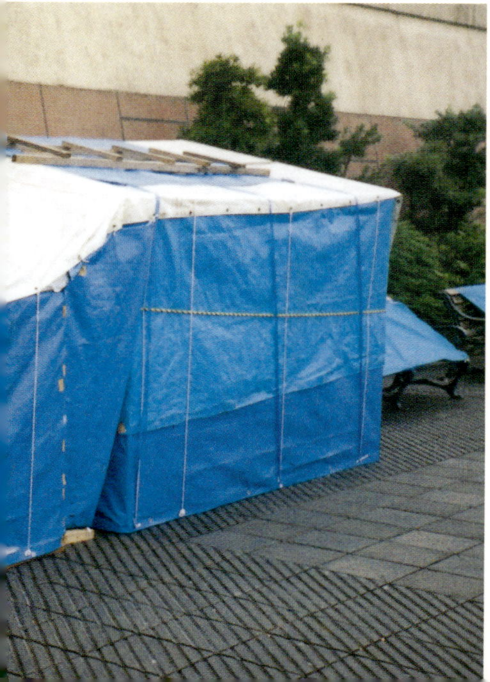
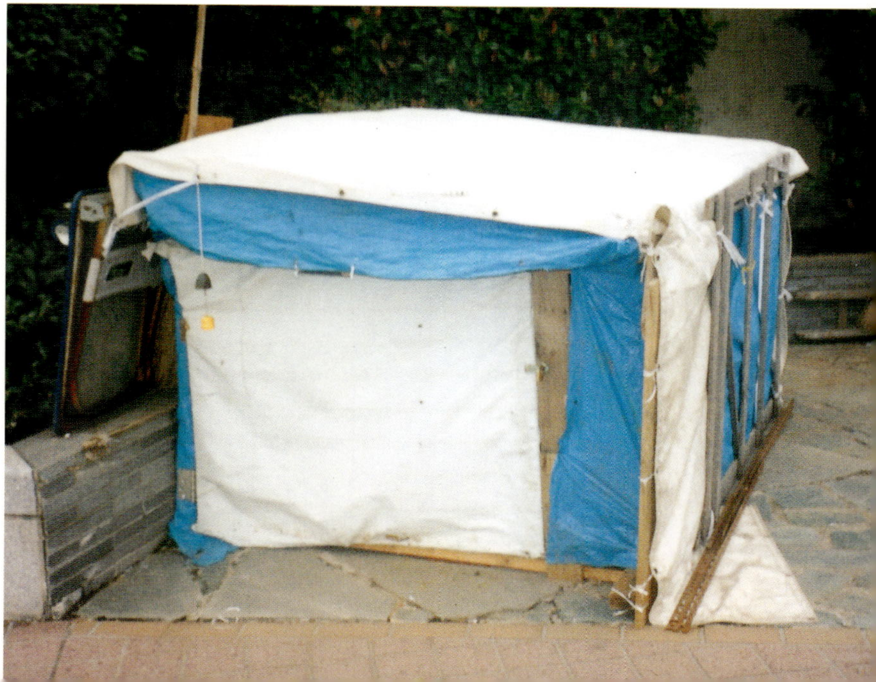

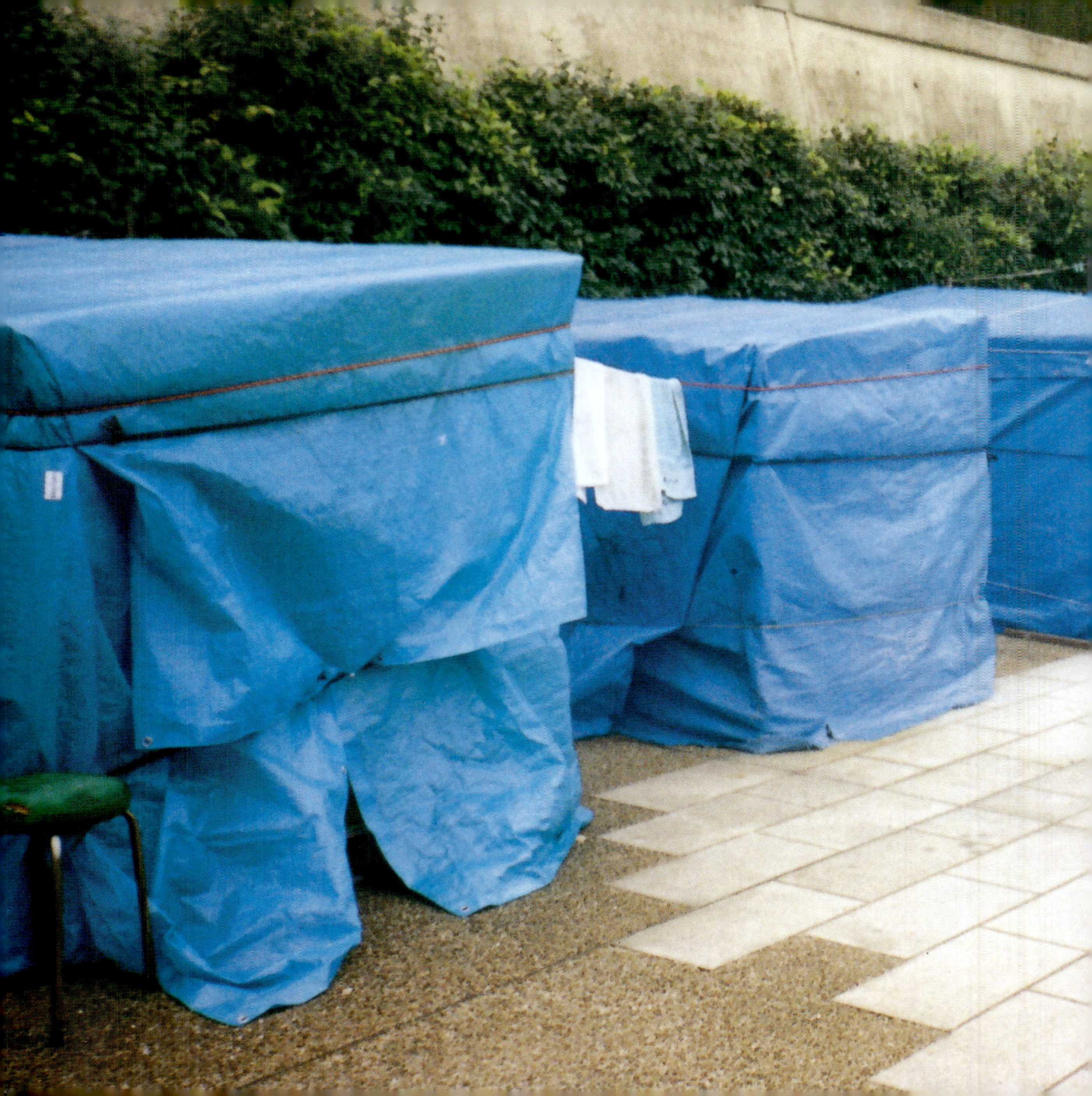

## Houses Built for Sale
建売住宅

まったく同じ作り、同じサイズの家が5軒建っている。どこかの建売住宅のような光景である。

Here are five houses of exactly the same size and structure. It looks like the ready-built housing communities that can be seen in many places.

# Flowers of Rubbish

## ゴミの花

隅田川沿いの住居群の中で一際異彩を放っていたのがこの家。家自体は他と変わらないが表に住人が作ったオブジェが飾られている。住んでいるのは30代後半の男性で、1日のほとんどをオブジェ作りに費やしている。すでに700個以上完成させたそうだ。オブジェは梱包に使用するプラスチック製のバンドで作られている。バンドを巻いて円状にしたものを幾つか重ねて土台を作り、その周りに拾ってきた造花などをコラージュしていく。1つ作るのに約20時間を要するという。バンドの色は青系だけでも10種類以上あると彼は熱弁をふるう。しかし最近では色のバリエーションが少なくなっており創作意欲をなくしている。

This is the most conspicuous house among the houses by the Sumidagawa River. The house itself is just like the others, except that it is decorated with objects created by its inhabitant. He is a man in his thirties who spends most of his day creating the objects, which are made of plastic packing bands. More than seven hundred objects have already been created, he says. Bands are rolled in a circular pattern, several are put together to form a base, and plastic flowers are added. He says it takes about twenty hours to make one. He speaks passionately about the fact that the bands come in more than ten different shades of blue alone. Recently, however, the number of color variations has decreased, and he is losing his desire to create.

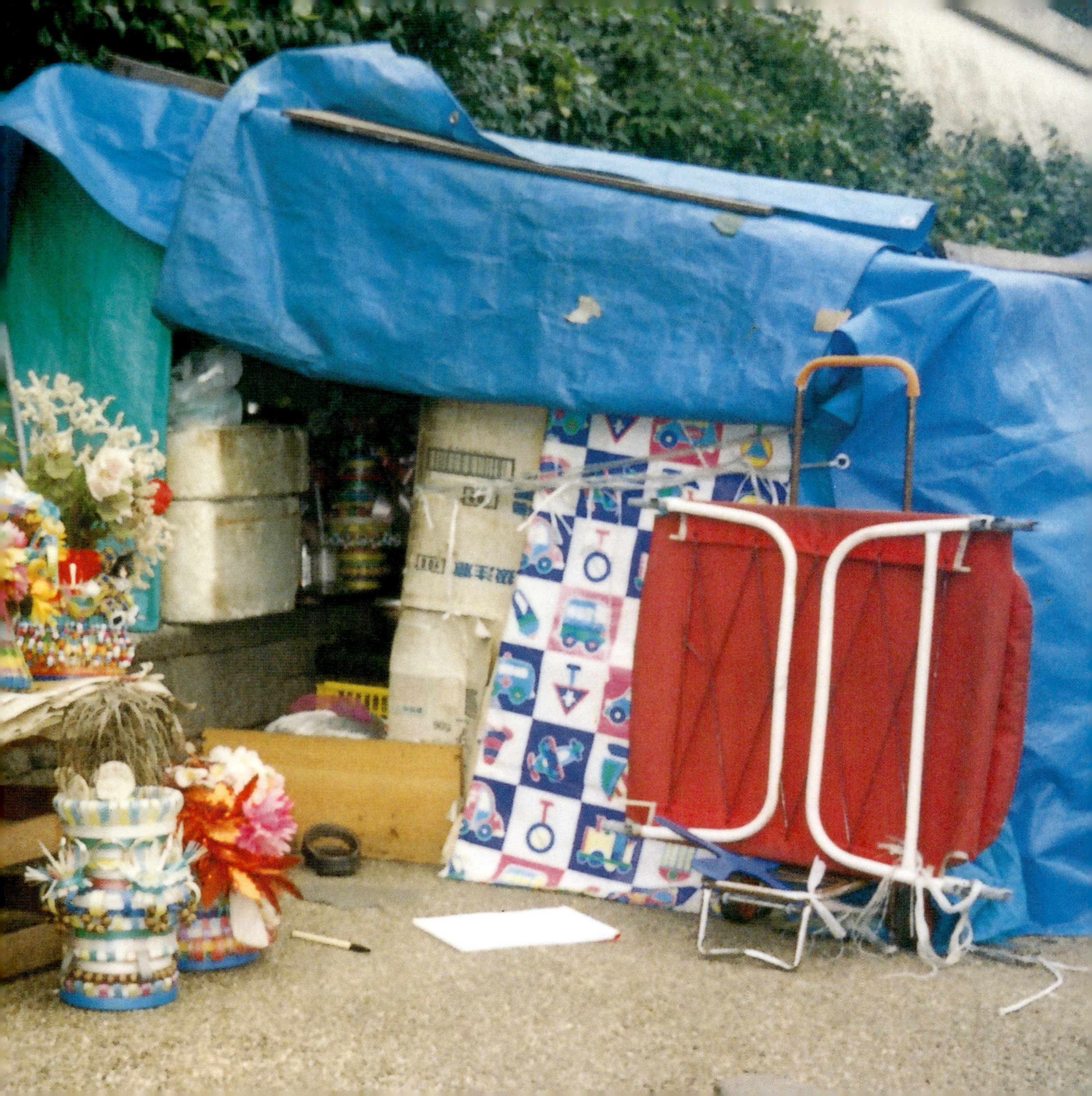

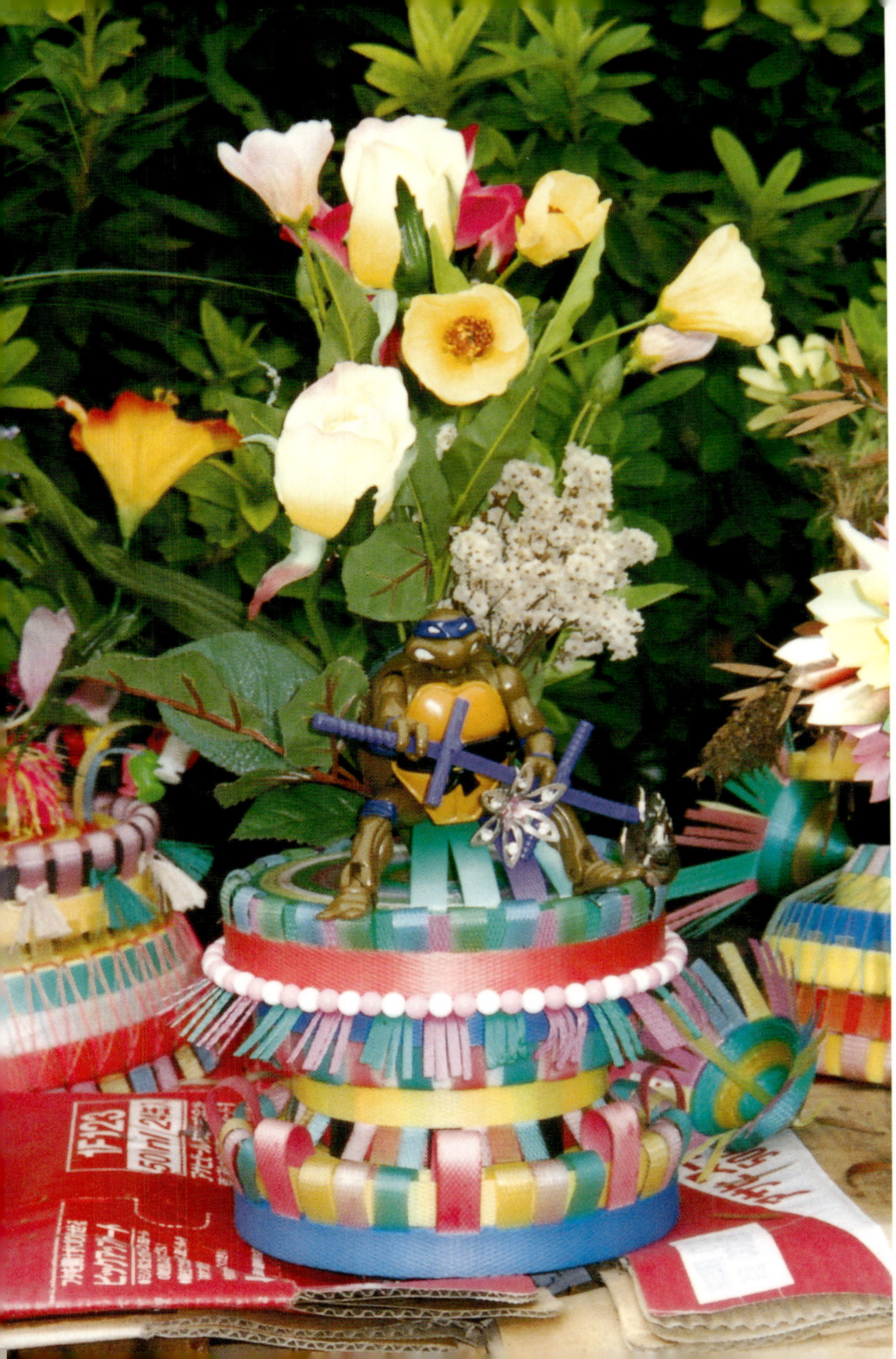

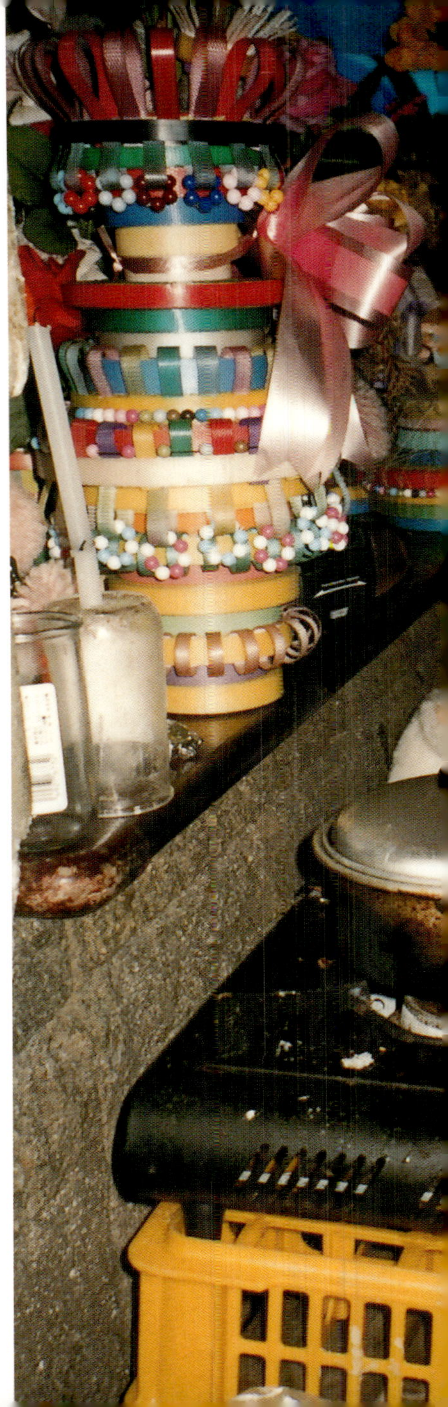

雪印コーヒー

## An Evolving House
進化する家

この家はすべて廃品で作られている。また屋根、居間、収納の3つに分解でき、容易に持ち運ぶことができる。極めつけは、ソーラーバッテリーで自家発電し、ラジオとテレビを使用していることだ。住人は生活しながらさらに家を改良し続けている。まさに、進化する家である。

This house is made of waste products only. And it can be dismantled into three pieces, the roof, the living room and storage area, for easy portability. The ultimate is that because this house has a solar electric generator, a T.V. and radio can be used here. The inhabitant continues to improve his house as he lives day to day. Certainly this is an evolving house.

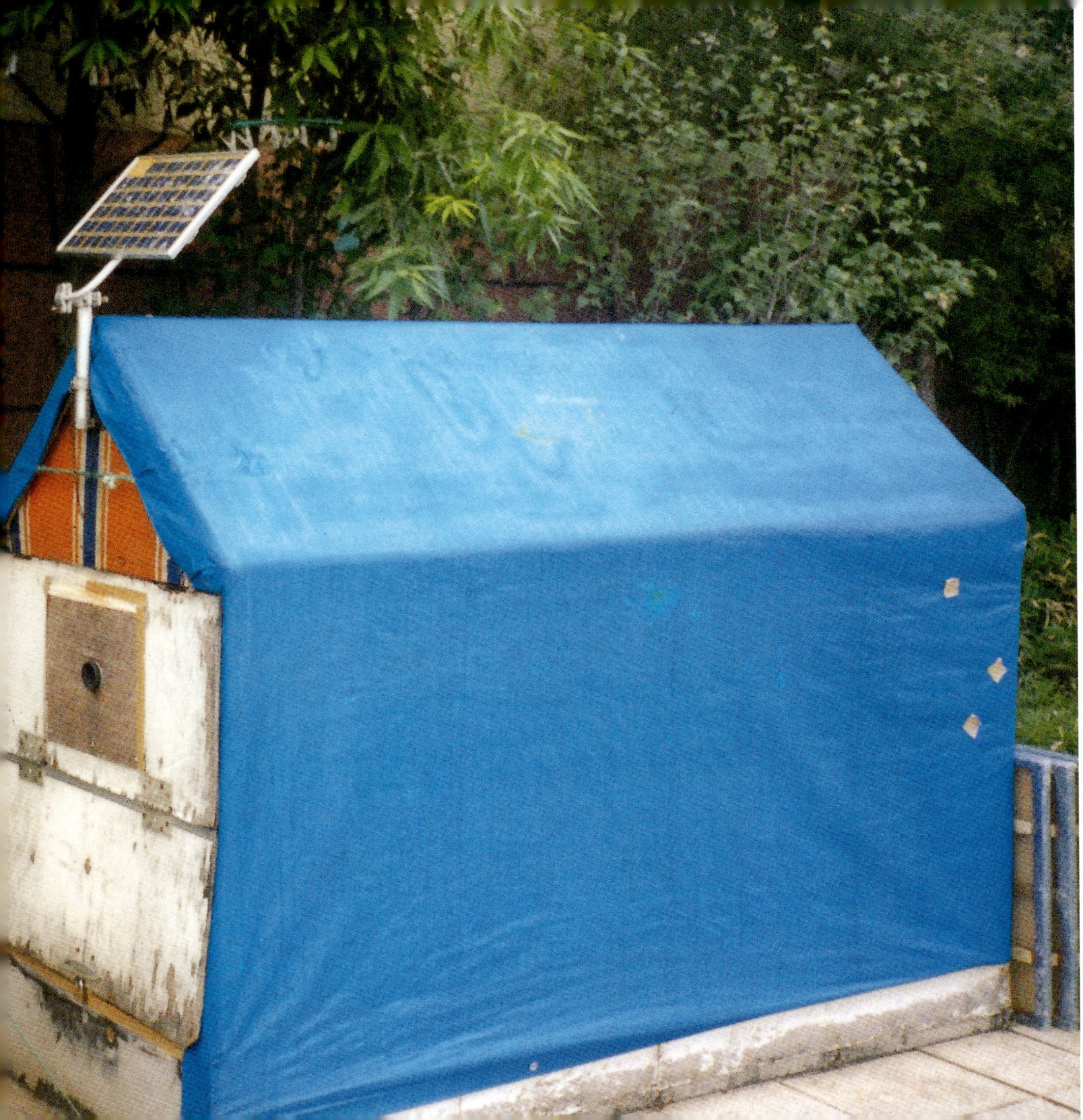

東京　2000年撮影

Tokyo, photographs taken in 2000.

# Sketch Book
スケッチ

# The Tamagawa

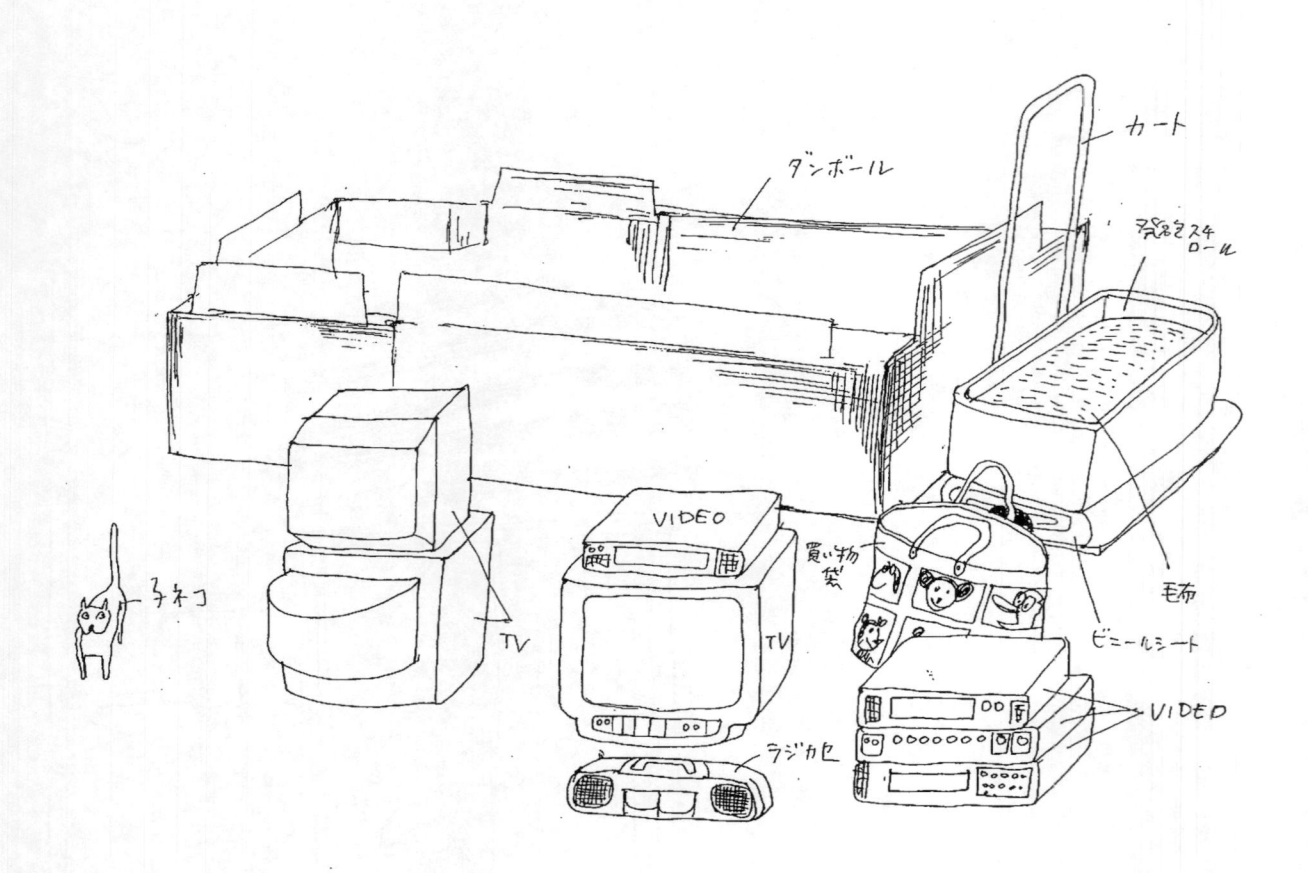

多摩川

単管　毛布　釣リザオ　なべ

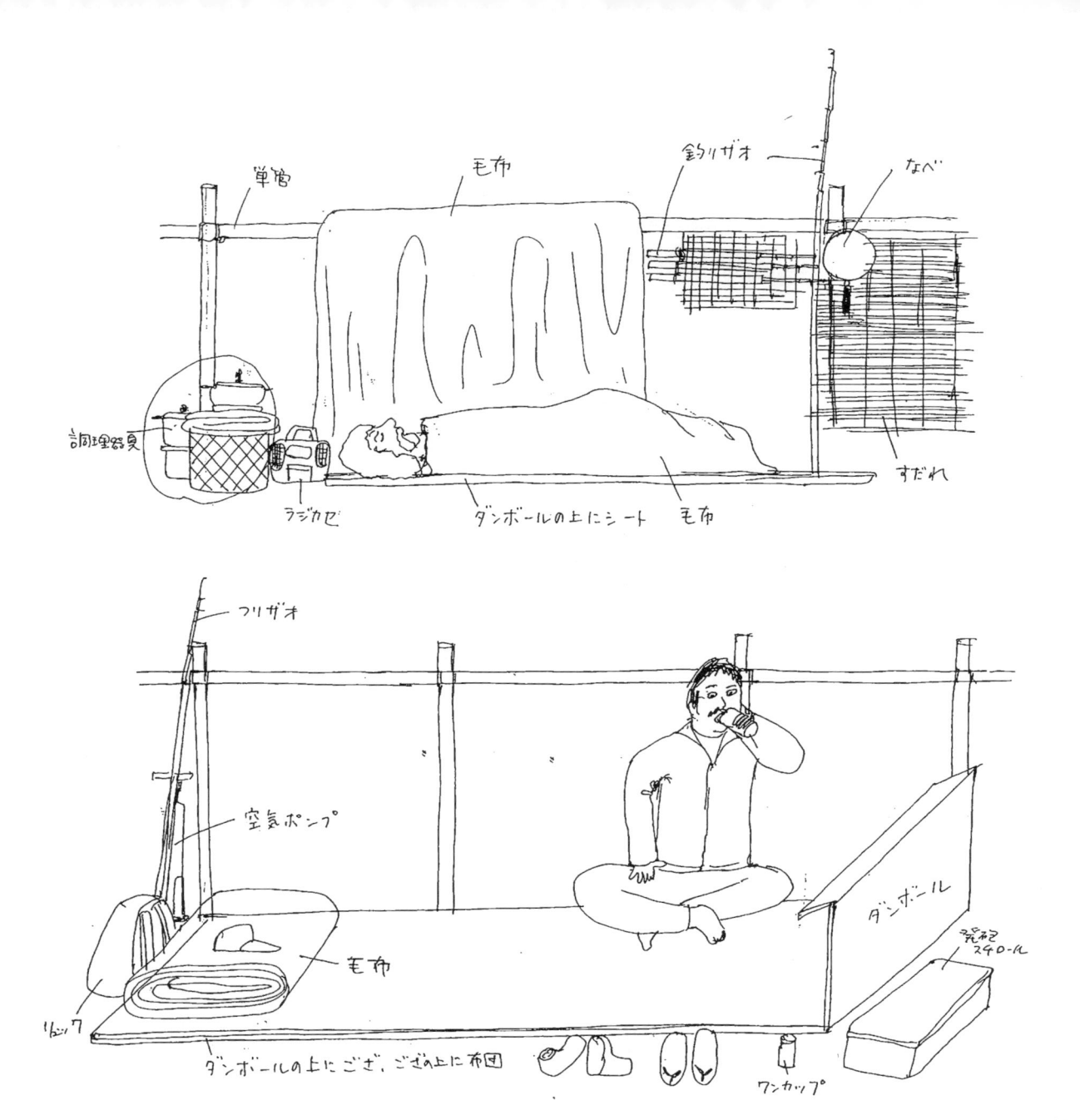

調理器具

ラジカセ　ダンボールの上にシート　毛布　すだれ

ツリザオ

空気ポンプ

毛布

リュック　ダンボール

ダンボールの上にござ、ござの上に布団　ワンカップ

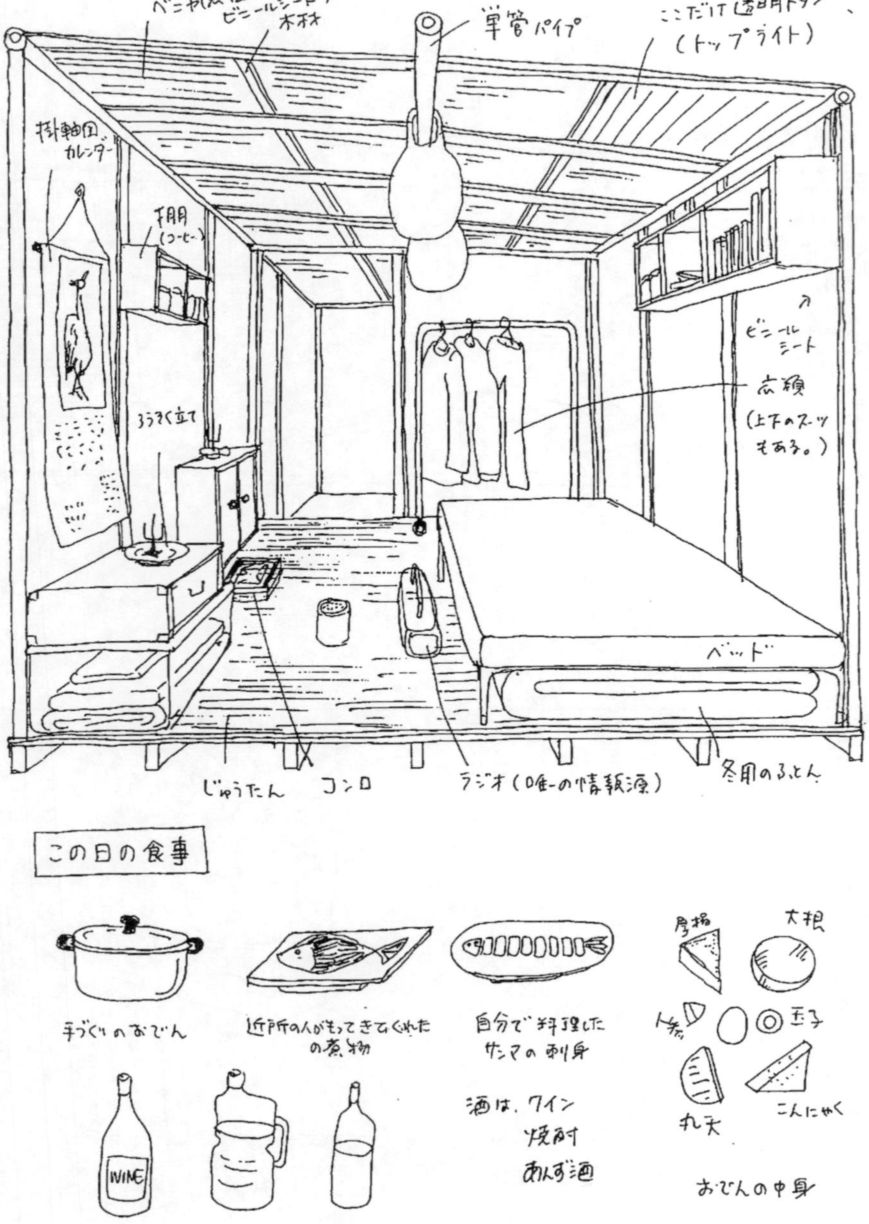

ベニヤ(表面にビニールシート)
木材
単管パイプ
ここだけ透明トタン、
(トップライト)
掛軸風カレンダー
棚(コーヒー)
ろうそく立て
ビニールシート
衣類(上下のスーツもある。)
ベッド
じゅうたん
コンロ
ラジオ(唯一の情報源)
冬用のふとん
この日の食事
手づくりのおでん
近所の人がもってきてくれたの煮物
自分で料理したサンマの刺身
厚揚
大根
玉子
丸天
こんにゃく
おでんの中身
WINE
酒は、ワイン
焼酎
あんず酒

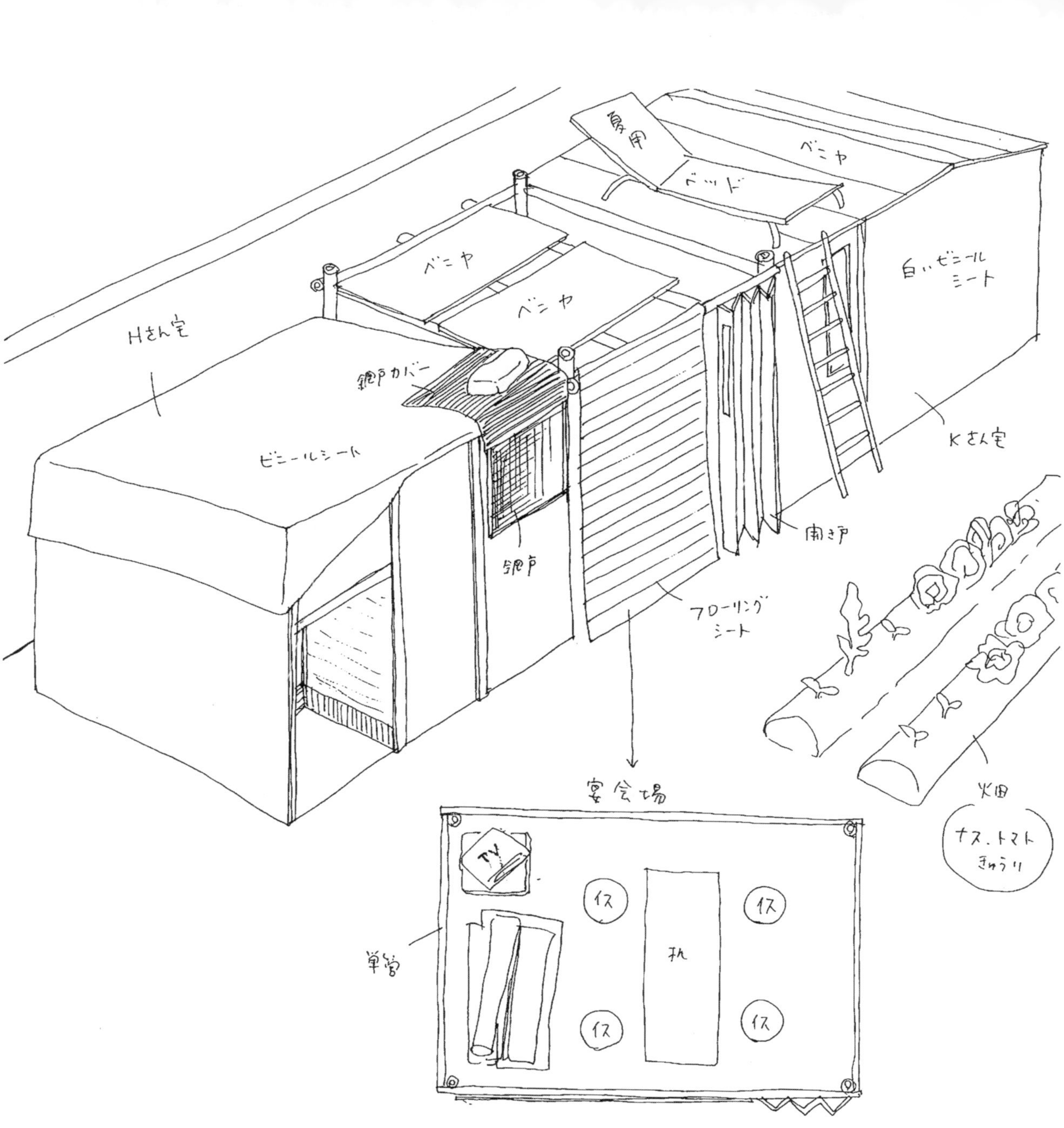
夏用
ベッド
ベニヤ
ベニヤ
ベニヤ
白いビニール
シート
Hさん宅
鎧戸カバー
ビニールシート
鎧戸
フローリング
シート
開き戸
Kさん宅
宴会場
TV
イス
イス
イス
イス
机
布団
畑
ナス、トマト
きゅうり

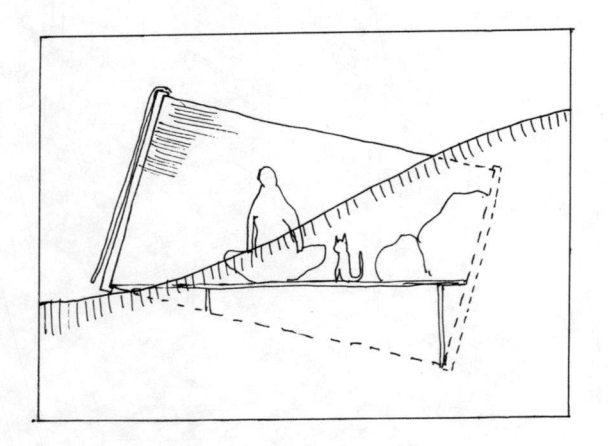

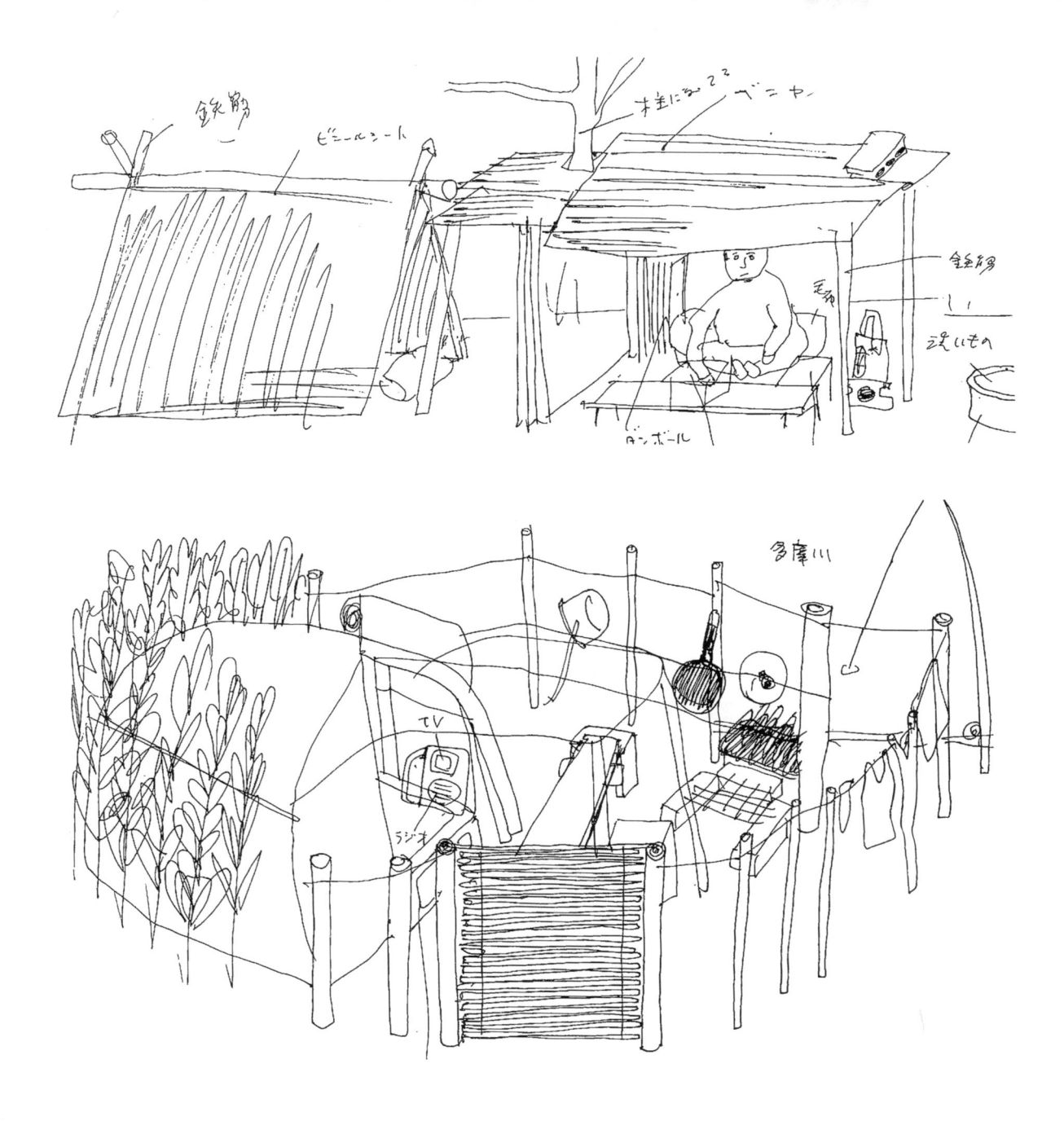

鉄筋　ビニールシート　柱になってる　ベニヤ

金網

毛布

ダンボール　洗いもの

多摩川

TV　ラジオ

〈おばさんの家〉

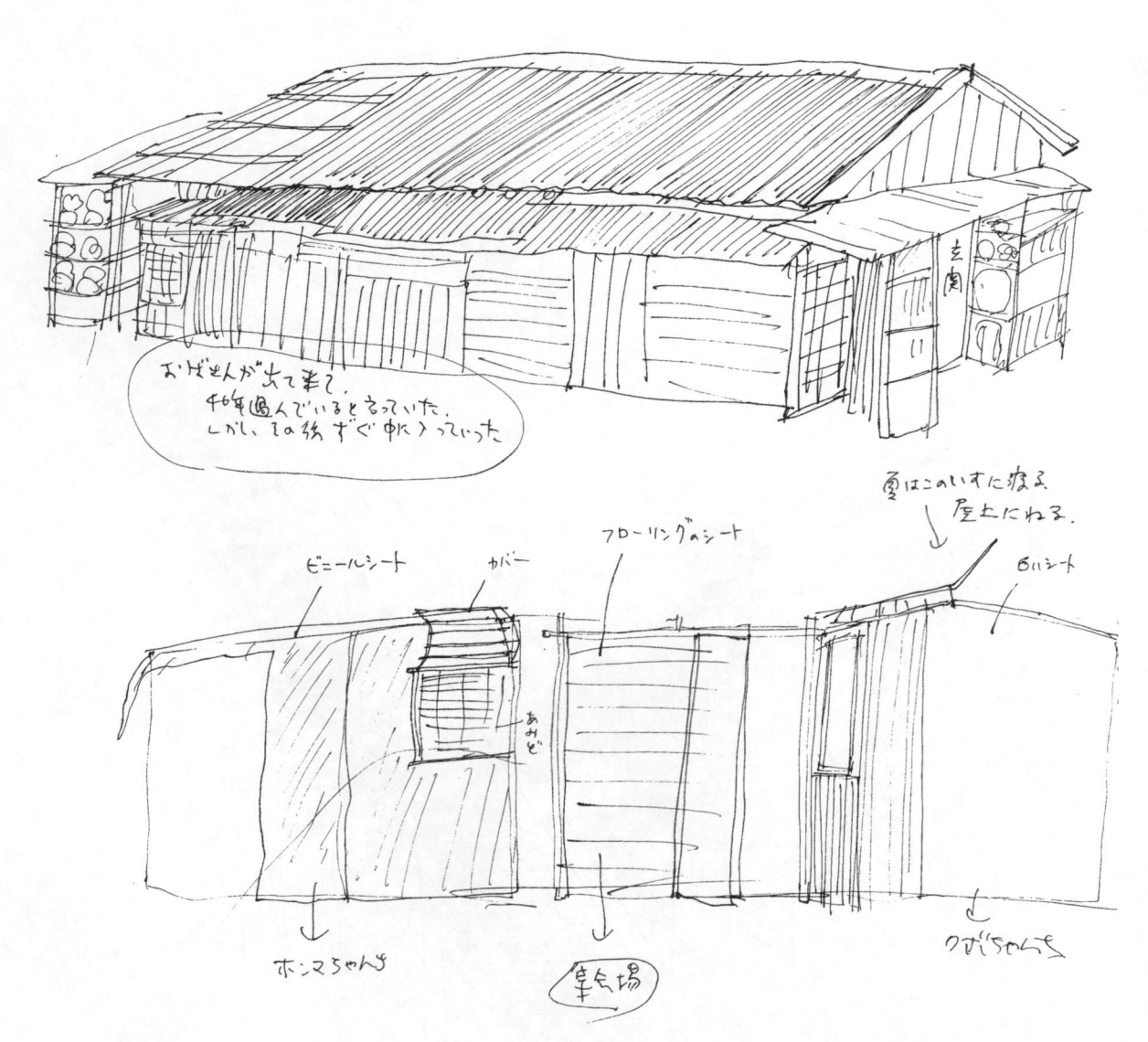

おばさんが出て来て、
40年過んでいると言っていた。
しかし、その後すぐ中に入っていった

夏はこのいすに寝る
屋上に寝る

ビニールシート　カバー　　フローリングのシート　　　　　　　Bシート

　　　　　　あみど

↓　　　　　↓　　　　　　↓
ホンマちゃんち　　寝る場　　　つびちゃんち

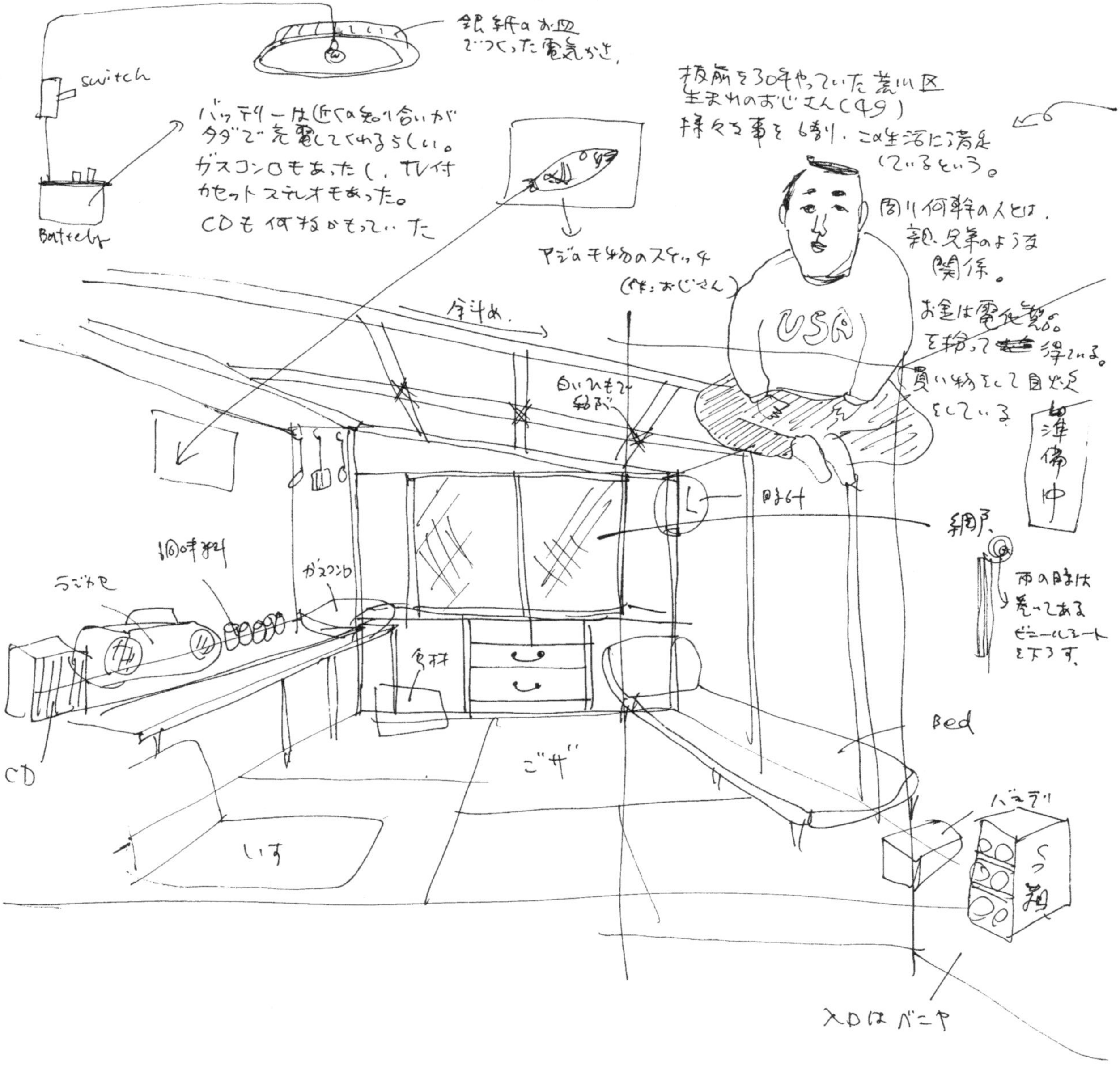

# Shinjuku Chuo Park

新宿中央公園

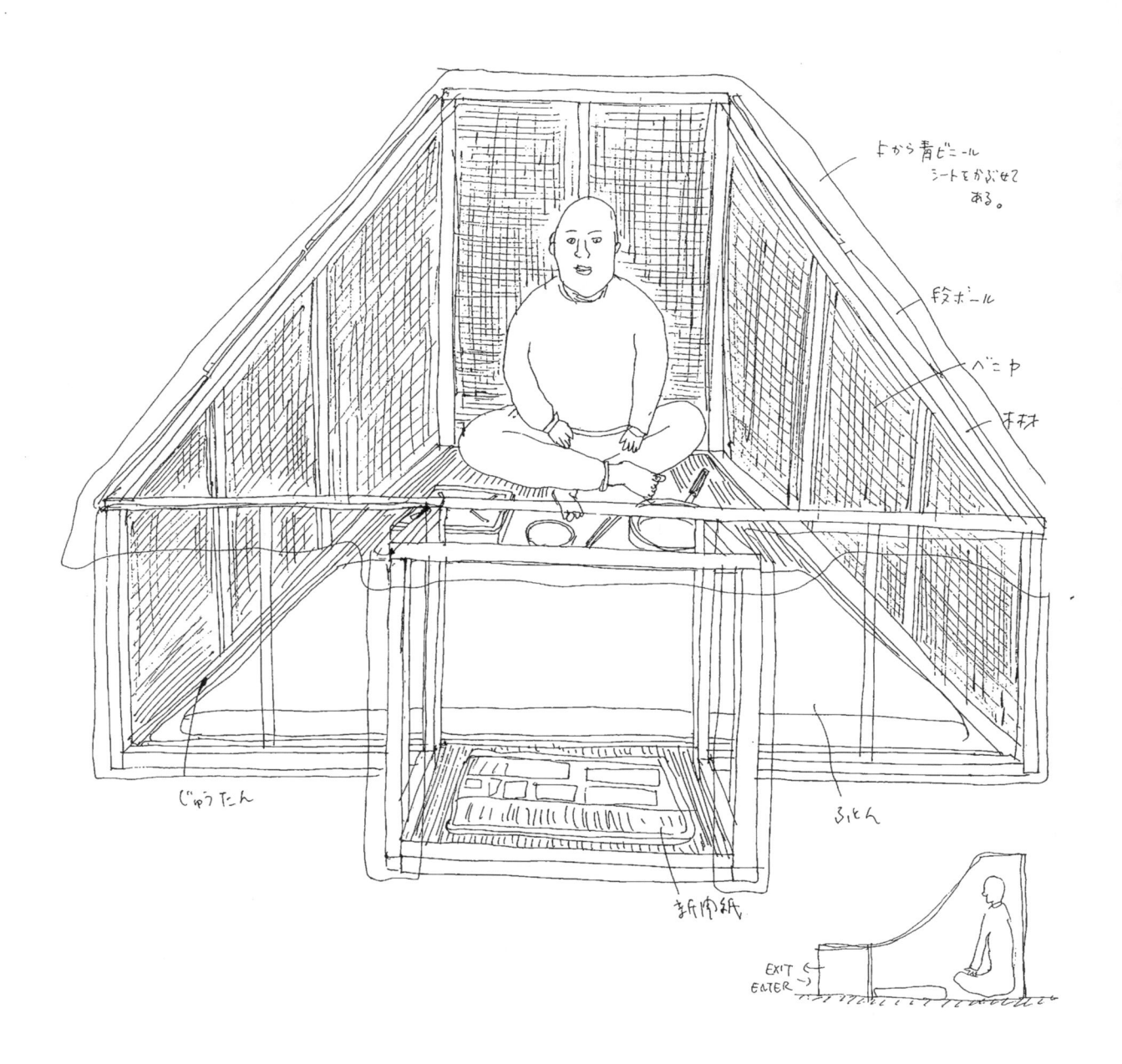

上から青ビニール
シートをかぶせて
ある。

段ボール

ベニヤ

木材

じゅうたん

ふとん

新聞紙

EXIT ←
ENTER →

白のビニール
シート

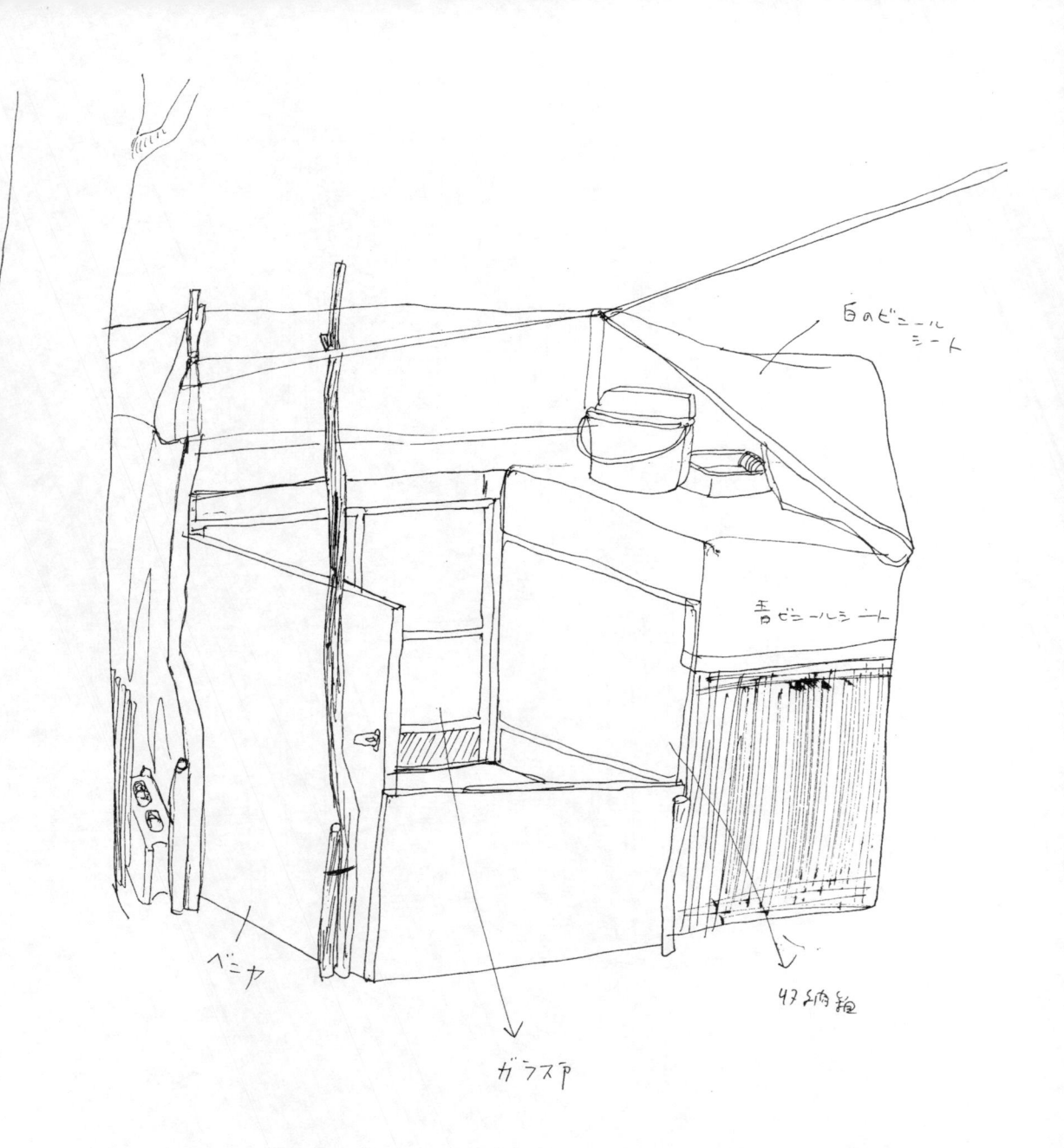

青ビニールシート

ベニア

ガラス戸

47 納箱

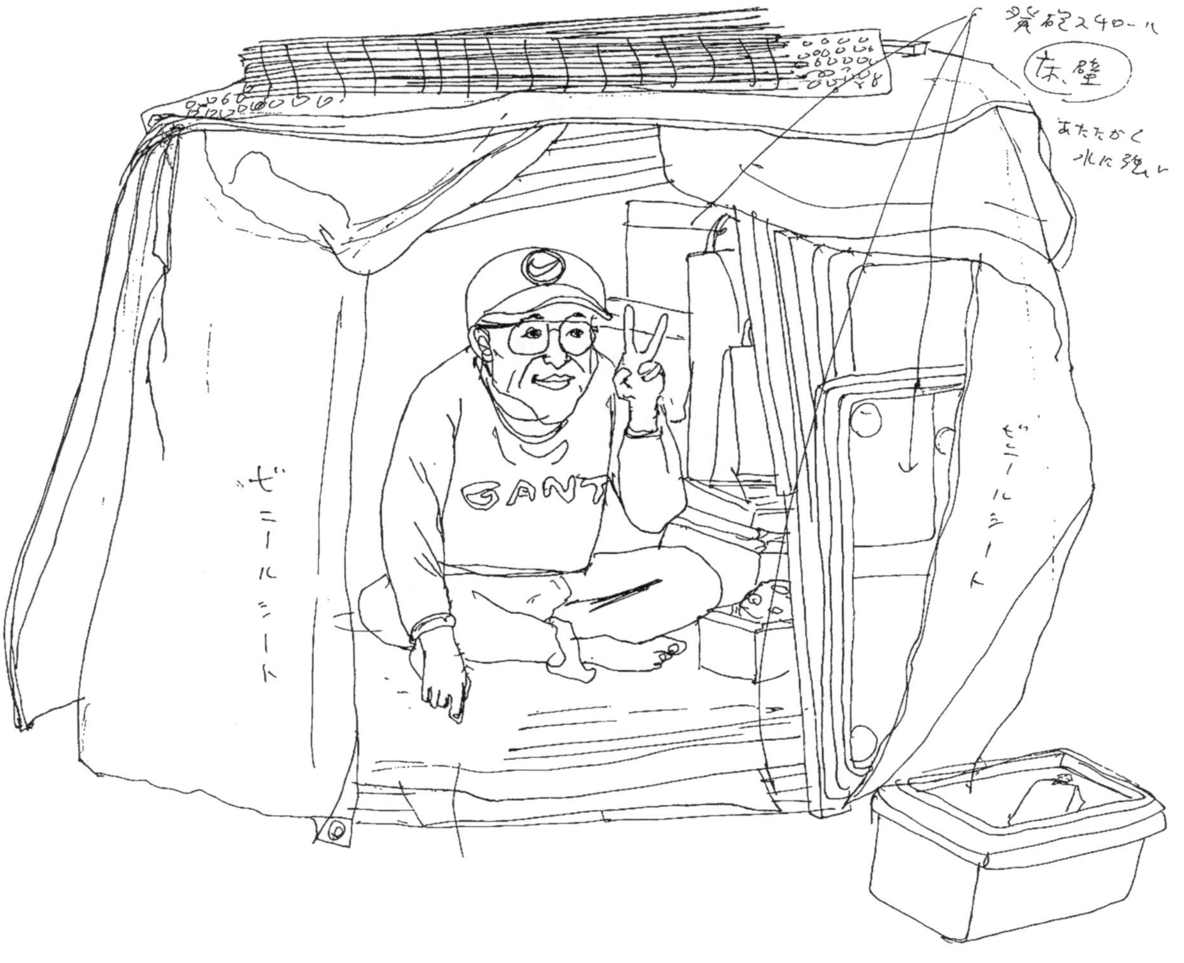
発砲スチロール
床、壁
あたたかく
水に強い
ビニールシート
GANT
ビニールシート

# The Sumidagawa
隅田川

僕がもらったオブゼ
彼は、1日1個これを作ってる
(1個につき20時間)
全てごみによって作られている

セシリアが取材した
切り込みを持っていた。

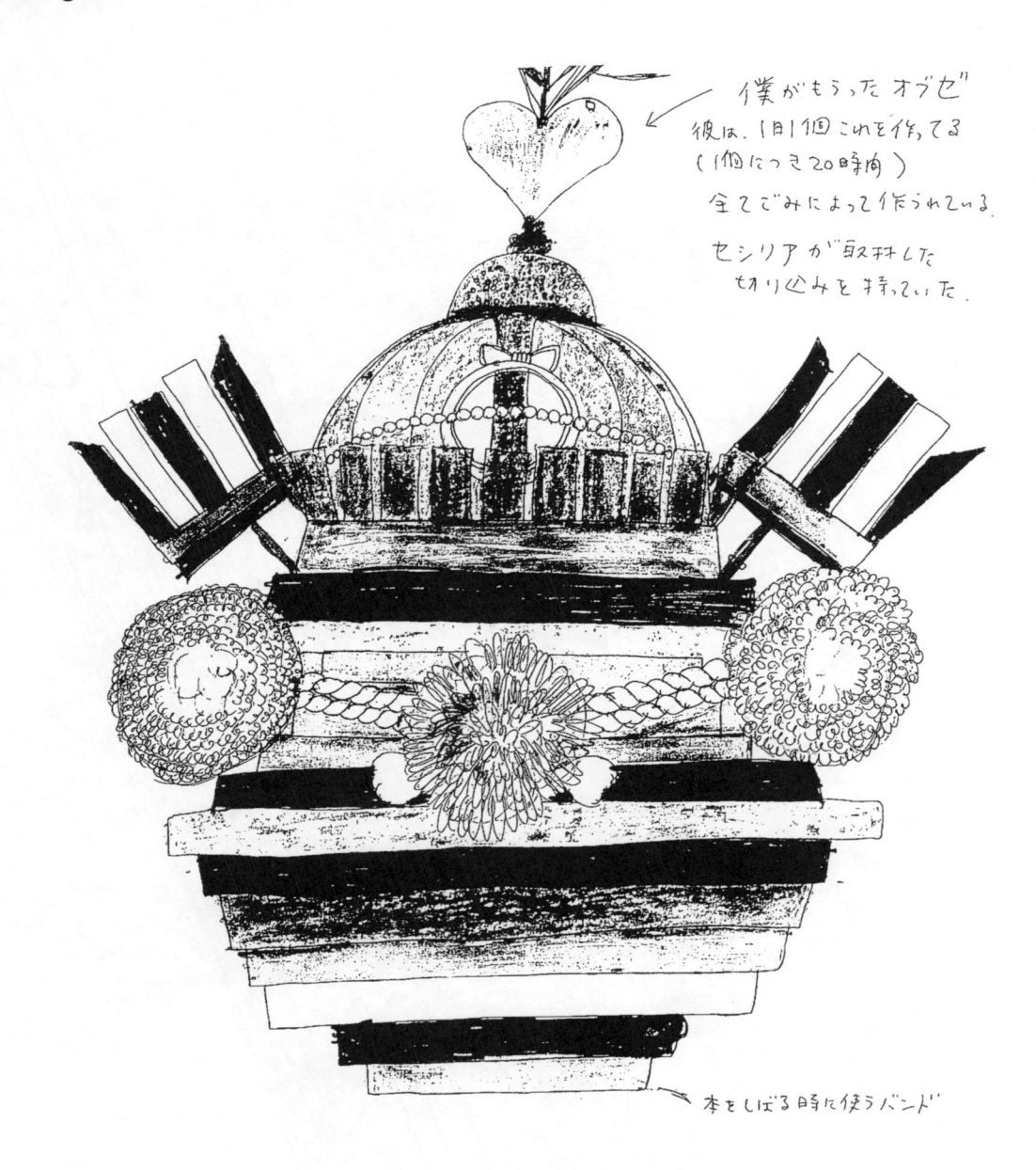

本をしばる時に使うバンド

## Postscript
## あとがき

坂口恭平
1978年 熊本県生まれ
2001年 早稲田大学理工学部建築学科卒業
URL http://www13.ocn.ne.jp/~kyodai/

Kyohei Sakaguchi
1978 Born in Kumamoto, Japan
2001 Graduated from the Department of Architecture, School of Science and Engineering, Waseda University
URL http://www13.ocn.ne.jp/~kyodai/

路上の家には創造性と現実性が同時に溢れかえっている。
どれ1つとして同じもののない家々の横を歩きながら、私はいつもそのことを感じていた。
住人自らが作った家というものは、絶えず運動と変化を繰り返し、秩序とずれが同居している。輪郭は常にゆらゆらと揺れ、しかもそれが調和を生み出している。その姿は建築物という3次元の世界を軽く飛び越えていく。
路上の家は、まさに人間の持っている柔軟で複雑な高次元の知覚そのものとなっていた。

Walking past the houses on the road, no two of which are alike, I always feel that they overflow with creativity and practicality at the same time. A house built by its inhabitant moves and changes in endless repetition. Order and divergence dwell together within. Its outline constantly wavers and yet produces a harmony. Its form easily leaps over the three-dimensional world of architecture.
The houses on the road embody the flexible and complex high-level knowledge and awareness of human beings.

本書185ページより198ページおよびカバー裏面のドローイングは坂口恭平自身によるものです。

Drawings shown on pages 185 to 198 and on the jacket are all the work of Kyohei Sakaguchi.

ゼロ円ハウス
坂口恭平

2004年7月22日初版第1刷発行
2012年6月20日初版第2刷発行

著者：坂口恭平
設計：宮川隆
翻訳：佐藤直子

編集：浅原裕久
発行人：孫家邦
発行所：株式会社リトルモア
〒151-0051 東京都渋谷区千駄ケ谷3-56-6
TEL：03-3401-1042
FAX：03-3401-1052
e-mail　info@littlemore.co.jp
URL　http://www.littlemore.co.jp

印刷・製本所：凸版印刷株式会社

©2004 Kyohei Sakaguchi / Little More
Printed in Japan
ISBN978-4-89815-117-4　C0072

乱丁・落丁本は送料小社負担にてお取り替えいたします。
本書の無断複写・複製・引用を禁じます。

## ZERO YEN HOUSES
### Kyohei Sakaguchi

Photographs, drawings and text by Kyohei Sakaguchi
Designed by Takashi Miyagawa
Translated by Naoko Sato
Edited by Hirohisa Asahara
Published by Sun Chiapang(Little More)

First Published in Japan in July 2004 by Little More Co.,Ltd.
3-56-6, Sendagaya, shibuya-Ku, Tokyo, 151-0051, Japan
TEL：+81-3-3401-1042
FAX：+81-3-3401-1052
e-mail　info@littlemore.co.jp
URL　http://www.littlemore.co.jp

Copyright©2004 Kyohei Sakaguchi / Little More
Printed and bound in Japan by Toppan Printing Co.,Ltd.
ISBN978-4-89815-117-4　C0072

All Rights Reserved.
No part of this book may be reproduced without written permission of the publisher.